The Waldorf Book of Poetry

Discover the Power of Imagination

The Waldorf Book of Poetry

Discover the Power of Imagination

Edited by David Kennedy

2012

2012 Living Arts Books Trade Paperback Edition

LIVING ARTS BOOKS

P.O. Box 221, Viroqua, WI 54665

www.livingartsbooks.com
www.waldorfpoetry.com

Cover design: Geri Shonka
Cover art: David Kennedy
Cover photography: Bronwyn Fargo

ISBN 978-0-9829905-1-3 (paperback)
Library of Congress Control Number 2010913218

Originally published in hardcover in the United States by Living Arts Books in 2012.

Printed and bound in the United States of America.

for Elise

Contents

Foreword

"Spring has returned. The Earth is like a child that knows poems."
-Rainer Maria Rilke

In my travels as a Waldorf consultant, I will now and then encounter a teacher who wistfully asks if I know of one all-purpose book that would show her the way to provide her children with the healthy rhythmic foundation they need to master their multiplication tables; that would map out a consistent approach to building vocabulary and improving spelling; that would cultivate good writing skills, style, and structure; and that would galvanize the teaching of history and geography, capturing the children's imaginative feeling for time and place.

A tall order, to be sure, yet I would venture to say that you are at this moment holding such a book. This unparalleled collection of poetry for Waldorf practitioners is at once an assemblage of powerful rhythmic exercises, a miniature dictionary/thesaurus of English usage and etymology, a manual of style by its most sensitive and trenchant masters, and an encyclopedic compendium of historical events and evocations of geographical settings (including a number of places that, technically, do not even exist). Read through these carefully selected and artfully categorized poems and you will receive the better part of a Waldorf education. If such a claim seems excessive, then please read on.

The memorization and recitation of great poetry was, for centuries, the mainstay of a good education. The image of an Athenian boy performing gymnastic exercises while his slave (pedagogue) recited the *Iliad* and the *Odyssey* has reverberated down the ages as the archetype of "a sound mind in a healthy body," and poetry was the elixir that provided this salutary wholeness.

In the early 1960s I attended a prestigious public high school in New York City. Once a month the 5000 boys who attended that school—most of them destined to be mathematicians, scientists, and engineers—would gather in its grand auditorium for an assembly. Although this was a public school, every assembly began with a specially chosen honor student reading from the Bible. The selection was always drawn from the *Psalms*, the contents of which were undoubtedly acceptable both to the predominantly Catholic school administration as well as the overwhelmingly Jewish faculty—and it was recited to an audience that sat rapt with silence and reverence. At the end of those assemblies, Mr. Wood, my homeroom teacher and an avowed atheist, would delightedly deconstruct the Psalm and show us how cleverly its honeyed surface was designed to open listeners up to its evocation of fear and trembling, guilt and mortification, and to effectively squelch anything individual or defiant from awakening within them.

In this way I was twice blessed. In the morning I learned to *appreciate* poetry, as I experienced the quiet power with which it could inspire inwardness and reverence, soothing the five thousand savage breasts of my boisterous and testosterone-driven schoolmates. In the afternoon, under Mr. Wood's incisive tutelage, I learned how to *analyze* poetry, to recognize that it was not the words alone, but also their placement and rhythm, that comprised the poem and that worked so profoundly upon the human psyche.

Alas, few such experiences are vouchsafed to schoolchildren anymore. This is not to say that children do not crave poetry: just witness the unprecedented proliferation of advertising jingles, mottos, and even the concise, iconic phrases that commonly accompany so many corporate logos in our time. As schools began to eschew immersion in literary and artistic pursuits in favor of subjects that were "relevant," children (and the adults they became) sought poetry wherever they could find it. Perhaps future sociologists will find a correlation between the twentieth century's supplanting of genuine poetry with its commercial caricatures and the substitution of genuine nourishment with fast food.

Fortunately, in this domain among many others, Waldorf education has a better idea. Rudolf Steiner, the progenitor of Waldorf methodology, had such a profound respect for poetry that he developed a new art of recitation, Sprachgestaltung, or "speech formation." Alongside this art he developed yet another, Eurythmy, or "beautiful movement." Eurythmy is performed not only to music but to the spoken word as well. Steiner's eurythmy choreography is replete with indications to performers concerning the sounds, meter, rhyme, and meaning of many great poems. This profound regard for poetry flowed into the life of the very first Waldorf school in 1919 and continues unabated to this day. Waldorf students begin to recite poetry in Nursery and Kindergarten as they imitate their teachers; by the middle and upper grades the more wakeful students may memorize hundreds of lines of poetry that they have read on their own, recited with classmates, or performed in eurythmy and school plays.

Over the course of the near-century since the first Waldorf school was founded, this poetic impulse has suffered at the hands of "school improvement." Even though Waldorf teachers may take pride in being removed from the fads and foibles of contemporary life, they have an uncanny knack for reflecting the cultural trends around them, and the treatment of poetry in the classroom is no exception to this rule. Through the first two-thirds of the twentieth century (the period in which my public high school still honored the *Psalms*), Waldorf teachers worked almost exclusively with poems drawn from the canon of European and nineteenth-century American literature. By the 1980s, as the Waldorf movement expanded exponentially into the western states, such poems appeared too Eurocentric, and the rapidly changing demographics of a state like California seemed to call for a more culturally diverse selection of poets and poetic experiences. While many of these changes were intended to "expand" the culture of the Waldorf school, all too often they diluted it.

At this time, too, teachers were encouraged to "write their own material" to suit the needs, temperaments, and ethnicities of their pupils. Without being able to draw upon their own recollections of hearing meaningful poetry, teachers responded heroically to the call, but their creations were usually jejune at best. With the onset of growing numbers of conferences—and, in time, the archival capacities of the Internet—such homegrown poems circulated so widely that their provenance became increasingly hazy. I recall how, several years after I had written the "Number Verses" that appear in this book, I mentored a first grade Waldorf teacher. Her class recited "Number Verses" with gusto, and I could not resist asking her if she knew who had written it. "I don't know the name," she replied, "But someone told me it was translated from the German."

Cultural trends aside, we must also recognize that Waldorf teachers are themselves the product of an educational system—usually the distinctly prosaic American system. Except for the small cadre of Waldorf practitioners who are Waldorf school graduates, most of today's teachers had little meaningful poetry as part of their own school experience on the elementary, secondary, or university level.

In the 1990s I would give my Sunbridge College Waldorf teacher trainees a short "entrance exam" on the first day of class. Among other things, trainees were asked to give the century of birth for ten poets (John Donne, Lord Byron, Alfred Tennyson, Walt Whitman, and Dylan Thomas among them) and to name one poem written by each. Foreign students might identify five or six of the poets, but Americans (English majors included) usually knew only one or two. Faced with a collection of poetry for children, such teachers would be likely to chose the "easier" poems for their classes, or to skip the anthologies altogether and use only the Waldorf verses they received as handouts in a summer conference.

Just when we have good cause to despair at the eclipse of great poetry in the Waldorf setting, David Kennedy has come to our rescue with this book. David's long experience as a Waldorf school class teacher, his skills as a writer, and what I can only term his enthusiastic discernment, make him the right person at the right time to resuscitate the barely breathing spirit of the Word in the classroom. He has arranged the poetry in a way that harmonizes with the structure and content of the Waldorf curriculum, yet leaves the reader free to meander at will. This is a collection of wonderful, classical, meaningful poems written by masters of the English language, or in masterful translations from ancient languages. Recycle those conference handouts, teachers, for herein lies eight years of nourishment and edification for your students!

Their poems are not merely main lesson content arranged to scan and rhyme. In many of the poems in this collection we all but meet the living and breathing poet, as well as the age in which that poet worked, and a world of soul and spirit that would otherwise have remained mute. We teachers and parents will teach these poems and be elevated, for we have heard the voice of an Initiate. Our students and our children, no less significantly, will speak these poems and be elevated as, for the first time, they hear their own voice.

In the first four grades, it is essential to choose and work with poems that have a regular, predictable rhyme scheme, e.g. rhyming couplets, and a strong and predictable rhythm. Both of these poetic qualities strengthen that part of the child termed by Rudolf Steiner the "etheric body," or "body of formative forces," or "life body." It is this aspect of the child's being that serves all later growth and health on a physiological basis, and serves the unfolding of the memory on the level of soul. In this respect, all poems are mnemonic devices, playing this role in branches of culture as diverse as religious ritual and modern advertising. And because the awakening of memory is so interwoven with poetic recitation, it is important that the primary grades child learns directly from the teacher's recitation of the poem, rather than by reading the poem. And it is no less important that the teacher learns the poem by heart, before bringing it to the child. In particular, what Steiner termed the "rhythmic-circulatory system," the interplay of breathing and the circulation of blood, is enlivened and regulated by this type of poetic recitation.

By fifth grade, the interplay of breathing and circulation is essentially stabilized, and it needs far less rhythmic support than in the earlier years. For the rest of the student's time in the grade school, the etheric body withdraws and what Rudolf Steiner described as the "astral body," or "soul body" assumes a position of growing importance. Now it is the life of feeling that must be educated along with the memory. The subtleties of meter (particularly iambic pentameter in English) and the nuanced harmonies of alternating rhymes (as in the abab/cdcd/efef/gg of the sonnet) intrigue and surprise the adolescent's burgeoning soul forces, giving form to otherwise stochastic emotions and elevating them to the level of conscious feelings. Meter, with its occasional irregularities and its connection to the spoken word, here may serve as a healthy antidote to the power of beat that plays such a commanding role in the life of the adolescent.

Given the central importance of the poetic experience for the child's growth and future learning, it is essential that poems not be taught hastily, superficially, or casually. If children do not get to savor every element of a poem, the poem may work upon them, but it will never come to fruition within them. As Alexander Pope (a poet that none of my teacher trainees could ever identify) said famously, "A little learning is a dangerous thing; drink deep, or taste not the Pierian spring."

With this in mind, I urge the teachers whom I mentor to stay with a poem for a month. Begin by learning it by heart, practicing its recitation at home, reciting it beautifully and clearly to your class (not just reading it aloud) and then, over the course of three days or more, have the students join you in its recitation. Whether you are teaching a short poem or dividing a longer piece into parts, never recite just once in a lesson; always repeat a poem two or three times. (And don't feel that you have to teach a dozen poems in every circle or warm-up; one or two meaningful poems a day may be plenty.) It has been my experience that the strongest spellers in a classroom are not necessarily the most voracious readers, but rather the children who recite the best. If we recall that the word "spell" originally mean a spoken invocation, we can understand the almost magical relationship between clear, well-enunciated poetic recitation and a preternatural sense for the structure of a word.

After three days, your recitation should be pared back, and the children should be reciting, as much as possible, without you. This way you can listen to them, providing constructive criticism, moving far away so that they must emote, or drawing very close so that they will whisper. Prepare every poem with your class as though you are rehearsing it for an assembly, or, better yet, for their eighth grade graduation, even if they are still in first grade. As you pull away and listen to your students, you may realize that some children have not been reciting at all. The shadow side of the Waldorf approach is that some children can hide in the group, appearing to be speaking a poem or chanting a multiplication table when, indeed, when quizzed by their parents one-on-one, they are clueless. By the time you are ready to move on to a new poem, you should have had many children recite the poem solo, or at least in a group no larger than two or three.

The past decade has seen a growing concern about the need for sufficient movement in the Waldorf main lesson. Unquestionably, poetry can be a springboard for movement, be it expressive or part of a game; this is especially true in the many American schools that lack a eurythmist. However, it is no less essential that children learn how to recite while standing still, as well, so that they are more awake to the inner movement that a poem may evoke. And poetry is not just about speaking—listening plays no less a role, and both are necessary if a class will recite with "one voice." Dividing the class into small groups, as described above, is an invaluable practice.

I would urge the teacher to set to work and read these poems twice, in two different ways. Firstly, study them in the way that David Kennedy presents them, according to the subjects taught from the lower to the higher grades. Secondly, with the help of a timeline or a book such as John Wulsin's *The Spirit of the English Language* (AWSNA Publications), experience them in the order in which they were written. The first reading will give you insight into the changing consciousness of the child; the second reading will allow you to experience the evolution of consciousness of humanity at large, and particularly of the English-speaking peoples. An understanding of both transformations of consciousness is sine qua non for a Waldorf teacher.

"Camerado!" Walt Whitman tells us in his masterpiece, *Leaves of Grass*, "This is no book; who touches this touches a man." In this book, David Kennedy shares with us the currents of sound and meaning that passed between him and his students in the course of his teaching career. His years of experience have helped to make his selection of poems and the order in which they appear a model that may be followed by any teacher wishing to encounter and honor the Word within the Waldorf curriculum. Touch this book, and you will touch and teach each child in your care.

EUGENE SCHWARTZ
Spring 2011

"Words are the voice of the heart."
-Confucius

Imagination

The Fairies

Rose Fyleman

The fairies have never a penny to spend,
    They haven't a thing put by,
But theirs is the dower of bird and flower
    And theirs is the earth and sky.
And though you should live in a palace of gold
    Or sleep in a dried up ditch,
You could never be as poor as the fairies are,
    And never as rich.

Since ever and ever the world began
    They danced like a ribbon of flame,
They have sung their song through the centuries long,
    And yet it is never the same.
And though you be foolish or though you be wise,
    With hair of silver or gold,
You can never be as young as the fairies are,
    And never as old.

A Cloak for a Fairy

Spider, spider, what are you spinning?
    A cloak for a fairy, I'm just beginning.
What is it made of, tell me true?
    Threads of moonshine, pearls of dew!
When will the fairy be wearing it?
    Tonight, when the glow worms' lamps are lit.
Can I see her if I come peeping?
    All good children must then be sleeping.

The Elf and the Dormouse

Oliver Herford

Under a toadstool crept a wee Elf,
Out of the rain to shelter himself.

Under the toadstool, sound asleep,
Sat a big Dormouse all in a heap.

Trembled the wee Elf, frightened, and yet
Fearing to fly away lest he get wet.

To the next shelter—maybe a mile!
Sudden the wee Elf smiled a wee smile,

Tugged till the toadstool toppled in two.
Holding it over him, gaily he flew.

Soon he was safe home, dry as could be.
Soon woke the Dormouse—"Good gracious me!

Where is my toadstool?" loud he lamented.
—And that's how umbrellas first were invented.

Some One

Walter de la Mare

Some one came knocking
    At my wee, small door;
Some one came knocking,
    I'm sure—sure—sure;
I listened, I opened,
    I looked to left and right,
But naught there was a-stirring
    In the still dark night;
Only the busy beetle
    Tap-tapping in the wall,
Only from the forest
    The screech-owl's call,
Only the cricket whistling
    While the dewdrops fall,
So I know not who came knocking,
    At all, at all, at all.

Little Dwarfs

Little dwarfs so short and strong
Heavy-footed march along;
Every head is straight and proud,
Every step is firm and loud.

Pick and hammer each must hold,
Deep in the earth to mine the gold
Ready over each one's back
Hangs a little empty sack.

When the hard day's work is done,
Home again they march as one.
Full sacks make a heavy load
As they tramp along the road.

I'd Love to Be a Fairy's Child

Robert Graves

Children born of fairy stock
Never need for shirt or frock,
Never want for food or fire,
Always get their heart's desire:

Jingle pockets full of gold,
Marry when they're seven years old.
Every fairy child may keep
Two strong ponies and ten sheep;

All have houses, each his own,
Built of brick or granite stone;
They live on cherries, they run wild—
I'd love to be a Fairy's child.

Fairy Shoes

Annette Wynne

The little shoes of fairies are
So light and soft and small
That though a million pass you by
You would not hear at all.

FROM THE FAIRIES

William Allingham

Up the airy mountain,
Down the rushy glen,
We daren't go a-hunting
For fear of little men;
Wee folk, good folk,
Trooping all together;
Green jacket, red cap,
And white owl's feather!

Down along the rocky shore
Some make their home,
They live on crispy pancakes
Of yellow tide-foam;
Some in the reeds
Of the black mountain lake,
With frogs for their watch-dogs,
All night awake.

By the craggy hill-side,
Through the mosses bare,
They have planted thorn-trees
For pleasure here and there.
If any man so daring
As dig them up in spite,
He shall find their sharpest thorns
In his bed at night.

Up the airy mountain,
Down the rushy glen,
We daren't go a-hunting
For fear of little men;
Wee folk, good folk,
Trooping all together;
Green jacket, red cap,
And white owl's feather!

The Cobbler

There once lived a cobbler and he was so wee
That he lived in a hole of a very big tree.

He had a neighbor and she was a mouse
And she did his wee washing and tidied his house.

Each morning at seven he heard a wee tap
And in came the mouse in her apron and cap.

She lit a small fire and fetched a wee broom
And she swept and she polished his little tree room.

To take any wages she always refused,
So the cobbler said, "Thank you," and mended her shoes.

The owl didn't eat her, not even the cat.
They said, "I wouldn't catch a kind mousie like that!"

from The Leprecaun or Fairy Shoemaker

William Allingham

"Tip-tap, rip-rap,
Tick-a-tack-too!
Scarlet leather, sewn together,
This will make a shoe.
    Left, right, pull it tight;
    Summer days are warm;
    Underground in winter,
    Laughing at the storm!"

"Big boots a-hunting,
Sandals in the hall,
White for a wedding-feast,
Pink for a ball.
    This way, that way,
    So we make a shoe;
    Getting rich every stitch,
    Tick-tack-too!"

Midsummer Night

Elizabeth Gould

The sun goes down,
The stars peep out,
And long slim shadows
Flit about.

In velvet shoes
The quiet dark
Comes stepping soft
O'er wood and park.

And now the world
Is fast asleep;
And fays and elves
Their revels keep.

They fly on the backs of the grey-winged moths,
They skim on the dragon-flies green and gold
On shimmering dew-wet grass they alight,
Tiny petal-skirts whirl, gauzy wings unfold.
The fairies are dancing beneath the moon
Hush! See the shimmer of their twinkling shoon!

Goblin Gold

Molly de Havas

Digging down in deepest dark and danger,
Gleeful goblins gather glittering gold.
High and hard a hundred heavy hammers
Clang and clash in columned caverns cold.

Little lamps their lengthy labours lighten
Shuddering shadows show, and shifting shine.
So they ceaseless search for silver secrets,
Midget men amid the mountain mine.

Treasures

Through echoing caves we run and glide,
Through cracks in the rocks we slip and slide,
Over great boulders we leap and bound;
Our little lamps show us where treasure is found.

We hammer, we hammer from morn till night,
We hammer together the treasure so bright,
Sparkling silver and glittering gold,
Crystals so pure and clear to behold.

Then up we fill our little sacks
And put them high upon our backs.
Down we go to the throne of our King,
To him our treasures we must bring.

Sir Nicketty Nox

Hugh Chesterman

Sir Nicketty Nox was an ancient knight,
So old was he that he'd lost his sight.
Blind as a mole, and slim as a fox,
And dry as a stick was Sir Nicketty Nox.

His sword and buckler were old and cracked,
So was his charger and that's a fact.
Thin as a rake from head to hocks,
Was this rickety nag of Sir Nicketty Nox.

A wife he had and daughters three,
And all were as old, as old could be.
They mended the shirts and darned the socks,
Of that old Antiquity, Nicketty Nox.

Sir Nicketty Nox would fly in rage
If anyone tried to guess his age.
He'd mouth and mutter and tear his locks,
This pernickety Nicketty Nox.

Danish Nursery Rhyme

There once was a King who had three daughters.
The oldest he called Sip!
The second he called Sip sippernip!
But the youngest of all he called Sip sippernip sip sirumsip!

Not far away lived another King who had three sons.
The oldest was called Skrat!
The second was called Skrat skratterat!
But the youngest of all was called Skrat skratterat skrat skrirumskrat!

Now by and by the two Kings got together, the King who had three daughters and the King who had three sons, and decided that their children should marry.

And married they were!

Sip got Skrat,

and Sipsippernip got Skratskratterat,

and Sipsippernipsipsirumsip got Skratskratteratskratskrirumskrat.

As simple as that!

Where Go the Boats?

Robert Louis Stevenson

Dark brown is the river.
Golden is the sand.
It flows along for ever,
With trees on either hand.

Green leaves a-floating,
Castles of the foam,
Boats of mine a-boating—
Where will all come home?

On goes the river
And out past the mill,
Away down the valley,
Away down the hill.

Away down the river,
A hundred miles or more,
Other little children
Shall bring my boats ashore.

The Knight

Molly de Havas

I ride on my horse with my sword in my hand,
I ride through the wooded and mountainous land.
I battle with dragons, with giants I fight;
Defending the weak and upholding the right.

My sword is of steel and my helmet of gold,
I dare all adventures, my heart is so bold.
My armor is shining as bright as the light,
And I am a gallant and glorious Knight.

A Song from the Suds

Louisa May Alcott

Queen of my tub, I merrily sing,
While the white foam raises high,
And sturdily wash, and rinse, and wring,
And fasten the clothes to dry;
Then out in the free fresh air they swing,
Under the sunny sky.

I wish we could wash from our hearts and our souls
The stains of the week away,
And let water and air by their magic make
Ourselves as pure as they;
Then on the earth there would be indeed
A glorious washing day!

Along the path of a useful life
Will heart's-ease ever bloom;
The busy mind has no time to think
Of sorrow, or care, or gloom;
And anxious thoughts may be swept away
As we busily wield a broom.

I am glad a task to me is given
To labor at day by day;
For it brings me health, and strength, and hope,
And I cheerfully learn to say,
"Head, you may think; heart, you may feel;
But hand, you shall work always!"

Introduction to Songs of Innocence

William Blake

Piping down the valleys wild,
Piping songs of pleasant glee,
On a cloud I saw a child,
And he laughing said to me:

"Pipe a song about a Lamb!"
So I piped with merry cheer.
"Piper, pipe that song again;"
So I piped: he wept to hear.

"Drop thy pipe, thy happy pipe;
Sing thy songs of happy cheer!"
So I sung the same again,
While he wept with joy to hear.

"Piper, sit thee down and write
In a book, that all may read."
So he vanished from my sight,
And I plucked a hollow reed,

And I made a rural pen,
And I stained the water clear,
And I wrote my happy songs
Every child may joy to hear.

There Was an Old Woman Tossed Up in a Basket

English Nursery Rhyme

There was an old woman tossed up in a basket
    Seventeen times as high as the moon;
Where she was going I couldn't but ask it,
    For in her hand she carried a broom.

"Old woman, old woman, old woman," quoth I,
    "Where are you going to up so high?"
"To brush the cobwebs off the sky!"
    "May I go with thee?" "Aye, by-and-by."

Dream Song

Walter de la Mare

Sunlight, moonlight,
Twilight, starlight—
Gloaming at the close of day,
And an owl calling,
Cool dews falling
In a wood of oak and may.

Lantern-light, taper-light,
Torchlight, no-light:
Darkness at the shut of day,
And lions roaring,
Their wrath pouring
In wild waste places far away.

Elf-light, bat-light,
Touchwood-light and toad-light,
And the sea a shimmering gloom of grey,
And a small face smiling
In a dream's beguiling
In a world of wonders far away.

A Fairy in Armor

Joseph Rodman Drake

He put his acorn-helmet on;
It was plum'd of the silk of the thistle down;
The corslet plate, that guarded his breast,
Was once the wild bees' golden vest;
His cloak, of a thousand mingled dyes,
Was form'd of the wings of butterflies;
His shield was the shell of a lady-bug queen,
Studs of gold on a ground of green;
And the quivering lance which he brandish'd bright,
Was the sting of a wasp he had slain in fight.
Swift he bestrode his fire-fly steed;
He bared his blade of the bent-grass blue;
He drove his spurs of the cockle-seed,
And away like a glance of thought he flew,
To skim the heavens, and follow far
The fiery trail of the rocket-star.

Time, You Old Gipsy Man

Ralph Hodgson

Time, you old gipsy man,
    Will you not stay,
Put up your caravan
    Just for one day?

All things I'll give you,
    Will you be my guest,
Bells for your jennet
    Of silver the best,
Goldsmiths shall beat you
    A great golden ring,
Peacocks shall bow to you,
    Little boys sing,
Oh, and sweet girls will
    Festoon you with may.
Time, you old gipsy,
    Why hasten away?

Last week in Babylon,
    Last night in Rome,
Morning, and in the crush
    Under Paul's dome;
Under Paul's dia
    You tighten your rein—
Only a moment,
    And off once again;
Off to some city
    Now blind in the womb,
Off to another
    Ere that's in the tomb.

Time, you old gipsy man,
    Will you not stay,
Put up your caravan
    Just for one day?

The Owl and the Pussycat

Edward Lear

The Owl and the Pussy-Cat went to sea
In a beautiful pea-green boat:
They took some honey, and plenty of money
Wrapped up in a five-pound note.
The Owl looked up to the stars above,
And sang to a small guitar,
"O lovely Pussy, O Pussy, my love,
What a beautiful Pussy you are,
    You are,
    You are!
What a beautiful Pussy you are!"

Pussy said to the Owl, "You elegant fowl,
How charmingly sweet you sing!
Oh! let us be married; too long we have tarried,
But what shall we do for a ring?"
They sailed away, for a year and a day,
To the land where the bong-tree grows;
And there in a wood a Piggy-wig stood,
With a ring at the end of his nose,
    His nose,
    His nose,
With a ring at the end of his nose.

"Dear Pig, are you willing to sell for one shilling
Your ring?" Said the Piggy, "I will."
So they took it away, and were married next day
By the turkey who lives on the hill.
They dined on mince and slices of quince,
Which they ate with a runcible spoon;
And hand in hand, on the edge of the sand,
They danced by the light of the moon,
    The moon,
    The moon,
They danced by the light of the moon.

Alms in Autumn

Rose Fyleman

Spindle-wood, spindle-wood, will you lend me pray,
A little flaming lantern to guide me on my way?
The fairies all have vanished from the meadow and the glen,
And I would fain go seeking till I find them once again.
Lend me now a lantern that I may bear a light,
To find the hidden pathways in the darkness of the night.

Ash-tree, ash-tree, throw me, if you please,
Throw me down a slender bunch of russet-gold keys,
I fear the gates of Fairyland all be shut so fast
That nothing but your magic keys will ever take me past.
I'll tie them to my girdle and as I go along,
My heart will find a comfort in the tinkle of their song.

Holly-bush, holly-bush, help me in my task,
A pocketfull of berries is all the alms I ask:
A pocketfull of berries to thread on golden strands,
(I would not go a-visiting with nothing in my hands).
So fine will be the rosy chains, so gay, so glossy bright,
They'll set the realms of Fairyland all dancing with delight.

The Song of the King of Ireland's Son

Padraic Colum

I put the fastenings on my boat
For a year and for a day,
And I went where the rowans grow,
And where the moorhens lay;

And I went over the stepping-stones
And dipped my feet in the ford,
And came at last to the Swineherd's house,—
The Youth without a Sword.

A swallow sang upon his porch
"Glu-ee, glu-ee, glu-ee,"
"The wonder of all wandering,
The wonder of the sea;"
A swallow soon to leave ground sang
"Glu-ee, glu-ee, glu-ee."

Puk-Wudjies

Patrick Reginald Chalmers

They live 'neath the curtain
Of fir woods and heather,
And never take hurt in
The wildest of weather,
But best they love Autumn—she's brown as themselves—
And they are the brownest of all the brown elves;
When loud sings the West Wind,
The bravest and best wind,
And puddles are shining in all the cart ruts,
They turn up the dead leaves,
The russet and red leaves,
Where squirrels have taught them to look out for nuts.

The hedge-cutters hear them
Where berries are glowing,
The scythe circles near them
At time of the mowing,
But most they love woodlands when Autumn's winds pipe.
And all through the cover the beechnuts are ripe,
And great spiky chestnuts,
The biggest and best nuts,
Blown down in the ditches, fair windfalls lie cast,
And no tree begrudges
The little Puk-Wudjies
A pocket of acorns, or handful of mast.

So should you be roaming
When branches are sighing,
When up in the gloaming
The moon-wrack is flying,
And hear through the darkness, again and again,
What's neither the wind nor the spatter of rain-
A flutter, a flurry,
A scuffle, a scurry,
A bump like the rabbits that bump on the ground,
A patter, a bustle,
Of small things that rustle,
You'll know the Puk-Wudjies are somewhere around.

Wynken, Blynken, and Nod

Eugene Field

Wynken, Blynken, and Nod one night
    Sailed off in a wooden shoe—
Sailed on a river of crystal light,
    Into a sea of dew.
"Where are you going, and what do you wish?"
    The old moon asked the three.
"We have come to fish for the herring fish
    That live in this beautiful sea;
    Nets of silver and gold have we!"
        Said Wynken,
        Blynken,
        And Nod.

The old moon laughed and sang a song,
    As they rocked in the wooden shoe,
And the wind that sped them all night long
    Ruffled the waves of dew.
The little stars were the herring fish
    That lived in that beautiful sea—
"Now cast your nets wherever you wish—
    Never afeard are we";
    So cried the stars to the fishermen three:
        Wynken,
        Blynken,
        And Nod.

All night long their nets they threw
    To the stars in the twinkling foam—
Then down from the skies came the wooden shoe,
    Bringing the fishermen home;
'T was all so pretty a sail it seemed
    As if it could not be,
And some folks thought 't was a dream they'd dreamed
    Of sailing that beautiful sea—
    But I shall name you the fishermen three:
        Wynken,
        Blynken,
        And Nod.

Wynken and Blynken are two little eyes,
  And Nod is a little head,
And the wooden shoe that sailed the skies
  Is a wee one's trundle-bed.
So shut your eyes while mother sings
  Of wonderful sights that be,
And you shall see the beautiful things
  As you rock in the misty sea,
  Where the old shoe rocked the fishermen three:
      Wynken,
      Blynken,
      And Nod.

The Jumblies

Edward Lear

They went to sea in a Sieve, they did,
  In a Sieve they went to sea:
In spite of all their friends could say,
On a winter's morn, on a stormy day,
  In a Sieve they went to sea!
And when the Sieve turned round and round,
And every one cried, 'You'll all be drowned!'
They called aloud, 'Our Sieve ain't big,
But we don't care a button! we don't care a fig!
  In a Sieve we'll go to sea!'
    Far and few, far and few,
      Are the lands where the Jumblies live;
    Their heads are green, and their hands are blue,
      And they went to sea in a Sieve.

They sailed away in a Sieve, they did,
  In a Sieve they sailed so fast,
With only a beautiful pea-green veil
Tied with a riband by way of a sail,
  To a small tobacco-pipe mast;
And every one said, who saw them go,
'O won't they be soon upset, you know!
For the sky is dark, and the voyage is long,
And happen what may, it's extremely wrong

In a Sieve to sail so fast!'
Far and few, far and few,
Are the lands where the Jumblies live;
Their heads are green, and their hands are blue,
And they went to sea in a Sieve.

The water it soon came in, it did,
The water it soon came in;
So to keep them dry, they wrapped their feet
In a pinky paper all folded neat,
And they fastened it down with a pin.
And they passed the night in a crockery-jar,
And each of them said, 'How wise we are!
Though the sky be dark, and the voyage be long,
Yet we never can think we were rash or wrong,
While round in our Sieve we spin!'
Far and few, far and few,
Are the lands where the Jumblies live;
Their heads are green, and their hands are blue,
And they went to sea in a Sieve.

And all night long they sailed away;
And when the sun went down,
They whistled and warbled a moony song
To the echoing sound of a coppery gong,
In the shade of the mountains brown.
'O Timballo! How happy we are,
When we live in a Sieve and a crockery-jar,
And all night long in the moonlight pale,
We sail away with a pea-green sail,
In the shade of the mountains brown!'
Far and few, far and few,
Are the lands where the Jumblies live;
Their heads are green, and their hands are blue,
And they went to sea in a Sieve.

They sailed to the Western Sea, they did,
To a land all covered with trees,
And they bought an Owl, and a useful Cart,
And a pound of Rice, and a Cranberry Tart,
And a hive of silvery Bees.
And they bought a Pig, and some green Jack-daws,
And a lovely Monkey with lollipop paws,
And forty bottles of Ring-Bo-Ree,

And no end of Stilton Cheese.
Far and few, far and few,
Are the lands where the Jumblies live;
Their heads are green, and their hands are blue,
And they went to sea in a Sieve.

And in twenty years they all came back,
In twenty years or more,
And every one said, 'How tall they've grown!
For they've been to the Lakes, and the Torrible Zone,
And the hills of the Chankly Bore!'
And they drank their health, and gave them a feast
Of dumplings made of beautiful yeast;
And every one said, 'If we only live,
We too will go to sea in a Sieve,—
To the hills of the Chankly Bore!'
Far and few, far and few,
Are the lands where the Jumblies live;
Their heads are green, and their hands are blue,
And they went to sea in a Sieve.

The Land of Counterpane

Robert Louis Stevenson

When I was sick and lay a-bed,
I had two pillows at my head,
And all my toys beside me lay,
To keep me happy all the day.

And sometimes for an hour or so
I watched my leaden soldiers go,
With different uniforms and drills,
Among the bed-clothes, through the hills;

And sometimes sent my ships in fleets
All up and down among the sheets;
Or brought my trees and houses out,
And planted cities all about.

I was the giant great and still
That sits upon the pillow-hill,
And sees before him, dale and plain,
The pleasant land of counterpane.

The Smithy

Magda Maier

The smithy, the smithy,
A little black house,
With a little black cat
And a little black mouse.

The blacksmith, the blacksmith,
So big and so strong,
With a fine leather apron
Both broad and long.

He hammers once,
He hammers twice,—
Out runs the cat,
And out runs the mice.

The Builder

I'm a builder, brisk and sturdy,
Working at my trade,
I can show how bricks and mortar
Always should be laid.

Lay the first brick, so, and tap it,
Then put mortar on,
Place the next brick square across it,
That's the way it's done.

When we go to build a mansion,
Cellars first we dig,
Put the walls up straight and steady
With our scaffolds big.

Bricks we carry up by loadfuls,
On our shoulders so,
Up and down the ladders quickly
See us come and go.

On the roof smooth slates we fasten,
Nailing them quite tight.
Fix the chimney-pots securely
From the north wind's might.

Then when all the house is finished,
Shining in the sun,
Flags we hoist to tell the people,
That our work is done.

The Carpenter

I'll be a carpenter,
Working in wood,
Trying my best
To be clever and good.
Give me a hammer
And give me some nails,
See how I'll turn
Little posts into rails.

Then when the hammering
Will not succeed,
Some other method
Of work we shall need.
Bring me a screwdriver,
Bring me some screws,
These I will show you
I know how to use.

Then, if a mighty beam
Smaller should be,
Give me a saw,
And a sight you shall see.
Upwards and downwards
The saw will be drawn,
Till into pieces
The log has been sawn.

But if the ruggedness
Still should annoy,
Planing will soon every
Blemish destroy.
Backwards and forwards
I work with my plane,
Till not a splinter
Or knot shall remain.

The Ancient Elf

James Stephens

I am the maker,
The builder, the breaker,
The eagle-winged helper,
The speedy forsaker!

The lance and the lyre,
The water, the fire,
The tooth of oppression,
The lip of desire!

The snare and the wing,
The honey, the sting!
When you seek for me—look
For a different thing!

I, careless and gay,
Never mean what I say,
For my thoughts and my eyes
Look the opposite way!

Cradle Song

Sarojini Naidu

From groves of spice,
O'er fields of rice,
Athwart the lotus-stream,
    I bring for you,
    Aglint with dew,
A little lovely dream.

Sweet, shut your eyes,
The wild fireflies
Dance through the fairy neem;
    From the poppybole
    For you I stole
A little lovely dream.

Dear eyes, good night,
In golden light
The stars around you gleam;
    On you I press
    With soft caress
A little lovely dream.

Windy Nights

Robert Louis Stevenson

Whenever the moon and stars are set,
    Whenever the wind is high,
All night long in the dark and wet,
    A man goes riding by.
Late in the night when the fires are out,
Why does he gallop and gallop about?

Whenever the trees are crying aloud,
    And ships are tossed at sea,
By, on the highway, low and loud,
    By at the gallop goes he.
By at the gallop he goes, and then
By he comes back at the gallop again.

In Days Gone By

Ida M. Mills

I feel that in the days gone by
    I did not live with walls and roofs.
Long years ago in deserts dry
I lived beneath the open sky
    And heard the roar of thundering hoofs,
        And I was racing madly,
        My head bent to the wind,
        And fifty thousand horsemen
            Galloping behind!

I feel that in that long ago
    I must have been a Nomad child
Feeling the desert sun's fierce glow,
And then, in saddle, head bent low,
    Heading a horde of Bedouins wild.
        I shut my eyes an instant
        And see them in my mind,
        These fifty thousand horsemen
            Galloping, galloping,
        Fifty thousand horsemen
            Galloping behind!

Meg Merrilees

John Keats

Old Meg she was a Gypsy,
And lived upon the Moors:
Her bed it was the brown heath turf,
And her house was out of doors.

Her apples were swart blackberries,
Her currants, pods o' broom;
Her wine was dew of the wild white rose,
Her book a churchyard tomb.

Her Brothers were the craggy hills,
Her Sisters larchen trees—
Alone with her great family
She lived as she did please.

No breakfast had she many a morn,
No dinner many a noon,
And 'stead of supper she would stare
Full hard against the Moon.

But every morn of woodbine fresh
She made her garlanding,
And every night the dark glen Yew
She wove, and she would sing.

And with her fingers, old and brown,
She plaited Mats o' Rushes,
And gave them to the Cottagers
She met among the Bushes.

Old Meg was brave as Margaret Queen,
And tall as Amazon:
An old red blanket cloak she wore;
A chip-hat had she on.
God rest her aged bones somewhere—

She died full long agone!

Grim

Walter de la Mare

Beside the blaze of forty fires
Giant Grim doth sit,
Roasting a thick-woolled mountain sheep
Upon an iron spit.
Above him wheels the winter sky,
Beneath him, fathoms deep,
Lies hidden in the valley mists
A village fast asleep—
Save for one restive hungry dog
That, snuffing towards the height,
Smells Grim's broiled supper-meat, and spies
His watch-fire twinkling bright.

At the Keyhole

Walter de la Mare

"Grill me some bones," said the Cobbler,
"Some bones, my pretty Sue;
I'm tired of my lonesome with heels and soles,
Springsides and uppers too;
A mouse in the wainscot is nibbling;
A wind in the keyhole drones;
And a sheet webbed over my candle, Susie,—
Grill me some bones!"

"Grill me some bones," said the Cobbler,
I sat at my tic-tac-to;
And a footstep came to my door and stopped,
And a hand groped to and fro;
And I peered up over my boot and last;
And my feet went cold as stones:
I saw an eye at the keyhole, Susie!—
Grill me some bones!"

The Ballad of Semmerwater

Sir William Watson

Deep asleep, deep asleep,
Deep asleep it lies,
The still lake of Semmerwater
Under the still skies.

And many a fathom, many a fathom,
Many a fathom below,
In a king's tower and a queen's bower
The fishes come and go.

Once there stood by Semmerwater
A mickle town and tall;
King's tower and queen's bower
And the wakeman on the wall.

Came a beggar halt and sore:
"I faint for lack of bread!"
King's tower and queen's bower
Cast him forth unfed.

He knock'd at the door of the eller's cot,
The eller's cot in the dale.
They gave him of their oatcake,
They gave him of their ale.
He has cursed aloud that city proud,
He has cursed it in its pride;
He has cursed it into Semmerwater
Down the brant hillside;
He has cursed it into Semmerwater
There to bide.

King's tower and queen's bower,
And a mickle town and tall;
By glimmer of scale and gleam of fin,
Folk have seen them all.

King's tower and queen's bower,
And weed and reed in the gloom;
And a lost city in Semmerwater,
Deep asleep till Doom.

The Fairies Dancing

Walter de la Mare

I heard along the early hills,
    Ere yet the lark was risen up,
Ere yet the dawn with firelight fills
    The night-dew of the bramble-cup,—
I heard the fairies in a ring
    Sing as they tripped a lilting round
Soft as the moon on wavering wing.
    The starlight shook as if with sound,
As if with echoing, and the stars
    Prankt their bright eyes with trembling gleams
While red with war the gusty Mars
    Rained upon earth his ruddy beams.
He shone alone, low down the West,
    While I, behind a hawthorn-bush,
Watched on the fairies flaxen-tressed
    The fires of the morning flush.
Till, as a mist, their beauty died,
    Their singing shrill and fainter grew;
And daylight tremulous and wide
    Flooded the moorland through and through;
Till Urdon's copper weathercock
    Was reared in golden flame afar,
And dim from moonlit dreams awoke
    The towers and groves of Arroar.

The Arrow and the Song

Henry Wadsworth Longfellow

I shot an arrow into the air,
It fell to earth, I knew not where;
For, so swiftly it flew, the sight
Could not follow it in its flight.

I breathed a song into the air,
It fell to earth, I knew not where;
For who has sight so keen and strong,
That it can follow the flight of song?

Long, long afterward, in an oak
I found the arrow, still unbroke;
And the song, from beginning to end,
I found again in the heart of a friend.

Antonio

Laura E. Richards

Antonio, Antonio
Was tired of living alonio.
    He thought he would woo
    Miss Lissamy Lu,
Miss Lissamy Lucy Molonio.

Antonio, Antonio,
Rode off on his polo-ponio.
    He found the fair maid
    In a bowery shade,
A-sitting and knitting alonio.

Antonio, Antonio,
Said, "If you will be my ownio,
    I'll love you true,
    And I'll buy for you
An icery creamery conio!"

"Oh, *no*nio, Antonio!
You're far too bleak and bonio!
    And all that I wish,
    You singular fish,
Is that you will quickly begonio."

Antonio, Antonio,
He uttered a dismal moanio;
    Then he ran off and hid
    (Or I'm told that he did)
In the Anticatarctical Zonio.

Little Things

For want of a nail the shoe was lost,
For want of a shoe the horse was lost,
For want of a horse the rider was lost,
For want of a rider the battle was lost,
For want of a battle the kingdom was lost,
And all for the want of a horseshoe nail.

The Modern Hiawatha

George A. Strong

He killed the noble Mudjokivis.
Of the skin he made him mittens,
Made them with the fur side inside,
Made them with the skin side outside.
He, to get the warm side inside,
Put the inside skin side outside.
He, to get the cold side outside,
Put the warm side fur side inside.
That's why he put the fur side inside,
Why he put the skin side outside,
Why he turned them inside outside.

Lobster Quadrille

Lewis Carroll

"Will you walk a little faster?" said a whiting to a snail,
"There's a porpoise close behind us, and he's treading on my tail.
See how eagerly the lobsters and the turtles all advance!
They are waiting on the shingle—will you come and join the dance?
Will you, won't you, will you, won't you,
will you join the dance?
Will you, won't you, will you, won't you,
won't you join the dance?

"You can really have no notion how delightful it will be
When they take us up and throw us, with the lobsters, out to sea!"
But the snail replied, "Too far, too far!" and gave a look askance—
Said he thanked the whiting kindly, but he would not join the dance.
Would not, could not, would not, could not,
would not join the dance.
Would not, could not, would not, could not,
could not join the dance.

"What matters it how far we go?" his scaly friend replied.
"There is another shore, you know, upon the other side.
The further off from England the nearer is to France—
Then turn not pale, beloved snail, but come and join the dance.
Will you, won't you, will you, won't you,
will you join the dance?
Will you, won't you, will you, won't you,
won't you join the dance?"

Jabberwocky

Lewis Carroll

'Twas brillig, and the slithy toves
Did gyre and gimble in the wabe;
All mimsy were the borogoves,
And the mome raths outgrabe.

"Beware the Jabberwock, my son!
The jaws that bite, the claws that catch!
Beware the Jubjub bird, and shun
The frumious Bandersnatch!"

He took his vorpal sword in hand:
Long time the manxome foe he sought—
So rested he by the Tumtum tree,
And stood awhile in thought.

And as in uffish thought he stood,
The Jabberwock, with eyes of flame,
Came whiffling through the tulgey wood,
And burbled as it came!

One, two! One, two! and through and through
The vorpal blade went snicker-snack!
He left it dead, and with its head
He went galumphing back.

"And hast thou slain the Jabberwock?
Come to my arms, my beamish boy!
O frabjous day! Callooh! Callay!"
He chortled in his joy.

'Twas brillig, and the slithy toves
Did gyre and gimble in the wabe;
All mimsy were the borogoves,
And the mome raths outgrabe.

Portmanteau (port-MAN-toh) words are made by combining the sounds and meanings of two words, resulting in words such as "smog" and "brunch". In "Through the Looking-Glass and What Alice Found There", Humpty Dumpty explains the meaning of some of the poem's portmanteau words. He says that "slithy" is a combination of "slimy" and "lithe" (active and graceful). Humpty Dumpty explains the practice of combining words in various ways by telling Alice, "You see it's like a portmanteau—there are two meanings packed up into one word."

For instance, take the two words "fuming" and "furious". Make up your mind that you will say both words, but leave it unsettled which you will say first, if you have the rarest of gifts, a perfectly balanced mind, you will say "fumious". The word "portmanteau" itself was coined by Carroll.

Ozymandias

Percy Bysshe Shelley

I met a traveler from an antique land
Who said: Two vast and trunkless legs of stone
Stand in the desert. Near them, on the sand,
Half sunk, a shattered visage lies, whose frown,
And wrinkled lip, and sneer of cold command,
Tell that its sculptor well those passions read
Which yet survive, stamped on these lifeless things,
The hand that mocked them, and the heart that fed;
And on the pedestal these words appear:
"My name is Ozymandias, king of kings:
Look on my works, ye Mighty, and despair!"
Nothing beside remains. Round the decay
Of that colossal wreck, boundless and bare
The lone and level sands stretch far away.

Ozymandias, another name for Ramesses the Great, Pharaoh of the nineteenth dynasty of ancient Egypt, represents a transliteration into Greek of a part of Ramesses' throne name, User-maat-re Setep-en-re. The sonnet paraphrases the inscription on the base of the statue; "King of Kings am I, Osymandias. If anyone would know how great I am and where I lie, let him surpass one of my works." The name Ozymandias should be pronounced with four syllables in the tenth line in order to fit the poem's meter.

The Kraken

Alfred, Lord Tennyson

Below the thunders of the upper deep;
Far, far beneath in the abysmal sea,
His ancient, dreamless, uninvaded sleep
The Kraken sleepeth: faintest sunlights flee
About his shadowy sides: above him swell
Huge sponges of millennial growth and height;
And far away into the sickly light,
From many a wondrous grot and secret cell
Unnumber'd and enormous polypi
Winnow with giant arms the slumbering green.
There hath he lain for ages and will lie
Battening upon huge seaworms in his sleep,
Until the latter fire shall heat the deep;
Then once by man and angels to be seen,
In roaring he shall rise and on the surface die.

A Song of Sherwood

Alfred Noyes

Sherwood in the twilight, is Robin Hood awake?
Grey and ghostly shadows are gliding through the brake;
Shadows of the dappled deer, dreaming of the morn,
Dreaming of a shadowy man that winds a shadowy horn.

Robin Hood is here again: all his merry thieves
Hear a ghostly bugle-note shivering through the leaves,
Calling as he used to call, faint and far away,
In Sherwood, in Sherwood, about the break of day.

Merry, merry England has kissed the lips of June:
All the wings of fairyland were here beneath the moon;
Like a flight of rose-leaves fluttering in a mist
Of opal and ruby and pearl and amethyst.

Merry, merry England is waking as of old,
With eyes of blither hazel and hair of brighter gold:
For Robin Hood is here again beneath the bursting spray
In Sherwood, in Sherwood, about the break of day.

Love is in the greenwood building him a house
Of wild rose and hawthorn and honeysuckle boughs;
Love it in the greenwood: dawn is in the skies;
And Marian is waiting with a glory in her eyes.

Hark! The dazzled laverock climbs the golden steep:
Marian is waiting: is Robin Hood asleep?
Round the fairy grass-rings frolic elf and fay,
In Sherwood, in Sherwood, about the break of day.

Oberon, Oberon, rake away the gold,
Rake away the red leaves, roll away the mould,
Rake away the gold leaves, roll away the red,
And wake Will Scarlett from his leafy forest bed.

Friar Tuck and Little John are riding down together
With quarter-staff and drinking-can and grey goose-feather;
The dead are coming back again; the years are rolled away
In Sherwood, in Sherwood, about the break of day.

Softly over Sherwood the south wind blows;
All the heart of England hid in every rose
Hears across the greenwood the sunny whisper leap,
Sherwood in the red dawn, is Robin Hood asleep?

Hark, the voice of England wakes him as of old
And, shattering the silence with a cry of brighter gold,
Bugles in the greenwood echo from the steep,
Sherwood in the red dawn, is Robin Hood asleep?

Where the deer are gliding down the shadowy glen
All across the glades of fern he calls his merry men;
Doublets of the Lincoln green glancing through the May,
In Sherwood, in Sherwood, about the break of day;

Calls them and they answer: from aisles of oak and ash
Rings the Follow! Follow! and the boughs begin to crash;
The ferns begin to flutter and the flowers begin to fly;
And through the crimson dawning the robber band goes by.

Robin! Robin! Robin! All his merry thieves
Answer as the bugle-note shivers through the leaves:
Calling as he used to call, faint and far away,
In Sherwood, in Sherwood, about the break of day.

Abou Ben Adhem

Leigh Hunt

Abou Ben Adhem (may his tribe increase!)
Awoke one night from a deep dream of peace,
And saw, within the moonlight in his room,
Making it rich, and like a lily in bloom,
An Angel writing in a book of gold:

Exceeding peace had made Ben Adhem bold,
And to the Presence in the room he said,
"What writest thou?" The Vision raised its head,
And with a look made of all sweet accord
Answered, "The names of those who love the Lord."

"And is mine one?" said Abou. "Nay, not so,"
Replied the Angel. Abou spoke more low,
But cheerily still; and said, "I pray thee, then,
Write me as one who loves his fellow men."

The Angel wrote, and vanished. The next night
It came again with a great wakening light,
And showed the names whom love of God had blessed,
And, lo! Ben Adhem's name led all the rest!

The Way Through the Woods

Rudyard Kipling

They shut the road through the woods
Seventy years ago.
Weather and rain have undone it again,
And now you would never know
There was once a road through the woods
Before they planted the trees.
It is underneath the coppice and heath,
And the thin anemones.
Only the keeper sees
That, where the ring-dove broods,
And the badgers roll at ease,
There was once a road through the woods.

Yet, if you enter the woods
Of a summer evening late,
When the night-air cools on the trout-ringed pools
Where the otter whistles his mate.
(They fear not men in the woods,
Because they see so few)
You will hear the beat of a horse's feet,
And the swish of a skirt in the dew,
Steadily cantering through
The misty solitudes,
As though they perfectly knew
The old lost road through the woods…
But there is no road through the woods.

Kubla Khan

Samuel Taylor Coleridge

Or a Vision in a Dream. A Fragment.

In Xanadu did Kubla Khan
A stately pleasure-dome decree:
Where Alph, the sacred river, ran
Through caverns measureless to man
Down to a sunless sea.
So twice five miles of fertile ground
With walls and towers were girdled round:
And there were gardens bright with sinuous rills,
Where blossomed many an incense-bearing tree;
And here were forests ancient as the hills,
Enfolding sunny spots of greenery.

But oh ! that deep romantic chasm which slanted
Down the green hill athwart a cedarn cover!
A savage place ! as holy and enchanted
As e'er beneath a waning moon was haunted
By woman wailing for her demon-lover!
And from this chasm, with ceaseless turmoil seething,
As if this earth in fast thick pants were breathing,
A mighty fountain momently was forced:
Amid whose swift half-intermitted burst
Huge fragments vaulted like rebounding hail,
Or chaffy grain beneath the thresher's flail:
And 'mid these dancing rocks at once and ever
It flung up momently the sacred river.
Five miles meandering with a mazy motion
Through wood and dale the sacred river ran,
Then reached the caverns measureless to man,
And sank in tumult to a lifeless ocean:
And 'mid this tumult Kubla heard from far
Ancestral voices prophesying war!
The shadow of the dome of pleasure
Floated midway on the waves;
Where was heard the mingled measure
From the fountain and the caves.
It was a miracle of rare device,
A sunny pleasure-dome with caves of ice!

A damsel with a dulcimer
In a vision once I saw:
It was an Abyssinian maid,
And on her dulcimer she played,
Singing of Mount Abora.
Could I revive within me
Her symphony and song,
To such a deep delight 'twould win me,
That with music loud and long,
I would build that dome in air,
That sunny dome ! those caves of ice!
And all who heard should see them there,
And all should cry, Beware! Beware!
His flashing eyes, his floating hair!
Weave a circle round him thrice,
And close your eyes with holy dread,
For he on honey-dew hath fed,
And drunk the milk of Paradise.

La Belle Dame sans Merci: A Ballad

John Keats

Oh what can ail thee, knight-at-arms,
Alone and palely loitering?
The sedge has withered from the lake,
And no birds sing.

Oh what can ail thee, knight-at-arms,
So haggard and so woe-begone?
The squirrel's granary is full,
And the harvest's done.

I see a lily on thy brow,
With anguish moist and fever-dew,
And on thy cheeks a fading rose
Fast withereth too.

I met a lady in the meads,
Full beautiful—a faery's child,
Her hair was long, her foot was light,
And her eyes were wild.

I made a garland for her head,
And bracelets too, and fragrant zone;
She looked at me as she did love,
And made sweet moan.

I set her on my pacing steed,
And nothing else saw all day long,
For sidelong would she bend, and sing
A faery's song.

She found me roots of relish sweet,
And honey wild, and manna dew,
And sure in language strange she said—
"I love thee true."

She took me to her elfin grot,
And there she wept and sighed full sore,
And there I shut her wild wild eyes
With kisses four.

And there she lulled me asleep
And there I dream'd—Ah! woe betide!
The latest dream I ever dream'd
On the cold hill's side.

I saw pale kings and princes too,
Pale warriors, death-pale were they all;
They cried—*La Belle Dame sans Merci*
Hath thee in thrall!'

I saw their starved lips in the gloam,
With horrid warning gaped wide,
And I awoke and found me here,
On the cold hill's side.

And this is why I sojourn here
Alone and palely loitering,
Though the sedge is wither'd from the lake,
And no birds sing.

The Listeners

Walter de la Mare

"Is there anybody there?" said the Traveller,
    Knocking on the moonlit door;
And his horse in the silence champed the grasses
    Of the forest's ferny floor:
And a bird flew up out of the turret,
    Above the Traveller's head:
And he smote upon the door again a second time;
    "Is there anybody there?" he said.
But no one descended to the Traveller;
    No head from the leaf-fringed sill
Leaned over and looked into his grey eyes,
    Where he stood perplexed and still.
But only a host of phantom listeners
    That dwelt in the lone house then
Stood listening in the quiet of the moonlight
    To that voice from the world of men:
Stood thronging the faint moonbeams on the dark stair,
    That goes down to the empty hall,
Hearkening in an air stirred and shaken
    By the lonely Traveller's call.
And he felt in his heart their strangeness,
    Their stillness answering his cry,
While his horse moved, cropping the dark turf,
    'Neath the starred and leafy sky;
For he suddenly smote on the door, even
    Louder, and lifted his head:—
"Tell them I came, and no one answered,
    That I kept my word," he said.
Never the least stir made the listeners,
    Though every word he spake
Fell echoing through the shadowiness of the still house
    From the one man left awake:
Ay, they heard his foot upon the stirrup,
    And the sound of iron on stone,
And how the silence surged softly backward,
    When the plunging hoofs were gone.

The Mermaid

Alfred, Lord Tennyson

Who would be
A mermaid fair,
Singing alone,
Combing her hair
Under the sea,
In a golden curl
With a comb of pearl,
On a throne?

I would be a mermaid fair;
I would sing to myself the whole of the day;
With a comb of pearl I would comb my hair;
And still as I comb'd I would sing and say,
'Who is it loves me? who loves not me?'
I would comb my hair till my ringlets would fall
Low adown, low adown,
From under my starry sea-bud crown
Low adown and around,
And I should look like a fountain of gold
Springing alone
With a shrill inner sound
Over the throne
In the midst of the hall;
Till that great sea-snake under the sea
From his coiled sleeps in the central deeps
Would slowly trail himself sevenfold
Round the hall where I sate, and look in at the gate
With his large calm eyes for the love of me.
And all the mermen under the sea
Would feel their immortality
Die in their hearts for the love of me.

A Smuggler's Song

Rudyard Kipling

If you wake at midnight, and hear a horse's feet,
Don't go drawing back the blind, or looking in the street.
Them that ask no questions isn't told a lie.
Watch the wall, my darling, while the Gentlemen go by!
    Five and twenty ponies,
    Trotting through the dark—
    Brandy for the Parson,
    'Baccy for the Clerk;
    Laces for a lady, letters for a spy,
And watch the wall, my darling, while the Gentlemen go by!

Running round the woodlump if you chance to find
Little barrels, roped and tarred, all full of brandy-wine,
Don't you shout to come and look, nor use 'em for your play.
Put the brushwood back again—and they'll be gone next day!

If you see the stable-door setting open wide;
If you see a tired horse lying down inside;
If your mother mends a coat cut about and tore;
If the lining's wet and warm—don't you ask no more!

If you meet King George's men, dressed in blue and red,
You be careful what you say, and mindful what is said.
If they call you "pretty maid," and chuck you 'neath the chin,
Don't you tell where no one is, nor yet where no one's been!

Knocks and footsteps round the house—whistles after dark—
You've no call for running out till the house-dogs bark.
Trusty's here, and *Pincher's* here, and see how dumb they lie—
They don't fret to follow when the Gentlemen go by!

If you do as you've been told, likely there's a chance,
You'll be given a dainty doll, all the way from France,
With a cap of Valenciennes, and a velvet hood—
A present from the Gentlemen, along o' being good!
    Five and twenty ponies,
    Trotting through the dark—
    Brandy for the Parson,
    'Baccy for the Clerk;
Them that asks no questions isn't told a lie—
Watch the wall, my darling, while the Gentlemen go by.

Sea-Fever

John Masefield

I must down to the seas again, to the lonely sea and the sky,
And all I ask is a tall ship and a star to steer her by,
And the wheel's kick and the wind's song and the white sail's shaking,
And a grey mist on the sea's face, and a grey dawn breaking.

I must down to the seas again, for the call of the running tide
Is a wild call and a clear call that may not be denied;
And all I ask is a windy day with the white clouds flying,
And the flung spray and the blown spume, and the sea-gulls crying.

I must down to the seas again, to the vagrant gypsy life,
To the gull's way and the whale's way where the wind's like a whetted knife;
And all I ask is a merry yarn from a laughing fellow-rover
And quiet sleep and a sweet dream when the long trick's over.

The Splendor Falls

Alfred, Lord Tennyson

The splendor falls on castle walls
    And snowy summits old in story:
The long light shakes across the lakes
    And the wild cataract leaps in glory.
Blow, bugle, blow, set the wild echoes flying,
Blow, bugle; answer, echoes dying, dying, dying.

O hark, O hear! how thin and clear,
    And thinner, clearer, farther going!
O sweet and far from cliff and scar
    The horns of Elfland faintly blowing!
Blow, let us hear the purple glens replying,
Blow, bugle; answer, echoes dying, dying, dying.

O love they die in yon rich sky,
    They faint on hill or field, or river:
Our echoes roll from soul to soul,
    And grow forever and forever.
Blow, bugle, blow, set the wild echoes flying,
And answer, echoes, answer, dying, dying, dying.

The Lake Isle of Innisfree

William Butler Yeats

I will arise and go now, and go to Innisfree,
And a small cabin build there, of clay and wattles made;
Nine bean rows will I have there, a hive for the honeybee,
And live alone in the bee-loud glade.

And I shall have some peace there, for peace comes dropping slow,
Dropping from the veils of the morning to where the cricket sings;
There midnight's all a-glimmer, and noon a purple glow,
And evening full of the linnet's wings.

I will arise and go now, for always night and day
I hear lake water lapping with low sounds by the shore;
While I stand on the roadway, or on the pavements gray,
I hear it in the deep heart's core.

Peace

Sara Teasdale

Peace flows into me
As the tide to the pool by the shore;
It is mine forevermore,
It ebbs not back like the sea.

I am the pool of blue
That worships the vivid sky;
My hopes were heaven-high,
They are all fulfilled in you.

I am the pool of gold
When sunset burns and dies,—
You are my deepening skies,
Give me your stars to hold.

Sun, Moon, Earth & Stars

Stars and Daisies

Frank Dempster Sherman

At evening when I go to bed
I see the stars shine overhead;
They are the little daisies white
That dot the meadow of the Night.

And often while I'm dreaming so,
Across the sky the Moon will go;
It is a lady, sweet and fair,
Who comes to gather daisies there.

For, when at morning I arise,
There's not a star left in the skies;
She's picked them all and dropped them down
Into the meadows of the town.

The Star

Jane Taylor

Twinkle, twinkle, little star,
How I wonder what you are!
Up above the world so high,
Like a diamond in the sky!

When the blazing sun is gone,
When he nothing shines upon,
Then you show your little light,
Twinkle, twinkle, all the night.

Then the traveller in the dark,
Thanks you for your tiny spark,
He could not see which way to go,
If you did not twinkle so.

In the dark blue sky you keep,
And often through my curtains peep,
For you never shut your eye,
Till the sun is in the sky.

As your bright and tiny spark,
Lights the traveller in the dark,—
Though I know not what you are,
Twinkle, twinkle, little star.

The Sun Is in My Heart

A. C. Harwood

The Sun is in my heart,
He warms me with his power,
And wakens, wakens life and love
In bird and beast and flower,
In bird and beast and flower.

The stars above my head
Are shining in my mind
As spirits, spirits of the world
That in my thought I find,
That in my thought I find.

The earth whereon I tread
Lets not my feet go through,
But strongly, strongly doth uphold
The weight of deeds I do,
The weight of deeds I do.

Then must I thankful be
That man on earth I dwell,
To know, to know and love the world,
And work all creatures well,
And work all creatures well.

The Early Morning

Hilaire Belloc

The moon on the one hand, the dawn on the other:
The moon is my sister, the dawn is my brother.
The moon on my left and the dawn on my right.
My brother, good morning: my sister, good night.

A Sun Like Thee

Eileen Hutchins

May our eyes shine
With light like thine,
May our hearts know
Thy warming glow,
May our hands give
Such strength to live,
That we may be
A sun like Thee.

Hymn to the Sun from Akbar's Dream

Alfred, Lord Tennyson

Once again thou flamest heavenward; once again we see thee rise.
Every morning is thy birthday gladdening human hearts and eyes.
Every morning here we greet it, bowing lowly down before thee,
Thee the Godlike, thee the changeless in thine ever-changing skies.

Shadow-maker, shadow-slayer, arrowing light from clime to clime,
Hear thy myriad laureates hail thee monarch in their woodland rhyme.
Warble bird, and open flower, and, men below the dome of azure
Kneel adoring Him the Timeless in the flame that measures Time!

Light—All Creating

Margaret Morgan

Into the world it streams—
Illuminating;
Directness it pursues—
Vindicating;
From captivity it escapes—
Liberating;
Illusion it loves to weave—
Intoxicating;
Life and warmth it bears—
Generating;
Into being it bursts—
Irradiating;

Light—all creating.

The Creation

Cecil Frances Alexander

All things bright and beautiful,
All creatures great and small,
All things wise and wonderful,
The Lord God made them all.

Each little flower that opens,
Each little bird that sings,
He made their glowing colours,
He made their tiny wings.

The rich man in his castle,
The poor man at his gate,
God made them, high or lowly,
And ordered their estate.

The purple-headed mountain,
The river running by,
The sunset, and the morning,
That brightens up the sky;

The cold wind in the winter,
The pleasant summer sun,
The ripe fruits in the garden,
He made them every one.

The tall trees in the greenwood,
The meadows where we play,
The rushes by the water,
We gather every day;—

He gave us eyes to see them,
And lips that we might tell,
How great is God Almighty,
Who has made all things well.

Song for the Sun That Disappeared Behind the Rainclouds

Khoikhoi Oral Tradition

The fire darkens, the wood turns black.
The flame extinguishes, misfortune upon us.
God sets out in search of the sun.
The rainbow sparkles in his hand,
The bow of the divine hunter.
He has heard the lamentations of his children.
He walks along the milky way, he collects the stars.
With quick arms he piles them into a basket
Piles them up with quick arms
Like a woman who collects lizards
And piles them into her pot, piles them
Until the pot overflows with lizards
Until the basket overflows with light.

O Lady Moon

Christina Rossetti

O Lady Moon, your horns point toward the east:
    Shine, be increased;
O Lady Moon, your horns point toward the west:
    Wane, be at rest.

What the Little Girl Said

Vachel Lindsay

The Moon's the North wind's cooky.
He bites it, day by day,
Until there's but a rim of scraps
That crumble all away.

The South wind is a baker.
He kneads clouds in his den,
And bakes a crisp new moon THAT . . . GREEDY
NORTH . . . WIND . . . EATS . . . AGAIN!

The Moon

Robert Louis Stevenson

The moon has a face like the clock in the hall;
She shines on thieves on the garden wall,
On streets and fields and harbour quays,
And birdies asleep in the forks of the trees.

The squalling cat and the squeaking mouse,
The howling dog by the door of the house,
The bat that lies in bed at noon,
All love to be out by the light of the moon.

But all of the things that belong to the day
Cuddle to sleep to be out of her way;
And flowers and children close their eyes
Till up in the morning the sun shall arise.

Lady Moon

Richard Monckton Milnes

"Lady Moon, Lady Moon, where are you roving?"
"Over the sea."
"Lady Moon, Lady Moon, whom are you loving?"
"All that love me."

"Are you not tired with rolling and never
Resting to sleep?
Why look so pale and so sad, as for ever
Wishing to weep?"

"Ask me not this, little child, if you love me;
You are too bold.
I must obey my dear Father above me,
And do as I'm told."

"Lady Moon, Lady Moon, where are you roving?"
"Over the sea."
"Lady Moon, Lady Moon, whom are you loving?"
"All that love me."

Silver

Walter de la Mare

Slowly, silently, now the moon
Walks the night in her silver shoon:
This way, and that, she peers and sees
Silver fruit upon silver trees;
One by one the casements catch
Her beams beneath the silvery thatch;
Couched in his kennel, like a log,
With paws of silver sleeps the dog
From their shadowy cote the white breasts peep
Of doves in a silver-feathered sleep;
A harvest mouse goes scampering by,
With silver claws and silver eye;
And moveless fish in the water gleam
By silver reeds in a silver stream.

The Wind and the Moon

George MacDonald

Said the Wind to the Moon, "I will blow you out,
    You stare
        In the air
            Like a ghost in a chair,
Always looking what I am about—
I hate to be watched; I'll blow you out."

The Wind blew hard, and out went the Moon.
    So, deep
        On a heap
            Of clouds, to sleep
Down lay the Wind, and slumbered soon,
Muttering low, "I've done for that Moon."

He turned in his bed; she was there again!
    On high
        In the sky,
            With her one ghost eye,
The Moon shone white and alive and plain.
Said the Wind, "I will blow you out again."

The Wind blew hard, and the Moon grew dim.
  "With my sledge
    And my wedge
      I have knocked off her edge!
If only I blow right fierce and grim,
The creature will soon be dimmer than dim."

He blew and he blew, and she thinned to a thread
  "One puff
    More's enough
      To blow her to snuff!
One good puff more where the last was bred,
And glimmer, glimmer glum will go the thread."

He blew a great blast, and the thread was gone;
  In the air
    Nowhere
      Was a moonbeam bare;
Far off and harmless the shy stars shone—
Sure and certain the Moon was gone!

The Wind he took to his revels once more:
  On down,
    In town,
      Like a merry-mad clown,
He leaped and hallooed with whistle and roar—
"What's that?" The glimmering thread once more!

He flew in a rage—he danced and blew;
  But in vain
    Was the pain
      Of his bursting brain;
For still the broader the Moon-scrap grew,
The broader he swelled his big cheeks and blew.

Slowly she grew—till she filled the night,
  And shone
    On her throne
      In the sky alone,
A matchless, wonderful, silvery light,
Radiant and lovely, the queen of the night.

Said the Wind: "What a marvel of power am I!
With my breath,
Good faith!
I blew her to death—
First blew her away right out of the sky—
Then blew her in; what a strength have I!"

But the Moon she knew nothing about the affair,
For, high
In the sky,
With her one white eye,
Motionless, miles above the air,
She had never heard the great Wind blare.

One Misty Moisty Morning

One misty moisty morning
When cloudy was the weather,
I met with an old man
A-clothèd all in leather,

He was clothèd all in leather
With a cap beneath his chin,
Singing, "How do you do
And how do you do
And how do you do again."

Whether the Weather

Whether the weather be fine,
Or whether the weather be not,
Whether the weather be cold,
Or whether the weather be hot,
We'll weather the weather
Whatever the weather,
Whether we like it or not!

Who Has Seen the Wind?

Christina Rossetti

Who has seen the wind?
Neither I nor you:
But when the leaves hang trembling
The wind is passing through.

Who has seen the wind?
Neither you nor I:
But when the trees bow down their heads
The wind is passing by.

An Emerald Is as Green as Grass

Christina Rossetti

An emerald is as green as grass;
    A ruby red as blood;
A sapphire shines as blue as heaven;
    A flint lies in the mud.

A diamond is a brilliant stone,
    To catch the world's desire;
An opal holds a fiery spark;
    But a flint holds fire.

Fog

Carl Sandburg

The fog comes
on little cat feet.

It sits looking
over harbor and city
on silent haunches
and then moves on.

This Is My Garden

This is my garden;
Extend one hand forward, palm up
I'll rake it with care,
Make raking motion on palm with other hand
And then some flower seeds,
I'll plant everywhere.
Planting motion

The sun will shine,
Make circle with hands
And the rain will fall,
Let fingers flutter down to lap
And my garden will blossom
Cup hands together, extend upward slowly
And grow straight and tall.

Farming

Margaret Morgan

To dig the ditch, to plough the land,
To this the farmer turns his hand.

To sow the seed, to hoe and weed,
To give the plants the light they need.

To milk the cows, to feed the hens,
To clean the pigs within their pens.

To cut the corn, to store the grain,
To bring the sheep to be sheared again.

To care for the soil, to let it rest,
To feed it—so it gives its best.

To grow good food for beast and man;
The farmer works as best he can.

The Ploughman's Charm

Traditional

Here is the remedy how thou mayest cure thy land if it refuses to bear or if ought untoward hath befallen it by way of witchcraft or sorcery. Strew seed on the body of the plough and repeat these words:

Erce, Erce, Erce, Mother of Earth!
May the Almighty Lord Everlasting
Grant thee fields, green and fertile,
Grant thee fields, fruitful and growing,
Hosts of spear shafts, shining harvests,
Harvest of barley the broad,
Harvest of wheat the white,
All the heaping harvests of Earth!

May the Almighty Lord Everlasting
And His holy saints in heaven above,
From friend and foe defend this land,
Keep it from blight and coming of harm,
From spell of witches, wickedly spread.
Now I pray the Almighty who made this work
That malice of man, or mouth of woman
Never may weaken the words I have spoken.

Start the plough and when the first furrow is turned, say:

Hail to thee, Earth, Mother of Men!
Grow and be great in God's embrace,
Filled with fruit for the food of men.

Knead a loaf of bread with milk and holy water, lay it under the first furrow and say:

Field, be full of food for men,
Blossom bright, for blessed thou art.
In the name of the Holy who made the heavens,
Created the earth whereon we live,
God who gavest this ground,
Grant us growth and increase.
Let each seed that is sown, sprout and be useful.

Vainamoinen's Sowing

from the Kalevala
translated by W. F. Kirby

Then he went to sow the country,
And to scatter seeds around him,
And he spoke the words which follow:
"Now I stoop the seeds to scatter,
As from the Creator's fingers,
From the hand of Him Almighty,
That the country may be fertile,
And the corn may grow and flourish.

"Patroness of lowland country,
Old one of the plains, Earth-Mother,
Let the tender blade spring upward,
Let the earth support and cherish.
Might of earth will never fail us,
Never while the earth existeth,
When the Givers are propitious,
And Creation's daughters aid us.

"Rise, O earth, from out thy slumber,
Field of the Creator, rouse thee,
Make the blade arise and flourish,
Let the stalks grow up and lengthen,
That the ears may grow by thousands,
Yet a hundredfold increasing,
By my ploughing and my sowing,
In return for all my labour.

"Ukko, thou of Gods the highest,
Father, thou in heaven abiding,
Thou to whom the clouds are subject,
Of the scattered clouds the ruler,
All thy clouds do thou assemble,
In the light make clear thy counsel,
Send thou forth a cloud from eastward,
In the north-west let one gather,
Send thou others from the westward,
Let them drive along from southward,
Send the light rain forth from heaven,
Let the clouds distil with honey,
That the corn may sprout up strongly,
And the stalks may wave and rustle."

Ukko, then, of Gods the highest,
Father of the highest heaven,
Heard, and all the clouds assembled,
In the light made clear his counsel,
And he sent a cloud from eastward,
In the north-west let one gather,
Others, too, he sent from westward,
Let them drive along from southward,
Linked them edge to edge together,
And he closed the rifts between them.
The he sent the rain from heaven,
And the clouds distilled sweet honey,
That the corn might sprout up stronger,
And the stalks might wave and rustle,
Thus the sprouting germ was nourished,
And the rustling stalks grew upward,
From the soft earth of the cornfield,
Through the toil of Väinämöinen.

The River

Molly de Havas

I spring within a moss-grown dell
on rugged mountain land,
Where only stunted pine trees,
shallow rooted stand,
And slow I grow with melted snow
from peaks on either hand.

I choose myself the quickest path
to find my way downhill,
And all the time from every side
new trickles swell my rill,
From sodden peat and cloudy mist
I draw the water chill.

I ripple over pebbles,
over waterfalls I leap,
I speed through narrow clefts where I
must dig my channel deep,
Then through the valley meadowlands
in placid curves I sweep.

Small fish live within me,
in my reeds the wildfowl nest;
Kingfisher, rat and otter
in my banks may safely rest,
And all poor weary creatures
are by crystal waters best.

Sometimes my sparkling clarity
is hidden by a frown,
Of dirt and oil and rubbish,
as I pass a busy town;
And sometimes little boats I bear
with sails of white or brown.

At last I reach a shady shore
whereon great waves foam,
By nature bound, yet ever free,
I need no longer roam,
The path designed I followed
to the sea which is my home.

The Brook

Alfred, Lord Tennyson

I come from haunts of coot and hern,
I make a sudden sally
And sparkle out among the fern,
To bicker down a valley.

By thirty hills I hurry down,
Or slip between the ridges,
By twenty thorps, a little town,
And half a hundred bridges.

Till last by Philip's farm I flow
To join the brimming river,
For men may come and men may go,
But I go on forever.

I chatter over stony ways,
In little sharps and trebles,
I bubble into eddying bays,
I babble on the pebbles.

With many a curve my banks I fret
    By many a field and fallow,
And many a fairy foreland set
    With willow-weed and mallow.

I chatter, chatter, as I flow
    To join the brimming river,
For men may come and men may go,
    But I go on forever.

I wind about, and in and out,
    With here a blossom sailing,
And here and there a lusty trout,
    And here and there a grayling,

And here and there a foamy flake
    Upon me, as I travel
With many a silvery waterbreak
    Above the golden gravel,

And draw them all along, and flow
    To join the brimming river
For men may come and men may go,
    But I go on forever.

I steal by lawns and grassy plots,
    I slide by hazel-covers;
I move the sweet forget-me-nots
    That grow for happy lovers.

I slip, I slide, I gloom, I glance,
    Among my skimming swallows;
I make the netted sunbeam dance
    Against my sandy shallows.

I murmur under moon and stars
    In brambly wildernesses;
I linger by my shingly bars;
    I loiter round my cresses;

And out again I curve and flow
    To join the brimming river,
For men may come and men may go,
    But I go on forever.

FROM The Cloud

Percy Bysshe Shelley

I bring fresh showers for the thirsting flowers,
From the seas and the streams;
I bear light shade for the leaves when laid
In their noonday dreams.
From my wings are shaken the dews that waken
The sweet buds every one,
When rocked to rest on their mother's breast,
As she dances about the sun.
I wield the flail of the lashing hail,
And whiten the green plains under,
And then again I dissolve it in rain,
And laugh as I pass in thunder.

I sift the snow on the mountains below,
And their great pines groan aghast;
And all the night 'tis my pillow white,
While I sleep in the arms of the blast.
Sublime on the towers of my skiey bowers,
Lightning my pilot sits,
In a cavern under is fretted the thunder,
It struggles and howls at fits;
Over earth and ocean, with gentle motion,
This pilot is guiding me,
Lured by the love of the genii that move
In the depths of the purple sea;
Over the rills, and the crags, and the hills,
Over the lakes and the plains,
Wherever he dream, under mountain or stream
The Spirit he loves remains;
And I all the while bask in Heaven's blue smile,
Whilst he is dissolving in rains.

from Ode to the West Wind

Percy Bysshe Shelley

O wild West Wind, thou breath of Autumn's being,
Thou from whose unseen presence the leaves dead
Are driven, like ghosts from an enchanter fleeing,

Yellow, and black, and pale, and hectic red,
Pestilence-stricken multitudes: O thou,
Who chariotest to their dark wintry bed

The wingèd seeds, where they lie cold and low,
Each like a corpse within its grave, until
Thine azure sister of the spring shall blow

Her clarion o'er the dreaming earth, and fill
(Driving sweet buds like flocks to feed in air)
With living hues and odours plain and hill:
Wild Spirit, which art moving every where;

Destroyer and Preserver; hear, O hear!
Drive my dead thoughts over the universe
Like withered leaves to quicken a new birth!
And, by the incantation of this verse,

Scatter, as from an unextinguished hearth
Ashes and sparks, my words among mankind!
Be through my lips to unawakened earth

The trumpet of a prophecy! O wind,
If Winter comes, can Spring be far behind?

Gold!

Thomas Hood

Gold! gold! gold! gold!
Bright and yellow, hard and cold,
Molten, graven, hammered and rolled;
Heavy to get, and light to hold;
Hoarded, bartered, bought, and sold,
Stolen, borrowed, squandered, doled:
Spurned by the young, but hugged by the old
To the very verge of the church-yard mould;
Price of many a crime untold:
Gold! gold! gold! gold!

Some Rivers

Frank Asch

Some rivers rush to the sea.
They push and tumble and fall.
But the Everglades is a river
with no hurry in her at all.
Soaking the cypress
that grows so tall;
nursing a frog,
so quiet and small;
she flows but a mile
in the course of a day,
with plenty of time
to think on the way.
But how can she cope
with the acres of corn
and sorrowful cities that drain her?
With hunters and tourists and levees
that chain and stain and pain her?
Does the half of her that's left
think only of the past?
Or does she think of her future
and how long it will last?
Some rivers rush to the sea.
They push and tumble and fall.
But the Everglades is a river
with no hurry in her at all.

Alaska

Joaquin Miller

Ice built, ice bound, and ice bounded,
Such cold seas of silence! such room!
Such snow-light, such sea-light, confounded
With thunders that smite like a doom!
Such grandeur! such glory! such gloom!
Hear that boom! Hear that deep distant boom
Of an avalanche hurled
Down this unfinished world!

Ice seas! and ice summits! ice spaces
In splendor of white, as God's throne!
Ice worlds to the pole! and ice places
Untracked, and unnamed, and unknown!
Hear that boom! Hear the grinding, the groan
Of the ice-gods in pain! Hear the moan
Of yon ice mountain hurled
Down this unfinished world!

Manahatta's Musings

Eugene Schwartz

I am the majestic Hudson,
Born out of fire and ice,
I am Manitou's daughter,
The Mother of Waters,
I greet Brother Sun at his rise.

I once was a river of fire,
Volcanoes ruled then—wild, untamed;
Molten stone flowed,
For ages untold,
And my blazing banks flickered, aflame.

Those smoldering peaks spewed and sputtered
Thick vapors of smothering smoke;
From my heights to my deeps
I shuddered in sleep
When with a loud CLAP! I awoke.

From the northlands grim glaciers descended,
In their grip all grew solid and still;
Cracking and crushing,
Pounding and pushing,
My mountains gave way to their will.

Those fierce frosty sculptors sliced through me,
Scooped stone and sand out of my depths,
In their pulverized play
They ground rocks into clay
As the Palisades rose in the west.

The ice melted and water coursed through me,
From bubbling brooks and swift streams,
It crashed in cascades,
Splashed past Palisades,
'Til into the sea it careened.

Though I now seem to stream so serenely,
Ice and fire wrestle still in my veins,
And when the salty sea's force
Mingles with my fresh source;
When the lightning's bright flash
And Storm King's cold crag clash;
When my brittle ice crumbles
And the Dunderberg rumbles,
You will hear my ancient name:
Manahatta, Mother of Waters,
Manitou's mighty daughter...
I am the majestic Hudson!

In the Mountains

Eugene Schwartz

Though dark the night, we move in light
Amidst the radiant mountain peaks;
Earth's crystal gaze, subdued by day,
At night reflecting starlight seeks.

This rock kingdom, seemingly dumb,
To wakeful ears is sounding;
Each crag to each thunderously speaks,
'Gainst vales each voice rebounding.

In limestone's chill and crystal's fire
The mountains brood o'er their abyss;
Intone in adamantine choir
Mysteries of their genesis.

The rocks, roused from long epochs' sleep,
Riddles solve of Space and Time,
While metals, gleaming in the deeps,
Harmoniously chime.

O seeker, slumbering in the haze,
Awaken with the stones!
Find crystal's flame within your gaze,
Lime's might in blood and bone.

This Land Is Your Land

"Woody" Guthrie

This land is your land, this land is my land
From California to the New York Island
From the Redwood Forest to the Gulf Stream waters
This land was made for you and me.

As I went walking that ribbon of highway
I saw above me that endless skyway
I saw below me that golden valley
This land was made for you and me.

I roamed and I rambled and I followed my footsteps
To the sparkling sands of her diamond deserts
While all around me a voice was sounding
This land was made for you and me.

When the sun came shining, and I was strolling
And the wheat fields waving and the dust clouds rolling
A voice was chanting, As the fog was lifting,
This land was made for you and me.

This land is your land, this land is my land
From California to the New York Island
From the Redwood Forest to the Gulf Stream waters
This land was made for you and me.

As I went walking I saw a sign there
And on the sign it said "No Trespassing."
But on the other side it didn't say nothing,
That side was made for you and me.

Nobody living can ever stop me,
As I go walking that freedom highway;
Nobody living can ever make me turn back
This land was made for you and me.

In the squares of the city, In the shadow of a steeple;
By the relief office, I'd seen my people.
As they stood there hungry, I stood there asking,
Is this land made for you and me?

Woodrow Wilson Guthrie wrote and sang hundreds of political, traditional and children's songs and ballads. In the 1930s, he joined the thousands of Okies migrating to California looking for work. Many of his songs are about his experiences in the Dust Bowl era during the Great Depression, earning him the nickname the "Dust Bowl Troubadour".

Spell of Creation

Kathleen Raine

Within the flower there lies a seed,
Within the seed there springs a tree,
Within the tree there spreads a wood.

In the wood there burns a fire,
And in the fire there melts a stone,
Within the stone a ring of iron.

Within the ring there lies an O,
Within the O there looks an eye,
In the eye there swims a sea,

And in the sea reflected sky,
And in the sky there shines the sun,
Within the sun a bird of gold.

Within the bird there beats a heart,
And from the heart there flows a song,
And in the song there sings a word.

In the word there speaks a world,
A world of joy, a world of grief,
From joy and grief there springs my love.

Oh love, my love, there springs a world,
And on the world there shines a sun,
And in the sun there burns a fire,

Within the fire consumes my heart,
And in my heart there beats a bird,
And in the bird there wakes an eye,

Within the eye, earth, sea and sky,
Earth, sky and sea within an O
Lie like the seed within the flower.

Wanderers

Walter de la Mare

Wide are the meadows of night,
And daisies are shining there,
Tossing their lovely dews,
Lustrous and fair;
And through these sweet fields go,
Wanderers amid the stars—
Venus, Mercury, Uranus, Neptune,
Saturn, Jupiter, Mars.

Tired in their silver, they move,
And circling, whisper and say,
Fair are the blossoming meads of delight
Through which we stray.

Star-Talk

Robert Graves

"Are you awake, Gemelli,
    This frosty night?"
"We'll be awake till reveillé,
Which is Sunrise," say the Gemelli,
"It's no good trying to go to sleep:
If there's wine to be got we'll drink it deep,
    But rest is hopeless to-night,
    But rest is hopeless to-night."

"Are you cold too, poor Pleiads,
    This frosty night?"
"Yes, and so are the Hyads:
See us cuddle and hug," say the Pleiads,
"All six in a ring: it keeps us warm:
We huddle together like birds in a storm:
    It's bitter weather to-night,
    It's bitter weather to-night."

"What do you hunt, Orion,
    This starry night?"
"The Ram, the Bull and the Lion,
And the Great Bear," says Orion,
"With my starry quiver and beautiful belt
I am trying to find a good thick pelt
    To warm my shoulders to-night,
    To warm my shoulders to-night."

"Did you hear that, Great She-bear,
    This frosty night?"
"Yes, he's talking of stripping me bare
Of my own big fur," says the She-bear,
"I'm afraid of the man and his terrible arrow:
The thought of it chills my bones to the marrow,
    And the frost so cruel to-night!
    And the frost so cruel to-night!"

"How is your trade, Aquarius,
    This frosty night?"
"Complaints is many and various
And my feet are cold," says Aquarius,
"There's Venus objects to Dolphin-scales,
And Mars to Crab-spawn found in my pails,
    And the pump has frozen to-night,
    And the pump has frozen to-night."

Gemmeli, a popular pasta in Italy, is Italian for "twins" and refers to the constellation Gemini. Pleiads refers to the constellation of the Pleiades, also called the Seven Sisters, and Hyads to the Hyades, a sisterhood of nymphs who bring rain.

When I Heard the Learn'd Astronomer

Walt Whitman

When I heard the learn'd astronomer,
When the proofs, the figures,
    were ranged in columns before me,
When I was shown the charts and diagrams,
    to add, divide, and measure them,
When I sitting heard the astronomer
    where he lectured with much applause in the lecture-room,
How soon unaccountable I became tired and sick,
Till rising and gliding out I wander'd off by myself,
In the mystical moist night-air, and from time to time,
Look'd up in perfect silence at the stars.

Seasons

The Seasons

The world is waking up again,
And *Spring* has just begun.
The catkins on the willow-tree
Turn yellow in the sun.
March brings us bright and windy days,
April gives us showers;
Then May puts green leaves everywhere,
Makes meadows full of flowers.

Now every day the *Summer* sun
Climbs higher in the sky;
The farmer's fields are stacked with hay
In June and July.
Long holidays are here again,
Blue sea and sandy beaches.
The time of sun-ripe fruit has come,
Of pears and golden peaches.

When *Autumn* comes, the weather's calm,
The sun is not so strong;
The days are shorter than before,
The nights are getting long.
Summer flowers are fading now
And die in late September;
Yellow and red October leaves
Must fall in grey November.

Winter is here; the days are cold;
The clouds bring rain and snow.
The roads are icy, slippery,
Our steps must be quite slow.
December brings us Christmas,
And January New Year;
Then snowdrops say in February
That *Spring* will soon be here.

A Calendar

Sara Coleridge

January brings the snow;
Makes our feet and fingers glow.
February brings the rain,
Thaws the frozen lake again.

March brings breezes, loud and shrill,
To stir the dancing daffodil.
April brings the primrose sweet,
Scatters daisies at our feet.

May brings flocks of pretty lambs
Skipping by their fleecy dams.
June brings tulips, lilies, roses,
Fills the children's hands with posies.

Hot July brings cooling showers,
Apricots and gillyflowers.
August brings the sheaves of corn,
Then the harvest home is borne.

Warm September brings the fruit;
Sportsmen then begin to shoot.
Fresh October brings the pheasant,
Then to gather nuts is pleasant.

Dull November brings the blast;
Then the leaves are whirling fast.
Chill December brings the sleet,
Blazing fire and Christmas treat.

The Morns Are Meeker Than They Were

Emily Dickinson

The morns are meeker than they were,
    the nuts are getting brown;
The berry's cheek is plumper,
    the rose is out of town.
The maple wears a gayer scarf,
    the field a scarlet gown.
Lest I should be old-fashioned,
    I'll put a trinket on.

Thirty Days Hath September

Thirty days hath September,
April, June, and November.
All the rest have thirty-one,
Except February alone,
Which has four and twenty-four
Till leap-year gives it one day more.

Thirty days hath September,
April, June, and November;
February has twenty-eight alone,
All the rest have thirty-one,
Except in leap-year, when's the time
That February has twenty-nine.

Through the Year

Flora Willis Watson

In January falls the snow,
In February cold winds blow,
In March peep out the early flowers,
And April comes with sunny showers.

In May the roses bloom so gay,
In June the farmer mows his hay,
In July brightly shines the sun,
In August harvest is begun.

September turns the green leaves brown,
October winds then shake them down,
November fills with bleak and drear,
December comes and ends the year.

Pirate Wind

Mary Jane Carr

The autumn wind's a pirate,
Blustering in from sea;
With a rollicking song, he sweeps along,
Swaggering boist'rously.

His skin is weather-beaten;
He wears a yellow sash,
With a handkerchief red about his head,
And a bristling black mustache.

He laughs as he storms the country,
A loud laugh and a bold;
And the trees all quake and shiver and shake,
As he robs them of their gold.

The autumn wind's a pirate,
Pillaging just for fun;
He'll snatch your hat as quick as that,
And laugh to see you run!

Red in Autumn

Elizabeth Gould

Tipperty-toes, the smallest elf,
Sat on a mushroom by himself,
Playing a little tinkling tune
Under the big round harvest moon;
And this is the song that Tipperty made
To sing to the little tune he played.

"Red are the hips, red are the haws,
Red and gold are the leaves that fall,
Red are the poppies in the corn,
Red berries on the rowan tall;
Red is the big round harvest moon,
And red are my new little dancing shoon."

When Mary Goes Walking

Patrick Reginald Chalmers

When Mary goes walking
The autumn winds blow,
The poplars they curtsey,
The larches bend low;

The oaks and the beeches
Their gold they fling down,
To make her a carpet,
To make her a crown.

O Come Little Leaves

George Cooper

"Come, little leaves," said the wind one day,
"Come o'er the meadows with me and play;
Put on your dresses of red and gold,
For summer's gone and the days grow cold."

Soon as the leaves heard the wind's loud call,
Down they came fluttering one and all;
Over the brown fields they danced and flew,
Singing the glad little songs they knew.

"Cricket, good-bye, we've been friends so long,
Little brook, sing us your farewell song;
Say you are sorry to see us go;
Ah, you will miss us, right well we know.

"Dear little lambs in your fleecy fold,
Mother will keep you from harm and cold;
Fondly we watched you in vale and glade,
Ay, will you dream of your loving shade?"

Dancing and whirling, the little leaves went,
Winter had called them and they were content;
Soon, fast asleep in their earthy beds,
The snow laid a coverlet over their heads.

Autumn Song

Margaret Rose

October is a piper,
Piping down the dell—
Sad sweet songs of sunshine—
Summer's last farewell,
He pipes till grey November
Comes in the mist and rain,
And then he puts his pipe away
Till Autumn comes again.

Sukkot

R. H. Marks

Here, where
we build our sukkah,
the air is sweet:
        Fragrant earth, our floor.

Here we
lay green bough and pine
to lace our roof:
        Sun shines through, and stars.

Here we
hang festoons of grape,
apple and pear:
        Fruits of late summer.

Here we
heap pumpkin and squash,
tall sheaves of corn:
        Gifts of autumn fields.

Here we
summon Abraham
and our fathers:
        Ancestors of old.

Here we
welcome in Sarah
and our mothers:
        All are exalted guests.

Here we
invite the hungry
to share our food:
        Let them enter in.

Winding
palm branch with willow
and green myrtle
        We weave our lulav.

Citron,
fragrantly scented
is our etrog:
        We wave it in prayer.

Here we
remember our past
and our people
        Who lived by the land.

Here we
will give thanks to God
for earth's bounty:
        Thanksgiving is ours.

October's Party

George Cooper

October gave a party.
    The leaves by hundreds came—
The Chestnuts, Oaks, and Maples,
    And leaves of every name.
The Sunshine spread a carpet,
    And everything was grand,
Miss Weather led the dancing;
    Professor Wind the band.

The Chestnuts came in yellow,
    The Oaks in crimson dressed;
The lovely Misses Maple,
    In purple, looked their best;
All balanced to their partners,
    And gaily fluttered by;
The sight was like a rainbow
    New fallen from the sky.

Then in the rustic hollows,
    At hide-and-seek they played.
The party closed at sundown
    And everybody stayed.
Professor Wind played louder;
    They flew along the ground,
And then the party ended
    In jolly "hands all round."

The Apple Tree

Here is a tree with leaves so green,
    Stretch arms with fingers spread.
Here are the apples that hang between.
    Clench fists for apples.
When the wind blows, the apples will fall,
    Wave arms in the wind and let apples drop suddenly.
Here is a basket to gather them all.
    Make a large circle with both arms in front of chest.

Autumn Leaves

The trees are saying "Goodbye" to their leaves
Stretch out arms and wave goodbye.
As they flutter and fly and float in the breeze.
Flutter fingers.
All golden, orange, and red, they sink softly off to bed.
Slowly bring fluttering fingers down to floor.
On Mother Earth's breast rests each leafy head.
Make sleeping gesture with palms together;
give a big, restful sigh.

Harvest

Molly de Havas

Fields of wheat and oats and barley
Bending in the summer breeze,
Sun and shadow, wave and ripple,
Chase across their golden seas.

Wheat stands tall and straight and heavy,
Oat grains hang in separate drops,
Barley's whiskered head curves over—
Gold, and brown, and yellow crops.

When the corn is fully ripened
Then the harvest is begun.
Reaping, binding, on the stubble
Stacking sheaves beneath the sun.

Now we load the great farm wagons
Working till the field is clear.
Stubble soon must turn to ploughland
Ready for another year.

The Scarecrow

Michael Franklin

A scarecrow stood in a field one day,
Stuffed with straw,
Stuffed with hay,
He watched the folk on the king's highway,
But never a word said he.

Much he saw but naught did heed,
Knowing not night,
Knowing not day,
For having naught, did nothing heed,
And never a word said he.

A little gray mouse had made its nest,
Oh so wee,
Oh so gray,
In the sleeve of a coat that was poor Tom's best,
But the scarecrow naught said he.

His hat was the home of a small jenny wren,
Ever so sweet,
Ever so gay,
A squirrel had put by his fear of men
And kissed him, but naught heeded he.

Ragged old man, I love him well,
Stuffed with straw,
Stuffed with hay,
Many's the tale that he could tell,
But never a word says he.

When the Frost Is on the Punkin

James Whitcomb Riley

When the frost is on the punkin and the fodder's in the shock,
And you hear the kyouck and gobble of the struttin' turkey-cock,
And the clackin' of the guineys, and the cluckin' of the hens,
And the rooster's hallylooyer as he tiptoes on the fence;
O, it's then's the times a feller is a-feelin' at his best,
With the risin' sun to greet him from a night of peaceful rest,
As he leaves the house, bareheaded, and goes to feed the stock,
When the frost is on the punkin and the fodder's in the shock.

They's something kindo' harty-like about the atmusfere
When the heat of summer's over and the coolin' fall is here—
Of course we miss the flowers, and the blossums on the trees,
And the mumble of the hummin'-birds and buzzin' of the bees;
But the air's so appetizin'; and the landscape through the haze
Of a crisp and sunny morning of the airly autumn days
Is a pictur' that no painter has the colorin' to mock—
When the frost is on the punkin and the fodder's in the shock.

The husky, rusty russel of the tossels of the corn,
And the raspin' of the tangled leaves, as golden as the morn;
The stubble in the furries—kindo' lonesome-like, but still
A-preachin' sermons to us of the barns they growed to fill;
The strawsack in the medder, and the reaper in the shed;
The hosses in theyr stalls below—the clover overhead!—
O, it sets my hart a-clickin' like the tickin' of a clock,
When the frost is on the punkin, and the fodder's in the shock!

Then your apples all is gethered, and the ones a feller keeps
Is poured around the celler-floor in red and yeller heaps;
And your cider-makin's over, and your wimmern-folks is through
With their mince and apple-butter, and theyr souse and saussage, too!
I don't know how to tell it—but ef sich a thing could be
As the Angles wantin' boardin', and they'd call around on me—
I'd want to 'commodate 'em—all the whole-indurin' flock—
When the frost is on the punkin and the fodder's in the shock!

Jack Frost

Eugene Schwartz

Jack Frost crept into my room,
Though the windows were shut tight;
Painting pictures on each pane,
Weaving worlds of glimmering ice.
Glowing on the gleaming glass,
Frosty flowers, snowy trees,
Crystal castles, icy grass—
Jack Frost painted all of these.
When the morning's rosy rays
Showed the power of the Sun,
Jack Frost laughingly erased
All the work that he had done!

Jack Frost

Cecily E. Pike

Look out! Look out!
Jack Frost is about!
He's after our fingers and toes;
And all through the night,
The gay little sprite
Is working where nobody knows.

He'll climb each tree,
So nimble is he.
His silvery powder he'll shake;
To windows he'll creep,
And while we're asleep,
Such wonderful pictures he'll make.

Across the grass
He'll merrily pass,
And change all its greenness to white.
Then home he will go;
And laugh, "Ho! Ho! Ho!
What fun I have had in the night!"

Goblins on the Doorstep

Dorothy Brown Thompson

Goblins on the doorstep,
Phantoms in the air,
Owls on witches' gateposts,
Giving stare for stare,

Cats on flying broomsticks,
Bats against the moon,
Stirrings round of fate-cakes,
With a solemn spoon.

Whirling apple parings,
Figures draped in sheets,
Dodging, disappearing,
Up and down the streets,

Jack-o-Lanterns grinning,
Shadows on a screen,
Shrieks and starts with laughter—
This is Halloween!

The Hag

Robert Herrick

The Hag is astride,
This night for to ride;
The Devill and shee together:
Through thick, and through thin,
Now out, and then in,
Though ne'r so foule be the weather.

A Thorn or a Burr
She takes for a Spurre:
With a lash of a Bramble she rides now,
Through Brakes and through Bryars,
O're Ditches, and Mires,
She followes the Spirit that guides now.

No Beast, for his food,
Dares now range the wood;
But husht in his laire he lies lurking:
While mischiefs, by these,
On Land and on Seas,
At noone of Night are working,

The storme will arise,
And trouble the skies;
This night, and more for the wonder,
The ghost from the Tomb
Affrighted shall come,
Cal'd out by the clap of the Thunder.

from The Broomstick Train

Oliver Wendell Holmes

Look out! Look out, boys! Clear the track!
The witches are here! They've all come back!
They hanged them high,—No use! No use!
What cares a witch for a hangman's noose?
They buried them deep, but they wouldn't lie still,
For cats and witches are hard to kill;
They swore they shouldn't and wouldn't die,—
Books said they did, but they lie! they lie!

The Ride-by-Nights

Walter de la Mare

Up on their brooms the Witches stream,
Crooked and black in the crescent's gleam;

One foot high, and one foot low,
Bearded, cloaked, and cowled, they go,

'Neath Charlie's Wain they twitter and tweet,
And away they swarm 'neath the Dragon's feet,

With a whoop and a flutter they swing and sway,
And surge pell-mell down the Milky Way.

Betwixt the legs of the glittering Chair
They hover and squeak in the empty air.

Then round they swoop past the glimmering Lion
To where Sirius barks behind huge Orion;

Up, then, and over to wheel amain,
Under the silver, and home again.

I Saw Three Witches

Walter de la Mare

I saw three witches
That bowed down like barley,
And straddled their brooms 'neath a louring sky,
And, mounting a storm-cloud,
Aloft on its margin,
Stood black in the silver as up they did fly.

I saw three witches
That mocked the poor sparrows
They carried in cages of wicker along,
Till a hawk from his eyrie
Swooped down like an arrow,
Smote on the cages, and ended their song.

I saw three witches
That sailed in a shallop,
All turning their heads with a snickering smile,
Till a bank of green osiers
Concealed their grim faces,
Though I heard them lamenting for many a mile.

I saw three witches
Asleep in a valley,
Their heads in a row, like stones in a flood,
Till the moon, creeping upward,
Looked white through the valley,
And turned them to bushes in bright scarlet bud.

November

Now it is November,
Trees are nearly bare;
Red and gold and brown leaves
Scatter everywhere.

Dark now, are the mornings,
Cold and frosty too;
Damp and misty evenings
Chill us through and through.

Busy are all creatures,
Winter food to hide;
Nests to make all cosy,
Warm and safe inside.

November

Elisabeth Gmeyner

Golden light is turning grey,
Mists begin to rule the day.
Bare the trees their branches lift,
Clouds of dead leaves earthward drift.

Through the field the farmer goes,
Seeds of ripened corn he sows,
Trusts the earth will hold it warm,
Shelter it from cold and harm.

For he knows that warmth and light
Live there, hidden from our sight,
And beneath a sheltering wing
Deep below new life will spring.

No!

Thomas Hood

No sun—no moon!
No morn—no noon!
No dawn--no dusk—no proper time of day—
No sky—no earthly view—
No distance looking blue—
No road—no street—no "t'other side this way"—
No end to any Row—
No indications where the Crescents go—
No top to any steeple—
No recognitions of familiar people—
No courtesies for showing 'em—
No knowing 'em!
No traveling at all—no locomotion—
No inkling of the way—no notion—
"No go" by land or ocean—
No mail—no post—
No news from any foreign coast—
No Park, no Ring, no afternoon gentility—
No company—no nobility—
No warmth, no cheerfulness, no healthful ease,
No comfortable feel in any member—
No shade, no shine, no butterflies, no bees,
No fruits, no flowers, no leaves, no birds—
November!

Thanksgiving

The year has turned its circle,
The seasons come and go.
The harvest is all gathered in
And chilly north winds blow.

Orchards have shared their treasures,
The fields, their yellow grain.
So open wide the doorway—
Thanksgiving comes again!

Thanksgiving Day

Lydia Maria Child

Over the river, and through the wood,
To Grandfather's house we go;
    The horse knows the way
    To carry the sleigh
Through the white and drifted snow.

Over the river, and through the wood—
Oh, how the wind does blow!
    It stings the toes
    And bites the nose
As over the ground we go.

Over the river, and through the wood,
To have a first-rate play.
    Hear the bells ring,
    "Ting-a-ling-ding",
Hurrah for Thanksgiving Day!

Over the river, and through the wood
Trot fast, my dapple-gray!
    Spring over the ground
    Like a hunting-hound,
For this is Thanksgiving Day.

Over the river, and through the wood—
And straight through the barnyard gate,
    We seem to go
    Extremely slow,
It is so hard to wait!

Over the river, and through the wood—
Now Grandmother's cap I spy!
    Hurrah for the fun!
    Is the pudding done?
Hurrah for the pumpkin pie!

Ice

Walter de la Mare

The North Wind sighed:
And in a trice
What was water
Now is ice.

What sweet rippling
Water was
Now bewitched is
Into glass.

White and brittle
Where is seen
The prisoned milfoil's
Tender green;

Clear and ringing
With sun aglow.
Where the boys sliding
And skating go.

Now furred ‘s each stick
And stalk and blade
With crystals out of
Dewdrops made.

Worms and ants
Flies, snails and bees
Keep close house-guard,
Lest they freeze;

Oh, with how sad
And solemn an eye
Each fish stares up
Into the sky.

In dread lest his
Wide watery home
At night shall solid
Ice become.

Snowflakes Falling

Snowflakes falling soft and light,
Snowflakes falling in the night,
Soft and light, pure and white.
When the sun shines out so bright
All the earth is dressed in white.

Stopping by Woods on a Snowy Evening

Robert Frost

Whose woods these are I think I know.
His house is in the village though;
He will not see me stopping here
To watch his woods fill up with snow.

My little horse must think it queer
To stop without a farmhouse near
Between the woods and frozen lake
The darkest evening of the year.

He gives his harness bells a shake
To ask if there is some mistake.
The only other sound's the sweep
Of easy wind and downy flake.

The woods are lovely, dark and deep.
But I have promises to keep,
And miles to go before I sleep,
And miles to go before I sleep.

A Winter Night

An Action Poem

Margaret Meyerkort

Snowflakes whirl through winter night,
Clothes the earth in glowing white,
Down beneath the snow so deep
Master Hare lies fast asleep.

Hark! What's that? A noise I hear,
Hide, now hide your head and ear.
Up above the snow-white ground
Hunterman walks with heavy sound,

Green his hat with flying feather,
Brown his coat for wintry weather.
Both his boots are big and black,
Bow and arrow on his back.

Slowly, softly place your boot,
Quietly if you want to shoot.
But alack! The ice goes crack.
Down a hole the Hunter rolls!

And master hare?
With a leap dee-lop-lop-lop,
Off he capers hop-hop-hop.
Laughing loud, "Ha-ha-hee-hee,
Hunter man, you can't catch me."

Then he nibbles at some hay,
Wipes and sweeps the snow away,
And once more falls fast asleep
'Neath the snow so white and deep.

Song 3rd by an Old Shepherd

William Blake

When silver snow decks Sylvio's clothes,
And jewel hangs at shepherd's nose,
We can abide life's pelting storm,
That makes our limbs quake, if our hearts be warm.

Whilst Virtue is our walking-staff,
And Truth a lantern to our path,
We can abide life's pelting storm,
That makes our limbs quake, if our hearts be warm.

Blow, boisterous wind, stern winter frown,
Innocence is a winter's gown,
So clad, we'll abide life's pelting storm,
That makes our limbs quake, if our hearts be warm.

Snowman

Once there was a snowman
Who stood outside the door.
He thought he'd like to come inside
And run around the floor.

He thought he'd like to warm himself
By the firelight red,
He thought he'd like to climb right up
Onto my big, white bed.

So he called the North Wind,
"Help me get away!
I'm completely frozen,
Standing here all day!."

So the North Wind came along
And blew him in the door.
And now there's only water left,
A puddle on the floor.

Stars Are Glowing

Softly, softly, through the darkness
    Snow is falling.
Meekly, meekly in the meadows
    Lambs are calling.
Coldly, coldly all around me
    Winds are blowing.
Brightly, brightly up above me
    Stars are glowing.

Adventsong

Eugene Schwartz

In the deep and dark wood's heart
Where moans the North Wind cold,
You will find a sun-filled cave
When you walk a spiral road.
Shimmering stars will sing above
To the crystals that glitter below,
While you draw your light from a flame so bright
Bringing warmth to the sparkling snow.

Advent Candles Verse

The first light of Advent,
it is the light of the stones,
Light that shines in crystals,
in seashells, and in bones.

The second light of Advent,
it is the light of the plants,
Plants that reach up to the sun,
and in the breezes dance.

The third light of Advent,
it is the light of the beasts,
The light of hope that we may see
in greatest and in least.

The fourth light of Advent,
it is the light of man,
The light of love, the light of thought,
to give and understand.

The Daffodil

Isabel Wyatt

Said a young star
To Father Sky:
"Would it be too far
For me to fly
To Mother Earth
For the Christ-Child's birth?"

Said Father Sky:
"Child, you may leave
Your home on high
On Christmas Eve,
With Earth to stay
Till the Three Kings' Day.

"Twelve Holy Nights
You may spend below.
But not as you are
Can you fly so far;
You can only go
As a flake of snow."

His six-winged crown
With its rays so bright,
The young star shrank
To a point of light.
His golden cup
He washed snow-white.

As a six-winged snowflake
He came to rest,
And sank with his warmth
In the Earth's bare breast
Till he kindled a bud
In a bulb's brown nest.

The star flew home
On Three Kings' Day;
And the bulb-bud opened
When the spring grew gay.

The flower smiled up
And her star smiled down
On his own gold cup
And his six-winged crown.

The Poem of Eva's Apple

Isabel Wyatt

Eva plucked the apple,
    And Earth was stricken sore;
The sword of flame was flickering
    At the Green Garden's door
As she came down the mountain,
    Carrying the apple's core.

Eva plucked the apple,
    And Earth's starlight paled;
Eva plucked the apple,
    And Earth's music failed;
And soil and stone and crystal
    And rain and river wailed.

Eva's tree bore apples
    Withered, hard and sour,
Till upon its branches
    At the first Christmas hour
A golden star descended,
    Enfolded in a flower.

Now Earth's pangs are lightened;
    The sword's fire backward blows;
Again is heard Earth's music;
    Again Earth's starlight glows.
There's a rose within the apple;
    There's a star within the rose.

In the Town

Old French Dialogue Carol

JOSEPH:
Take heart, the journey's ended:
I see the twinkling lights,
Where we shall be befriended
On this night of nights.

MARY:
Now praise the Lord that led us
So safe into the town,
Where men will feed and bed us,
And I can lay me down.

JOSEPH:
And how then shall we praise him?
Alas, my heart is sore
That we no gifts can raise him,
We are so very poor.

MARY:
We have as much as any
That on the earth do live,
Although we have no penny,
We have ourselves to give.

JOSEPH:
Look yonder, wife, look yonder!
A hostelry I see,
Where travelers that wander
Will very welcome be.

MARY:
The house is tall and stately,
The door stands open thus;
Yet husband, I fear greatly
That inn is not for us.

JOSEPH:
God save you, gentle master!
Your littlest room indeed
With plainest walls of plaster
Tonight will serve our need.

HOST:
For lordlings and for ladies
I've lodgings and to spare;
For you and yonder maid is
No closet anywhere.

JOSEPH:
Take heart, take heart, sweet Mary,
Another inn I spy,
Whose host will not be chary
To let us easy lie.

MARY:
Oh, aid me, I am ailing,
My strength is nearly gone;
I feel my limbs are failing,
And yet we must go on.

JOSEPH:
God save you, Hostess, kindly!
I pray you, house my wife,
Who bears beside me blindly
The burden of her life.

HOSTESS:
My guests are rich men's daughters,
And sons, I'd have you know!
Seek out the poorer quarters,
Where ragged people go.

JOSEPH:
Good sir, my wife's in labor,
Some corner let us keep.

HOST:
Not I: knock on my neighbor's door,
And as for me, I'll sleep.

MARY:
In all the lighted city
Where rich men welcome win,
Will not one house for pity
Take two poor strangers in?

JOSEPH:
Good woman, I implore you,
Afford my wife a bed.

HOSTESS:
Nay, nay, I've nothing for you
Except the cattle shed.

MARY:
Then gladly in the manger
Our bodies we will house,
Since men tonight are stranger
Than donkeys, sheep and cows.

JOSEPH:
Take heart, take heart, sweet Mary,
The cattle are our friends.
Lie down, lie down, sweet Mary,
For here our journey ends.

MARY:
Now praise the Lord that found me
This shelter in the town,
Where I with friends around me
May lay my burden down.

The Friendly Beasts

An Old Carol from France

Jesus, our brother, kind and good,
Was humbly born in a stable rude;
And the friendly beasts around Him stood,
Jesus, our brother, kind and good.

"I," said the donkey, shaggy and brown,
"I carried His mother uphill and down;
I carried His mother to Bethlehem town;
I," said the donkey, shaggy and brown.

"I," said the cow, all white and red,
"I gave Him my manger for His bed;
I gave Him hay to pillow His head;
I," said the cow, all white and red.

"I," said the sheep with curly horn,
"I gave Him my wool for His blanket warm.
He wore my coat on Christmas morn.
I," said the sheep with curly horn.

"I," said the dove, from the rafters high,
"I cooed Him to sleep that He should not cry,
We cooed Him to sleep, my mate and I.
I," said the dove, from the rafters high.

Thus all the beasts, by some good spell,
In the stable dark were glad to tell
Of the gifts they gave Emmanuel,
The gifts they gave Emmanuel.

A Visit from Saint Nicholas

Clement Clark Moore

'T was the night before Christmas, when all through the house
Not a creature was stirring, not even a mouse;
The stockings were hung by the chimney with care,
In hopes that St. Nicholas soon would be there.

The children were nestled all snug in their beds,
While visions of sugar-plums danced in their heads;
And mamma in her 'kerchief, and I in my cap,
Had just settled our brains for a long winter's nap,

When out on the lawn there arose such a clatter,
I sprang from the bed to see what was the matter.
Away to the window I flew like a flash,
Tore open the shutters and threw up the sash.

The moon on the breast of the new-fallen snow
Gave the lustre of mid-day to objects below,
When, what to my wondering eyes should appear,
But a miniature sleigh, and eight tiny reindeer,

With a little old driver, so lively and quick,
I knew in a moment it must be St. Nick.
More rapid than eagles his coursers they came,
And he whistled, and shouted, and called them by name.

"Now, Dasher! now, Dancer! now, Prancer and Vixen!
On, Comet! on, Cupid! on, Donder and Blitzen!
To the top of the porch! to the top of the wall!
Now dash away! dash away! dash away all!"

As dry leaves that before the wild hurricane fly,
When they meet with an obstacle, mount to the sky;
So up to the house-top the coursers they flew,
With the sleigh full of Toys, and St. Nicholas too.

And then, in a twinkling, I heard on the roof
The prancing and pawing of each little hoof.
As I drew in my head, and was turning around,
Down the chimney St. Nicholas came with a bound.

He was dressed all in fur, from his head to his foot,
And his clothes were all tarnished with ashes and soot;
A bundle of Toys he had flung on his back,
And he looked like a pedlar just opening his pack.

His eyes—how they twinkled! his dimples how merry!
His cheeks were like roses, his nose like a cherry!
His droll little mouth was drawn up like a bow
And the beard of his chin was as white as the snow;

The stump of a pipe he held tight in his teeth,
And the smoke it encircled his head like a wreath;
He had a broad face and a little round belly,
That shook when he laughed, like a bowlful of jelly.

He was chubby and plump, a right jolly old elf,
And I laughed when I saw him, in spite of myself;
A wink of his eye and a twist of his head,
Soon gave me to know I had nothing to dread;

He spoke not a word, but went straight to his work,
And filled all the stockings; then turned with a jerk,
And laying his finger aside of his nose,
And giving a nod, up the chimney he rose;

He sprang to his sleigh, to his team gave a whistle,
And away they all flew like the down of a thistle,
But I heard him exclaim, ere he drove out of sight,
"Happy Christmas to all, and to all a good-night."

Ring Out, Wild Bells

Alfred, Lord Tennyson

Ring out, wild bells, to the wild sky,
The flying cloud, the frosty light;
The year is dying in the night;
Ring out, wild bells, and let him die.

Ring out the old, ring in the new,
Ring, happy bells, across the snow;
The year is going, let him go;
Ring out the false, ring in the true.

Ring out the grief that saps the mind,
For those that here we see no more,
Ring out the feud of rich and poor,
Ring in redress to all mankind.

Ring out a slowly dying cause,
And ancient forms of party strife;
Ring in the nobler modes of life,
With sweeter manners, purer laws.

Ring out the want, the care, the sin,
The faithless coldness of the times;
Ring out, ring out my mournful rhymes,
But ring the fuller minstrel in.

Ring out false pride in place and blood,
The civic slander and the spite;
Ring in the love of truth and right,
Ring in the common love of good.

Ring out old shapes of foul disease,
Ring out the narrowing lust of gold;
Ring out the thousand wars of old,
Ring in the thousand years of peace.

Ring in the valiant man and free,
The larger heart, the kindlier hand;
Ring out the darkness of the land,
Ring in the Christ that is to be.

The Three Kings

Henry Wadsworth Longfellow

Three Kings came riding from far away,
Melchior and Gaspar and Baltasar;
Three Wise Men out of the East were they,
And they travelled by night and they slept by day,
For their guide was a beautiful, wonderful star.

The star was so beautiful, large and clear,
That all the other stars of the sky
Became a white mist in the atmosphere,
And by this they knew that the coming was near
Of the Prince foretold in the prophecy.

Three caskets they bore on their saddle-bows,
Three caskets of gold with golden keys;
Their robes were of crimson silk with rows
Of bells and pomegranates and furbelows,
Their turbans like blossoming almond-trees.

And so the Three Kings rode into the West,
Through the dusk of the night, over hill and dell,
And sometimes they nodded with beard on breast,
And sometimes talked, as they paused to rest,
With the people they met at some wayside well.

"Of the child that is born," said Baltasar,
"Good people, I pray you, tell us the news;
For we in the East have seen his star,
And have ridden fast, and have ridden far,
To find and worship the King of the Jews."

And the people answered, "You ask in vain;
We know of no King but Herod the Great!"
They thought the Wise Men were men insane,
As they spurred their horses across the plain,
Like riders in haste, who cannot wait.

And when they came to Jerusalem,
Herod the Great, who had heard this thing,
Sent for the Wise Men and questioned them;
And said, "Go down unto Bethlehem,
And bring me tidings of this new king."

So they rode away; and the star stood still,
The only one in the grey of morn;
Yes, it stopped—it stood still of its own free will,
Right over Bethlehem on the hill,
The city of David, where Christ was born.

And the Three Kings rode through the gate and the guard,
Through the silent street, till their horses turned
And neighed as they entered the great inn-yard;
But the windows were closed, and the doors were barred,
And only a light in the stable burned.

And cradled there in the scented hay,
In the air made sweet by the breath of kine,
The little child in the manger lay,
The child, that would be king one day
Of a kingdom not human, but divine.

His mother Mary of Nazareth
Sat watching beside his place of rest,
Watching the even flow of his breath,
For the joy of life and the terror of death
Were mingled together in her breast.

They laid their offerings at his feet:
The gold was their tribute to a King,
The frankincense, with its odor sweet,
Was for the Priest, the Paraclete,
The myrrh for the body's burying.

And the mother wondered and bowed her head,
And sat as still as a statue of stone;
Her heart was troubled yet comforted,
Remembering what the Angel had said
Of an endless reign and of David's throne.

Then the Kings rode out of the city gate,
With a clatter of hoofs in proud array;
But they went not back to Herod the Great,
For they knew his malice and feared his hate,
And returned to their homes by another way.

Two Verses for Candlemas

If Candlemas Day be fair and bright,
  Winter will have another flight.
But if Candlemas Day be clouds and rain,
  Winter is gone, and will not come again.

If Candlemas Day be fair and clear,
  There'll be two winters in that one year.

Seeds

Molly de Havas

After Christmas it's time to be thinking of Spring,
And the flowers and vegetables springtime will bring.
We must go to a shop and choose packets of seeds
To be sown in the garden to fill all our needs.

First the weeds must be pulled and the clean earth laid bare,
Then dug over, and broken, and levelled with care;
Next in furrows and holes that we've made in the earth
We will plant the brown seeds, and with joy wait their birth.

King Winter

King Winter sat in his hall one day,
And he said to himself, said he,
"I must admit I've had some fun,
I've chilled the Earth and cooled the Sun,
And not a flower or tree
But wishes that my reign were done.
As long as time and tide shall run,
I'll go on making everyone
As cold as cold can be."

There came a knock at the outer door;
"Who's there?" King Winter cried;
"Open your palace gates," said Spring.
"For you can reign no more as King,
No longer here abide;
This message from the sun I bring,
"The trees are green, the birds do sing;
The hills with joy are echoing:
So pray, Sir—step outside!"

A Little Brown Bulb

A little brown bulb went to sleep in the ground.
There she slept very sound.
While Old King Winter raged and roared overhead,
The little brown bulb did not stir in her bed.
Then came Lady Spring tip-toeing over the lea,
Fingers to lips as soft as can be.
And the little brown bulb just lifted her head,
Slipped off her nightie and jumped out of bed.

The Merry Month of March

William Wordsworth

The cock is crowing,
The stream is flowing,
The small birds twitter,
The lake doth glitter,
The green field sleeps in the sun;
The oldest and youngest
Are at work with the strongest;
The cattle are grazing,
Their heads never raising;
There are forty feeding like one!

Like an army defeated
The snow hath retreated,
And now doth fare ill
On the top of the bare hill;
The ploughboy is whooping—anon—anon:
There's joy in the mountains;
There's life in the fountains;
Small clouds are sailing,
Blue sky prevailing;
The rain is over and gone!

Wild Geese

Celia Thaxter

The wind blows, the sun shines, the birds sing loud,
The blue, blue sky is flecked with fleecy dappled cloud,
Over earth's rejoicing fields the children dance and sing,
And the frogs pipe in chorus, "It is spring! It is spring!"

The grass comes, the flower laughs where lately lay the snow,
O'er the breezy hill-top hoarsely calls the crow,
By the flowing river the alder catkins swing,
And the sweet song sparrow cries, "Spring! It is spring!"

Hark, what a clamor goes winging through the sky!
Look, children! Listen to the sound so wild and high!
Like a peal of broken bells,—kling, klang, kling,—
Far and high the wild geese cry, "Spring! It is spring!"

Bear the winter off with you, O wild geese dear!
Carry all the cold away, far away from here;
Chase the snow into the north, O strong of heart and wing,
While we share the robin's rapture, crying, "Spring! It is spring!"

Spring Work at the Farm

Thirza Wakely

What does the farmer do in the spring?
He sows the seed that harvests bring;
But first he wakes the earth from sleep
By ploughing it well and harrowing deep.

And busy must be the farmer's boy!
To care for the lambs that leap for joy.
To feed the calves so tender and young
He rises as soon as the day's begun.

And then the farmer's wife so kind,
Food for the ducklings and chicks will find.
And, hark! what the queer little piggy-wigs say,
"Don't forget me, I'm hungry today."

Spring

William Blake

Sound the flute!
Now it's mute.
Birds delight
Day and night.
Nightingale
In the dale,
Lark in the sky,
Merrily,
Merrily, merrily to welcome in the year.

Little boy
Full of joy,
Little girl
Sweet and small.
Cock does crow,
So do you.
Merry voice,
Infant noise,
Merrily, merrily to welcome in the year.

Little lamb
Here I am
Come and lick
My white neck.
Let me pull
Your soft wool.
Let me kiss
Your soft face,
Merrily, merrily we welcome in the year.

'Tis Merry in Greenwood

Sir Walter Scott

'Tis merry in Greenwood—thus runs the old lay,—
In the gladsome month of lively May,
When the wild birds' song on stem and spray
    Invites to forest bower;
Then rears the ash his airy chest,
Then shines the birch in silver vest,
And the beech in glistening leaves is drest,
And dark between shows the oak's proud breast,
    Like a chieftan's frowning tower;
Though a thousand branches join their screen,
Yet the broken sunbeams glance between,
And tip the leaves with lighter green,
    With brighter tints the flowers;
Dull is the heart that loves not then
The deep recess of the wildwood glen,
Where roe and red-deer find sheltering den,
    When the sun is in his power.

from Song

Thomas Hood

'Tis like the birthday of the world,
    When earth was born in bloom;
The light is made of many dyes,
    The air is all perfume;
There's crimson buds, and white and blue—
    The very rainbow showers
Have turned to blossoms where they fell,
    And sown the earth with flowers.

Summer Comes

The little darling Spring has run away,
The sunshine grew too hot for her to stay.
She kissed her sister, Summer, and she said,
"When I am gone, you must be Queen instead."
Now reigns the Lady Summer, round whose feet
A thousand fairies flock with blossoms sweet.

Saints

Five Verses for Michaelmas

Sword of Micha-el brightly gleaming,
Down to earth its light is streaming;—
May we see its shining rays
In the winter's darkest days.

St. Micha-el, brave and bright
Who loves to live in the light,
The fierce foe to fight,
And smite with swinging sword
The dragon dark and dread—
Defeat is his reward.

There lived a noble prince,
St. Micha-el was his name.
He held a shining sword,
And mighty was his fame.

Think wisely,
Speak well,
Stand upright,
And Micha-el will lead me
From darkness to light.

Earth is dark
And fear is lurking.
O St. Micha-el, Heaven's knight,
Go before us now and lead us
Out of darkness, into light.

St. George

Eugene Schwartz

(For Michaelmas, September 29 or St. George's Day, April 23)

(The children form a circle, which becomes the battlements of the town wall. Within is the princess or prince, and outside of the circle are St. George and the Dragon.)

In a swamp, dark and dank,
Lived a Dragon most wild,
Who devoured the crops
Every lamb and each child.

(The Dragon breaks into the circle and pursues the princess or prince.)

All folk trembled in fear
When he rose from the mire,
Like a fierce flying snake,
Belching smoke, breathing fire!

(St. George enters and battles the Dragon.)

Oh St. George, Come! Advance!
'Gainst the Dragon to fight,
With your horse and your lance
And your conquering might!

St. George battled the beast,
Till the rays of the sun
As it rose in the east
Showed our knight to have won!

St. Jerome and the Lion

Eugene Schwartz

(Expansion and Contraction)

(The children form a very quiet circle of monks. Jerome sits on a stool in the center of the circle; the Lion is outside the circle.)

Quietly working, the monks did not look
Backwards or sidewards or up from their books;
When in strode a lion, ferocious and rough,
Who they were certain would eat them all up!

(Children run to farthest corners of the room)

Help! Help! Help! Help! Help! Help! Help! Help! Help! Help!

(The Lion approaches Jerome; the children reform their circle and slowly walk towards the center.)

Mild St. Jerome neither faltered nor feared;
He did not flee when the Lion appeared—
He kindly cared for the poor limping beast,
And tended his paw till his suffering ceased.

(Children again run to farthest corners of room)

Ceased! Ceased! Ceased! Ceased! Ceased! Ceased! Ceased!
Ceased! Ceased! Ceased!

(As Jerome cares for the Lion's paw, the children slowly approach the center of the circle again)

Later that day, all bedraggled and beaten,
The monks returned, certain Jerome had been eaten.
They found, when they timidly peered in his cell,
That the Lion was purring—Jerome was quite well!

(Children again run to farthest corners of room)

Well! Well! Well! Well! Well! Well! Well! Well! Well! Well!

The Rune of St. Patrick

At Tara today in this fateful hour
I place all Heaven with its power,
And the sun with its brightness,
And the snow with its whiteness,
And fire with all the strength it hath,
And lightning with its rapid wrath,
And the winds with their swiftness along their path,
And the sea with its deepness,
And the rocks with their steepness,
And the earth with its starkness
All these I place,
By God's almighty help and grace,
Between myself and the powers of darkness.

from The Deer's Cry
(The Breastplate of Saint Patrick)

I arise today
Through the strength of heaven;
Light of sun,
Radiance of moon,
Splendor of fire,
Speed of lightning,
Swiftness of wind,
Depth of sea,
Stability of earth,
Firmness of rock.

I arise today
Through God's strength to pilot me,
Might to uphold me,
Wisdom to guide me,
Eye to look before me,
Ear to hear me,
Word to speak for me,
Hand to guard me,
Shield to protect me,
Host to save me,
From snares of devils,
From temptations of vices,
From everyone who shall wish me ill,
Afar and anear,
Alone and in a multitude.

This very old rune, which has survived from the Seventh century, was sung by St. Patrick on his way to Tara, the capital of Ireland. High-King Loeguire (Leary) had assassins lying in ambush, ready to kill him and his followers that they would not reach Tara to sow the faith of Christianity. As St. Patrick chanted these words, it seemed to those lying in ambush that he and his monks were wild deer with a fawn following them.

Canticle to the Sun

St. Francis of Assisi
translated by Lawrence Edwards

Praised be God for brother Sun,
Who shines with splendid glow,
He brings the golden day to us,
Thy glory does he show!

Praised be God for sister Moon
And every twinkling star,
They shine in heaven most bright and clear,
All glorious they are.

Praised be God for brother Wind
That storms across the skies,
And then grows still and silent moves
And sweetly sings and sighs.

Praised be God for Water pure,
Her usefulness we tell,
So humble, precious, clean and good,
She works for us so well.

Praised be God for brother Fire
Friendly and wild and tame,
Tender and warm, mighty and strong,
A flashing, flaring, flame.

Praised be God for Mother Earth
Who keeps us safe and well,
Whose Mother heart, all warm with love,
Dark in her depths doth dwell.

from St. Francis' Sermon to the Birds

Henry Wadsworth Longfellow

Around Assisi's convent gate
The birds, God's poor who cannot wait,
From moor and mere and darksome wood
Come flocking for their dole of food.

"O brother birds," St. Francis said,
"Ye come to me and ask for bread,
But not with bread alone to-day
Shall ye be fed and sent away.

"Ye shall be fed, ye happy birds,
With manna of celestial words;
Not mine, though mine they seem to be,
Not mine, though they be spoken through me.

"Oh, doubly are ye bound to praise
The great Creator in your lays;
He giveth you your plumes of down,
Your crimson hoods, your cloaks of brown.

"He giveth you your wings to fly
And breathe a purer air on high,
And careth for you everywhere,
Who for yourselves so little care!"

With flutter of swift wings and songs
Together rose the feathered throngs,
And singing scattered far apart;
Deep peace was in St. Francis' heart.

He knew not if the brotherhood
His homily had understood;
He only knew that to one ear
The meaning of his words was clear.

St. Martin

Eugene Schwartz

St. Martin, St. Martin, a Roman soldier bold,
Swiftly on his snow-white steed through icy streets once rode,
Not fearing bleak November skies nor numbing winds so cold!

An aged, ailing beggar Martin met upon his way,
"Oh, could you spare a coin for one so poor, my lord, I pray?
"Oh, would you save a soul who suffers from the chill this day?"

Martin drew his cloak more tightly 'round his shoulders broad;
Bright red was the woolen cloak that stretched from helm to sword;
Only Roman soldiers wore such warmth as their reward.

Yet the wind cut keenly through the rags the beggar wore;
Beneath the soldier's Roman garb a Christian heart grew sore—
From his armor Martin now the woolen mantle tore.

With his sword he cut the bright red cloak in pieces two:
"What was one I'll double so that it may be shared with you!"
(Multiplying by dividing was a secret Martin knew!)

Martin dreamed a wondrous dream upon that icy night:
Hosts of angels drew him upwards to the starry heights,
Where the Lord his mantle wore, wrapped in radiance of light.

"It was I in beggar's guise who asked your charity;
You were wise to trust to heart and give so graciously—
For what you do to any one you do so unto Me."

It is four hundred years since the life of Christ. Vandals surge across the frozen Rhine, the Goths stamp at the gates of Rome. The classical world collapsing into the dark ages. It was then that Martin came, the last soldier of Rome, obedient, poor, chaste, packed off to the army by his father angry at the boy's love of religion.

By the end of his life you find a thousand men, like sand martins, in caves by the River Loire, living the discipline of Martin. His long life is caught in the deed of sharing, when he met the beggar at the city gate and cut his cloak in two. The bystanders laughed. They did not recognize the stranger Christ.

Eight hundred years later another angry father, Pietro Bernadone, in the Piazza del Commune, in Assisi, saw his son, Francis, the poverello, strip off all his clothes. His cloak, the whole of it, he had already given to a poor knight. From Martin we learn sharing, from Francis the unconditional gift.

We need to know both, how to give and how to share, for both are healing, both kindle the light which lets us see the meaning in our lives. -from "Shaping the Flame"

Fables

The Hare and the Tortoise

Aesop

Said the Tortoise one day to the Hare,
"I'll run you a race if you dare.
  I'll bet you cannot
  Arrive at that spot
As quickly as *I* can get there."

Quoth the Hare, "You are surely insane.
Pray, *what* has affected your brain?
  You seem pretty sick.
  Call a doctor in—quick,
And let him prescribe for your pain."

"Never mind," said the Tortoise. "Let's run!
Will you bet me?" "Why, certainly." "Done!"
  While the slow Tortoise creeps,
  Mr. Hare makes four leaps,
And then loafs around in the sun.

It seemed such a one-sided race,
To win was almost a disgrace.
  So he frolicked about
  Then at last he set out—
As the Tortoise was nearing the place.

Too late! Though he sped like a dart,
The Tortoise was first. She was smart:
  "You can surely run fast,"
  She remarked. "Yet you're last.
It is better to get a good start."

A Fable

Ralph Waldo Emerson

The mountain and the squirrel
Had a quarrel;
And the former called the latter "Little Prig."

Bun replied,
"You are doubtless very big;
But all sorts of things and weather
Must be taken in together,
To make up a year
And a sphere.
And I think it no disgrace
To occupy my place.
If I'm not so large as you,
You are not so small as I,
And not half so spry.
I'll not deny you make
A very pretty squirrel track;
Talents differ; all is well and wisely put;
If I cannot carry forests on my back,
Neither can you crack a nut."

The Fox and the Grapes

Aesop

"What luscious grapes," mused a hungry fox;
"Fine, good grapes," said he.
"If I jump as high as a clever fox can,
I'll have those grapes for me."

He jumped and he leaped and he snapped with his teeth,
But only the air did he bite,
While the grapes, sweet and juicy, dangled above,
And swayed at a lofty height.

The fox grew mad, turn'd scarlet red,
But tossing his head, said he:
"Those grapes are sour and full of worms—
Who wants those grapes? *Not me!"*

The Shepherd Boy and the Wolf

Aesop

A shepherd boy beside a stream,
"The wolf, the wolf," was wont to scream;
And when the villagers appeared
He'd laugh and call them silly-eared.

A wolf at last came down the steep:
"The wolf, the wolf, my legs, my sheep!"
The creature had a jolly feast,
Quite undisturbed, on boy and beast.
For none believes the liar forsooth,
Even when the liar speaks the truth.

The Lion and the Mouse

Aesop, William Ellery Leonard

Lion, dreaming in his pride of place,
Was waked by Mouse who cross'd his face.
The mouse he caught and was about
To claw and kill, when Mouse cried out,
"Spare my life! I'll repay you well."
Lion laughed and loosed him. It befell
A little later some hunters bound
This king of beasts upon the ground.
When Mouse, who heard his roar, in glee
Soon gnawed the ropes and set him free.
Scorn no man's friendship,
Howso small he be.

The Oak and the Reed

Aesop

The great oak tree thinks he's the strongest,
As he's been standing there the longest.
The wind it blew, the rain came lashing;
And down the great oak tree came crashing.
The slender reed, she knows much better,
For she can bend in stormy weather.
The slender reed swayed in the weather,
And at the dawn was strong as ever.

"I Bend and Break Not"

The Wolf and His Shadow

Aesop, William Ellery Leonard

A Wolf, who roamed the mountain side,
Beheld his Shadow stretching wide,
Considerably magnified,
Because 'twas nearing eventide.
Then said the Wolf, the while he eyed
That shadow with increasing pride:
"Why thus should I in fear abide
Of Lion's roar or Lion's stride—
Could I not eat him hair and hide?"
Meanwhile the hungry Lion spied
This most complacent Wolf and tried
The matter out, and Wolf he died,
And dying mournfully he cried:
"Woe worth the fool self-satisfied."

The Country Mouse and the City Mouse

Richard Schrafton Sharpe

In a snug little cot lived a fat little mouse,
Who enjoyed, unmolested, the range of the house;
With plain food content, she would breakfast on cheese,
She dined upon bacon, and supped on grey peas.

A friend from the town to the cottage did stray,
And he said he was come a short visit to pay;
So the mouse spread her table as gay as you please,
And brought the nice bacon and charming grey peas.

The visitor frowned, and he thought to be witty:
Cried he, "You must know, I am come from the city,
Where we all should be shocked at provisions like these,
For we never eat bacon and horrid grey peas.

"To town come with me, I will give you a treat:
Some excellent food, most delightful to eat.
With me shall you feast just as long as you please;
Come, leave this fat bacon and shocking grey peas."

This kind invitation she could not refuse,
And the city mouse wished not a moment to lose;
Reluctant she quitted the fields and the trees,
The delicious fat bacon and charming grey peas.

They slily crept under a gay parlour door,
Where a feast had been given the evening before;
And it must be confessed they on dainties did seize,
Far better than bacon, or even grey peas.

Here were custard and trifle, and cheesecakes good store,
Nice sweetmeats and jellies, and twenty things more;
All that art had invented the palate to please,
Except some fat bacon and smoking grey peas.

They were nicely regaling, when into the room
Came the dog and the cat, and the maid with a broom:
They jumped in a custard both up to their knees;
The country mouse sighed for her bacon and peas.

Cried she to her friend, "Get me safely away,
I can venture no longer in London to stay;
For if oft you receive interruptions like these,
Give me my nice bacon and charming grey peas.

"Your living is splendid and gay, to be sure,
But the dread of disturbance you ever endure;
I taste true delight in contentment and ease,
And I feast on fat bacon and charming grey peas."

The Crow and the Fox

Aesop

A crow, with some cheese, sat down at her ease
  to eat it upon a high tree;
A fox passing by, who did this espy, said,
  "That must be mine speedily!"

"Oh! crow!" he exclaimed, "I'm really ashamed,
  I've never yet heard how you sing!
When ev'rywhere 'round the praises resound
  of your beauteous voice in the spring!"

The crow, full of pride, at this opened wide
  her beak and cawed loudly and shrill;
While fox, with a smile, rejoiced at his guile,
  and swallowed the cheese with a will.

And swallowed the cheese with a will.

The Wind and the Sun

Aesop, Walter Crane

The Wind and the Sun had a bet,
The wayfarers' cloak which should get:
    Blew the Wind—the cloak clung:
    Shone the Sun—the cloak flung
Showed the Sun had the best of it yet.

"True Strength Is Not Bluster"

The Peacock's Complaint

Aesop, Walter Crane

The Peacock considered it wrong
That he had not the nightingale's song;
    So to Juno he went,
    She replied, "Be content
With thy having, and hold thy fool's tongue!"

"Do Not Quarrel with Nature"

The Fox and the Stork

Aesop, Jean de la Fontaine

Old Father Fox, who was known to be mean,
Invited Dame Stork in to dinner.
There was nothing but soup that could scarcely be seen:—
Soup *never* was served any thinner.
And the worst of it was, as I'm bound to relate,
Father Fox dished it up on a *flat* china plate.

Dame Stork, as you know, has a very long beak:
Not a crumb or drop could she gather
Had she pecked at the plate every day in the week.
But as for the Fox—sly old Father:
With his tongue lapping soup at a scandalous rate,
He licked up the last bit and polished the plate.

Pretty soon Mistress Stork spread a feast of her own;
Father Fox was invited to share it.
He came, and he saw, and he gave a great groan:
The stork had known how to prepare it.
She had meant to get even, and now was *her* turn:
Father Fox was invited to *eat from an urn.*

The urn's mouth was small, and it had a long neck;
The food in it smelled most delightful.
Dame Stork, with her beak in, proceeded to peck;
But the Fox found that fasting is frightful.
Home he sneaked. On his way there he felt his ears burn
When he thought of the Stork and her tall, tricky urn.

The Butterfly and the Caterpillar

Joseph Lauren

A butterfly, one summer morn,
Sat on a spray of blossoming thorn
And, as he sipped and drank his share
Of honey from the flowered air,
Below, upon a garden wall,
A caterpillar chanced to crawl.
"Horrors!" the butterfly exclaimed,
"This must be stopped! I am ashamed
That such as I should have to be
In the same world with such as he.
Preserve me from such hideous things!
Disgusting shape! Where are his wings!
Fuzzy and gray! Eater of clay!
Won't someone take the worm away!"
The caterpillar crawled ahead,
But, as he munched a leaf, he said,
"Eight days ago, young butterfly,
You wormed about, the same as I;
Within a fortnight from today
Two wings will bear me far away,
To brighter blooms and lovelier lures,
With colors that outrival yours.
"So, flutter-flit, be not so proud;
Each caterpillar is endowed
With power to make him by and by,
A blithe and brilliant butterfly.
While you, who scorn the common clay,
You, in your livery so gay,
And all the gaudy moths and millers,
Are only dressed up caterpillars."

The Spider and the Fly

Mary Howitt

"Will you walk into my parlor?"
  Said the Spider to the Fly;
"'Tis the prettiest little parlor
  That ever you did spy.

"The way into my parlor
  Is up a winding stair,
And I have many curious things
  To show when you are there."

"Oh no, no," said the little Fly;
  "To ask me is in vain,
For who goes up your winding stair
  Can ne'er come down again."

"I'm sure you must be weary, dear,
  With soaring up so high;
Well you rest upon my little bed?"
  Said the Spider to the Fly.

"There are pretty curtains drawn around;
  The sheets are fine and thin,
And if you like to rest a while,
  I'll snugly tuck you in!"

"Oh no, no," said the little Fly,
  "For I've often heard it said,
They never, never wake again
  Who sleep upon your bed!"

Said the cunning Spider to the Fly:
  "Dear friend, what can I do
To prove the warm affection
  I've always felt for you?

"I have within my pantry
  Good store of all that's nice;
I'm sure you're very welcome—
  Will you please to take a slice?"

"Oh no, no," said the little Fly;
  "Kind sir, that cannot be:
I've heard what's in your pantry,
  And I do not wish to see!"

"Sweet creature!" said the Spider,
"You're witty and you're wise;
How handsome are your gauzy wings;
How brilliant are your eyes!

"I have a little looking-glass
Upon my parlor shelf;
If you'll step in one moment, dear,
You shall behold yourself."

"I thank you, gentle sir," she said,
"For what you're pleased to say,
And, bidding you good morning now,
I'll call another day."

The Spider turned him round about,
And went into his den,
For well he knew the silly Fly
Would soon come back again;

So he wove a subtle web
In a little corner sly,
And set his table ready
To dine upon the Fly;

Then came out to his door again
And merrily did sing:
"Come hither, hither, pretty Fly,
With pearl and silver wing;

"Your robes are green and purple—
There's a crest upon your head;
Your eyes are like diamond bright,
But mine are dull as lead!"

Alas, alas! how very soon
This silly little Fly,
Hearing his wily, flattering words,
Came slowly flitting by;

With buzzing wings she hung aloft,
Then near and nearer grew,
Thinking only of her brilliant eyes,
And green and purple hue—

Thinking only of her crested head—
    Poor, foolish thing! At last
Up jumped the cunning Spider,
    And fiercely held her fast.

He dragged her up his winding stair,
    Into his dismal den,
Within his little parlor—
    But she ne'er came out again!

And now, dear little children,
    Who may this story read,
To idle, silly flattering words
    I pray you ne'er give heed;

Unto an evil counselor
    Close heart and ear and eye,
And take a lesson from this tale
    Of the Spider and the Fly.

Flowers, Plants & Trees

The Little Plant

Kate Louise Brown

In the heart of a seed,
Buried deep so deep,
A tiny plant
Lay fast asleep.

"Wake," said the sunshine,
"And creep to the light."
"Wake," said the voice
Of the raindrops bright.

The little plant heard
And it rose to see,
What the wonderful,
Outside world might be.

The Harvest

Alice C. Henderson

The silver rain, the shining sun,
The fields where scarlet poppies run,
And all the ripples of the wheat
Are in the bread that I do eat.

So when I sit for every meal
And say a grace, I always feel
That I am eating rain and sun,
And fields where scarlet poppies run.

Pretty Flower Elves Are We

Pretty flower elves are we,
Dancing to and fro,
Peeping out from 'neath our buds
As round and round we go.

Sleepy, sleepy snails are we;
Our steps are long and slow.
We drag our feet along the ground
As round and round we go.

Butterflies from the air are we;
Our wings are fairy light.
We dance before the King and Queen
Upon the flowers bright.

Funny little gnomes are we;
Our beards are long and white.
Towards the rocks our footsteps turn
To tap from morn till night.

Long green snakes in the grass are we;
Our tails are far away.
We wriggle and wriggle and twist and turn
As in and out we sway.

The Butterbean Tent

Elizabeth Madox Roberts

All through the garden I went and went,
And I walked in under the butterbean tent.
The poles leaned up like a good tepee
And made a nice little house for me.

I had a hard brown clod for a seat,
And all outside was a cool green street.
A little green worm and a butterfly
And a cricket-like thing that could hop went by.

Hidden away there were flocks and flocks
Of bugs that could go like little clocks.
Such a good day it was when I spent
A long, long while in the butterbean tent.

Baby Seed Song

Edith Nesbit

Little brown brother, oh! little brown brother,
Are you awake in the dark?
Here we lie cosily, close to each other:
Hark to the song of the lark—

"Waken!" the lark says, "waken and dress you;
Put on your green coats and gay,
Blue sky will shine on you, sunshine caress you
Waken! 'tis morning 'tis May!"

Little brown brother, oh! little brown brother,
What kind of a flower will you be?
I'll be a poppy all white, like my mother;
Do be a poppy like me.

What! You're a sunflower! How I shall miss you
When you're grown golden and high!
But I shall send all the bees up to kiss you;
Little brown brother, good-bye.

April Fools

Emily Huntington Miller

Shy little pansies tucked away to sleep,
Wrapped in brown blankets piled snug and deep,
Heard in a day-dream a bird singing clear:
"Wake, little sweethearts; the springtime is here!"

Glad little pansies, stirring from their sleep,
Shook their brown blankets off for a peep,
Put on their velvet hoods, purple and gold,
And stood all a-tremble abroad in the cold.

Snowflakes were flying, skies were grim and gray,
Bluebird and robin had scurried away;
Only a cruel wind laughed as it said,
"Poor little April fools, hurry back to bed!"

Soft chins a-quiver, dark eyes full of tears,
Brave little pansies, spite of their fears,
Said, "Let us wait for the sunshiny weather;
Take hold of hands, dears, and cuddle up together."

FROM FLOWER CHORUS

Ralph Waldo Emerson

O Such a commotion under the ground,
When March called, "Ho there! ho!"
Such spreading of rootlets far and wide,
Such whisperings to and fro!
"Are you ready?" the Snowdrop asked,
"Tis time to start, you know."
"Almost, my dear!" the Scilla replied,
"I'll follow as soon as you go."
Then "Ha! ha! ha!" a chorus came
Of laughter sweet and low,
From millions of flowers under the ground,
Yes, millions beginning to grow.

"I'll promise my blossoms," the Crocus said,
"When I hear the blackbird sing."
And straight thereafter Narcissus cried,
"My silver and gold I'll bring."
"And ere they are dulled," another spoke,
"The Hyacinth bells shall ring."
But the Violet only murmured, "I'm here,"
And sweet grew the air of Spring.
Then "Ha! ha! ha!" a chorus came
Of laughter sweet and low,
From millions of flowers under the ground,
Yes, millions beginning to grow.

MINNIE AND MATTIE

Christina Rossetti

Minnie and Mattie
And fat little May,
Out in the country,
Spending a day.

Such a bright day,
With the sun glowing,
And the trees half in leaf,
And the grass growing.

Pinky white pigling
    Squeals through his snout,
Woolly white lambkin
    Frisks all about.

Cluck! cluck! the nursing hen
    Summons her folk,—
Ducklings all downy soft
    Yellow as yolk.

Cluck! cluck! the mother hen
    Summons her chickens
To peck the dainty bits
    Found in her pickings.

Minnie and Mattie
    And May carry posies,
Half of sweet violets,
    Half of primroses.

Give the sun time enough,
    Glowing and glowing,
He'll rouse the roses
    And bring them blowing.

Don't wait for roses
    Losing to-day,
O Minnie, Mattie,
    And wise little May.

Violets and primroses
    Blossom to-day
For Minnie and Mattie
    And fat little May.

White Coral Bells

White coral bells upon a slender stalk,
Lilies of the valley deck my garden walk.

Oh, don't you wish that you could hear them ring?
That will only happen when the fairies sing.

The City Child

Alfred, Lord Tennyson

Dainty little maiden, whither would you wander?
Whither from this pretty home, the home where mother dwells?
"Far and far away," said the dainty little maiden,
"All among the gardens, auriculas, anemones,
Roses and lilies and Canterbury-bells."

Dainty little maiden, whither would you wander?
Whither from this pretty house, this city-house of ours?
"Far and far away," said the dainty little maiden,
"All among the meadows, the clover and the clematis,
Daisies and kingcups and honeysuckle-flowers."

Mother Earth

Eileen Hutchins

Mother Earth, Mother Earth,
Take our seed and give it birth.

Father Sun, gleam and glow
Until the roots begin to grow.

Sister Rain, Sister Rain,
Shed thy tears to swell the grain.

Brother Wind, breathe and blow,
Then the blade green will grow.

Earth and Sun and Wind and Rain
Turn to gold the living grain.

The Lily

William Blake

The modest Rose puts forth a thorn,
The humble sheep a threat'ning horn:
While the Lily white shall in love delight,
Nor a thorn nor a threat stain her beauty bright.

In My Little Garden

In my little garden
By the apple tree,
Daffodils are dancing—
One, two, three!

In my little garden
By the kitchen door,
Daisies red are smiling—
Two, three, four!

In my little garden
By the winding drive,
Roses bright are climbing—
Three, four, five!

In my little garden
By the pile of bricks,
Hollyhocks are growing—
Four, five, six!

In my little garden
Down in sunny Devon,
Violets are hiding—
Five, six, seven!

In my little garden
By the cottage gate,
Pansies gay are shining—
Six, seven, eight!

Daffodils in golden gowns,
Daisies all red,
Hollyhocks so very tall
By the garden shed,

Roses in the sunshine,
Violets dewy bright,
Pansies smiling gaily—
What a lovely sight!

Snowdrops

Laurence Alma Tadema

Little ladies, white and green,
With your spears about you,
Will you tell us where you've been
Since we lived without you?

You are sweet, and fresh, and clean,
With your pearly faces;
In the dark earth where you've been
There are wondrous places:

Yet you come again, serene,
When the leaves are hidden;
Bringing joy from where you've been
You return unbidden—

Little ladies, white and green,
Are you glad to cheer us ?
Hunger not for where you've been,
Stay till Spring be near us!

Dandelion, Yellow as Gold

Noreen Bath

O Dandelion, yellow as gold,
what do you do all day?
"I just wait here in the tall, green grass,
till the children come to play."

O Dandelion, yellow as gold,
what do you do all night?
"I wait and wait, till the cool dew falls,
and my hair grows long and white."

And what do you do when your hair grows white,
and the children come to play?
"They take me in their dimpled hands,
and blow my hair away!"

Fern Song

John B. Tabb

Dance to the beat of the rain, little Fern,
And spread out your palms again,
  And say, "Tho' the Sun
  Hath my vesture spun,
He hath labored, alas, in vain,
  But for the shade
  That the Cloud hath made,
And the gift of the Dew and the Rain."
  Then laugh and upturn
  All your fronds, little Fern,
And rejoice in the beat of the rain!

Cosmic Dance

Dennis Klocek

A stately lily in a field
Was dancing with a breeze;
As they went 'round the love they knew
Expanded to the trees.
The trees bestowed it on the clouds,
The clouds they touched the moon.
The moon embraced the planets,
The planets kissed the sun,
The sun it served the cosmos,
The cosmos it loved God.
Then God reflected all this love
Back to a piece of sod,
Where playful breezes dance around
And grateful flowers nod.

I Know a Little Pussy

I know a little pussy
Her coat is silver gray
She lives down in the meadow
Not very far away.

Though she is a pussy
She'll never be a cat.
She is a pussy willow.
Now what do you think of that!

Pussy Willow

Marian Douglass

The brook is brimmed with melting snow,
    The maple sap is running,
And on the highest elm a crow
    His coal-black wings is sunning.
A close, green bud, the Mayflower lies
    Upon its mossy pillow;
And sweet and low the south wind blows,
And through the brown fields calling goes,
    "Come, Pussy! Pussy Willow!
Within your close, brown wrapper stir;
Come out and show your silver fur;
    Come, Pussy! Pussy Willow!"

Soon red will bud the maple trees,
    The bluebirds will be singing,
And yellow tassels in the breeze
    Be from the poplars swinging;
And rosy will the Mayflower lie
    Upon its mossy pillow;
"But you must come the first of all,—
Come, Pussy!" is the south wind's call,—
    "Come, Pussy! Pussy Willow!
A fairy gift to children dear,
The downy firstling of the year,—
    Come, Pussy! Pussy Willow!"

Trees

Joyce Kilmer

I think that I shall never see
A poem as lovely as a tree,
A tree whose hungry mouth is pressed
Against the earth's sweet flowing breast
A tree that looks at God all day
And lifts her leafy arms to pray.
A tree that may, in summer, wear
A nest of robins in her hair
Upon whose bosom snow has lain
Who intimately lives with rain.
Poems are made by fools like me,
But only God can make a tree.

The Acorn

In small green cup an acorn grew
On tall and stately oak:
The spreading leaves the secret knew,
And hid it like a cloak.
The breezes rocked it tenderly,
The sunbeams whispered low,
"Some day the smallest acorn here
Will make an oak, you know."

The little acorn heard it all,
And thought it quite a joke:
How could he dream an acorn small
Would ever be an oak?
He laughed so much that presently
He tumbled from his cup,
And rolled a long way from the tree,
Where no one picked him up.

Close by him was a rabbit hole,
And when the wind blew high,
Down went the acorn with a roll
For weeks in gloom to lie.
But, one bright day, a shoot of green
Broke from his body dry,
And pushed its way with longing keen
To see the glorious sky.

It grew and grew, with all its might,
As weeks and months rolled on:
The sunbeam's words were proving right.
For, ere a year had gone,
The shoot became a sturdy plant,
While now the country folk
Can sit beneath the spreading leaves
Of a mighty forest oak.

I Wandered Lonely as a Cloud

William Wordsworth

I wandered lonely as a cloud
That floats on high o'er vales and hills,
When all at once I saw a crowd,
A host of golden daffodils;
    Beside the lake, beneath the trees,
    Fluttering and dancing in the breeze.

Continuous as the stars
That shine and twinkle on the Milky Way,
They stretched in never-ending line
Along the margin of a bay:
    Ten thousand saw I at a glance,
    Tossing their heads in sprightly dance.

The waves beside them danced; but they
Out-did the sparkling waves in glee:
A poet could not but be gay,
In such a jocund company:
    I gazed—and gazed—but little thought
    What wealth the show to me had brought:

For oft, when on my couch I lie
In vacant or in pensive mood,
They flash upon that inward eye
Which is the bliss of solitude;
    And then my heart with pleasure fills,
    And dances with the daffodil.

Autumn Fancies

The maple is a dainty maid,
    The pet of all the wood,
Who lights the dusky forest glade
    With scarlet cloak and hood.

The elm a lovely lady is,
    In shimmering robes of gold,
That catch the sunlight when she moves,
    And glisten, fold on fold.

The sumac is a gypsy queen,
  Who flaunts in crimson dressed,
And wild along the roadside runs,
  Red blossoms in her breast.

And towering high above the wood,
  All in his purple cloak,
A monarch in his splendor is
  The round and princely oak.

Trees

Sara Coleridge

The Oak is called the King of Trees,
The Aspen quivers in the breeze,
The Poplar grows up straight and tall,
The Pear tree spreads along the wall,
The Sycamore gives pleasant shade,
The Willow droops in watery glade,
The Fire tree useful timber gives,
The Beech amid the forest lives.

The Willows

Walter Prichard Eaton

By the little river,
  Still and deep and brown,
Grow the graceful willows,
  Gently dipping down.

Dipping down and brushing
  Everything that floats—
Leaves and logs and fishes,
  And the passing boats.

Were they water maidens
  In the long ago,
That they lean out sadly
  Looking down below?

In the misty twilight
  You can see their hair,
Weeping water maidens
  That were once so fair.

In France

Frances Cornford

The poplars in the fields of France
Are golden ladies come to dance;
But yet to see them there is none
But I and the September sun.

The girl who in their shadow sits
Can only see the sock she knits;
Her dog is watching all the day
That not a cow shall go astray.

The leisurely contented cows
Can only see the earth they browse;
Their piebald bodies through the grass
With busy, munching noses pass.

Alone the sun and I behold
Processions crowned with shining gold—
The poplars in the fields of France,
Like glorious ladies come to dance.

What Do We Plant?

Henry Abbey

What do we plant when we plant the tree?
We plant the ship, which will cross the sea.
We plant the mast to carry the sails;
We plant the planks to withstand the gales—
The keel, the keelson, and the beam and knee;
We plant the ship when we plant the tree.

What do we plant when we plant the tree?
We plant the houses for you and me.
We plant the rafters, the shingles, the floors.
We plant the studding, the lath, the doors,
The beams, and siding, all parts that be;
We plant the house when we plant the tree.

What do we plant when we plant the tree?
A thousand things that we daily see;
We plant the spire that out-towers the crag,
We plant the staff for our country's flag,
We plant the shade, from the hot sun free;
We plant all these when we plant the tree.

Timber

With oak, the old-time ships were laid,
The round-back chairs of ash were made.
Of birch the brooms to sweep the floor,
The furniture was sycamore.
Clogs were of alder, bows of yew,
And fishing rods of bright bamboo.
Willow was used for cricket bats,
And ash again for tubs and vats.
Of pine, the roof beams and the floor
Or for the window frames and door.
Elm made a wagon or a cart,
And maple was for the carver's art.
Beech was for bowls, pipes were of briar.
Many a wood would make a fire.
But in the cottage or the hall,
Ash made the brightest fire of all.

A Seed

William Allingham

See how a Seed, which Autumn flung down,
　　And through the Winter neglected lay,
Uncoils two little green leaves and two brown,
　　With tiny root taking hold on the clay,
　　As, lifting and strengthening day by day,
It pushes red branchlets, sprouts new leaves,
And cell after cell the Power in it weaves
Out of the storehouse of soil and clime,
To fashion a Tree in due course of time;
Tree with rough bark and boughs' expansion,
Where the Crow can build his mansion,
Or a Man, in some new May,
Lie under whispering leaves and say,
"Are the ills of one's life so very bad
When a Green Tree makes me deliciously glad?"
As I do now. But where shall I be
When this little Seed is a tall green Tree?

The Metaphor of a Plant

The plant, a being that always grows,
Stands alone, somehow it knows
And in the end beauty shows
The way that life can be.

Yet surrounded with love and care and tending
Its journey really never-ending
Will find the way in each days rending
To be what's meant to be.

Plants

Johann Wolfgang von Goethe

If Nature Study be your goal,
Take note: a single part reflects the whole.
Nought is within and nought without,
For what is in is also out.
So grasp without delay this prize:
That here a holy public secret lies.
Rejoice in true illusion's fame,
Rejoice in Nature's serious game.
No living thing alone can be—
It only exists in company.

Nature

Ralph Waldo Emerson

The rounded world is fair to see,
Nine times folded in mystery:
Though baffled seers cannot impart
The secret of its laboring heart,
Throb thine with Nature's throbbing breast,
And all is clear from east to west.
Spirit that lurks each form within
Beckons to spirit of its kin;
Self-kindled every atom glows,
And hints the future which it owes.

Animals

They Shall Teach Thee

Job 12:7,8

But ask now the beasts, and they shall teach thee;
And the fowls of the air and they shall teach thee:
Or speak to the earth, and it shall teach thee;
And the fishes of the sea shall declare unto thee.

The Butterfly

I know a little butterfly
With tiny golden wings;
He plays among the summer flowers,
And up and down he swings.

He dances on their honey cups
So happy all the day;
And then he spreads his tiny wings,
And softly flies away.

Peacocks

Rose Fyleman

Peacocks sweep the fairies' rooms;
They use their folded tails for brooms;
But fairy dust is brighter far
Than any mortal colours are;
And all about their tails it clings
In strange designs of rounds and rings;
And that is why they strut about
And proudly spread their feathers out.

Answer to a Child's Question

Samuel Taylor Coleridge

Do you ask what the birds say? The Sparrow, the Dove,
The Linnet and Thrush say, "I love and I love!"
In the winter they're silent—the wind is so strong;
What it says, I don't know, but it sings a loud song.
But green leaves, and blossoms, and sunny warm weather,
And singing, and loving—all come back together.
But the Lark is so brimful of gladness and love,
The green fields below him, the blue sky above,
That he sings, and he sings; and for ever sings he—
"I love my Love, and my Love loves me!"

How Doth the Little Busy Bee

Isaac Watts

How doth the little busy bee
  Improve each shining hour,
And gather honey all the day
  From every passing flower!

How skilfully she builds her cell!
  How neat she spreads the wax!
And labours hard to store it well
  With the sweet food she makes.

No Shop Does the Bird Use

Elizabeth Coatsworth

No shop does the bird use,
No counter nor baker,
But the bush is his orchard,
The grass is his acre;
The ant is his quarry,
The seed is his bread,
And a star is his candle
To light him to bed.

The Cow

Robert Louis Stevenson

The friendly cow, all red and white,
I love with all my heart:
She gives me cream with all her might,
To eat with apple-tart.

She wanders lowing here and there,
And yet she cannot stray,
All in the pleasant open air,
The pleasant light of day;

And blown by all the winds that pass,
And wet with all the showers,
She walks among the meadow grass
And eats the meadow flowers.

An Old Rat's Tale

Laura E. Richards

He was a rat, and she was a rat,
And down in one hole they did dwell.
And each was as black as a witch's cat,
And they loved one another well.

He had a tail, and she had a tail,
Both long and curling and fine.
And each said, "Yours is the finest tail
In the world, excepting mine!"

He smelt the cheese, and she smelt the cheese,
And they both pronounced it good;
And both remarked it would greatly add
To the charm of their daily food.

So he ventured out and she ventured out;
And I saw them go with pain.
But what them befell I never can tell,
For they never came back again.

The Rabbits' Song Outside the Tavern

Elizabeth Coatsworth

We, who play under the pines,
We, who dance in the snow
That shines blue in the light of the moon,
Sometimes halt as we go—
Stand with our ears erect,
Our noses testing the air,
To gaze at the golden world
Behind the windows there.

Suns they have in a cave,
Stars, each on a tall white stem,
And the thought of a fox or an owl
Seems never to trouble them.
They laugh and eat and are warm,
Their food is ready at hand,
While hungry out in the cold
We little rabbits stand.

But they never dance as we dance!
They haven't the speed nor the grace.
We scorn the dog and the cat
Who lie by their fireplace.
We scorn them licking their paws
Their eyes on an upraised spoon—
We who dance hungry and wild
Under a winter's moon.

Grasshopper Green

Grasshopper Green is a comical chap;
He lives on the best of fare.
Bright little trousers, jacket and cap,
These are his summer wear.

Out in the meadow he loves to go,
Playing away in the sun;
It's hopperty, skipperty, high and low—
Summer's the time for fun.

Grasshopper Green has a quaint little house:
It's under the hedgerow gay.
Grandmother Spider, as still as a mouse,
Watches him over the way.

Gladly he's calling the children, I know,
Out in the beautiful sun;
It's hopperty, skipperty, high and low—
Summer's the time for fun.

The Kind Mousie

Natalie Joan

There once was a cobbler,
  And he was so wee
That he lived in a hole
  In a very big tree.
He had a good neighbor,
  And she was a mouse;
She did his wee washing
  And tidied his house.

Each morning at seven
  He heard a wee tap,
And in came the mouse
  In her apron and cap.
She lighted his fire
  And she fetched a wee broom,
And she swept and she polished
  His little Tree-room.

To take any wages
  She'd always refuse,
So the cobbler said, "Thank you!"
  And mended her shoes;
And the owl didn't eat her,
  And even the cat
Said, "I never would catch
  A kind mousie like that!"

The Two Kittens

Two little kittens, one stormy night,
Began to quarrel and to fight.
One had a mouse, the other had none,
This was the way the fight had begun:

"I'll have that mouse," said the bigger cat.
"You'll have that mouse? We'll see about that!"
"I will have that mouse!" said the older one.
"You shan't have that mouse!" said the little one.

I told you before 'twas a stormy night
When these two little kittens began to fight.
The old woman took her sweeping broom,
And swept the kittens right out of the room.

The ground was covered with frost and snow,
And the poor little kittens had nowhere to go.
So they both lay down on the mat at the door,
While the old woman finished sweeping the floor.

Then they both crept in, as quiet as mice,
All wet with snow, and cold as ice,
For they found it was better, that stormy night,
To lie down and sleep than to quarrel and fight.

Duck's Ditty

Kenneth Grahame

All along the backwater,
    Through the rushes tall,
Ducks are a-dabbling,
    Up tails all!

Ducks' tails, drake's tails,
    Yellow feet a-quiver,
Yellow bills all out of sight,
    Busy in the river!

Slushy green undergrowth
    Where the roach swim—
Here we keep our larder,
    Cool and full and dim!

Everyone for what he likes!
  WE like to be
Heads down, tails up,
  Dabbling free!

High in the blue above
  Swifts whirl and call -
WE are down a-dabbling,
  Up tails all!

The Lamb

William Blake

Little lamb, who made thee?
Dost thou know who made thee?
Gave thee life, and bid thee feed
By the stream and o'er the mead;
Gave thee clothing of delight,
Softest clothing, woolly, bright;
Gave thee such a tender voice,
Making all the vales rejoice?
Little lamb, who made thee?
Dost thou know who made thee?

Little lamb, I'll tell thee,
Little lamb, I'll tell thee:
He is called by thy name,
For He calls Himself a lamb.
He is meek, and He is mild;
He became a little child.
I a child, and thou a lamb,
We are called by His name.
Little lamb, God bless thee!
Little lamb, God bless thee!

What Robin Told

George Cooper

How do the robins build their nests?
    Robin Redbreast told me.
First a wisp of amber hay
In a pretty round they lay;
Then some shreds of downy floss,
Feathers, too, and bits of moss,
Woven with a sweet, sweet song,
This way, that way, and across;
    That's what Robin told me.

Where do the robins hide their nests?
    Robin Redbreast told me.
Up among the leaves so deep,
Where the sunbeams rarely creep;
Long before the winds are cold,
Long before the leaves are gold,
Bright-eyed stars will peep and see
Baby robins—one, two, three;
    That's what Robin told me.

Whisky Frisky

Whisky, frisky,
Hippity hop;
Up he goes
To the tree top!

Whirly, twirly,
Round and round,
Down he scampers
To the ground.

Furly, curly
What a tail!
Tall as a feather
Broad as a sail!

Where's his supper?
In the shell,
Snappy, cracky,
Out it fell!

The Song of the Robin

Beatrice Bergquist

The cows low in the pasture on the hill,
The blue bird sings, building a nest,
The water is singing down by the mill—
But the robin's song is the best!

The squirrels are chattering in the trees,
The wind is blowing toward the west,
Around the flowers are humming bees—
But the robin's song is the best!

The dogwood trees are blossoming white,
The plow horse is neighing for rest,
The song sparrow is singing with all his might—
But the robin's song is the best!

The Robin

The robin is the fairies' page;
They keep him neatly dressed
For country service or for town
In dapper livery of brown
And little scarlet vest.

On busy errands all day long
He hurries to and fro
With watchful eyes and nimble wings
There are not very many things.
The robin doesn't know.

And he can tell you, if he will,
The latest fairy news:
The quaint adventures of the King,
And whom the Queen is visiting,
And where she gets her shoes.

And lately, when the Fairy Court
Invited me to tea,
He stood behind the Royal Chair
And here, I solemnly declare,
When he discovered I was there,
That robin winked at me.

The Frog

Hillaire Belloc

Be kind and tender to the Frog,
And do not call him names,
As "Slimy skin," or "Polly-wog,"
Or likewise "Ugly James,"
Or "Gap-a-grin," or "Toad-gone-wrong,"
Or "Bill Bandy-knees":
The Frog is justly sensitive
To epithets like these.

No animal will more repay
A treatment kind and fair;
At least so lonely people say
Who keep a frog (and, by the way,
They are extremely rare).

The Owl

Molly de Havas

When night is falling in the wood,
The Owl wakes up and cries, "Tu-whoo!
Dear children, you must go to bed,
Your day is done, Goodnight to you.

For me the darkness is the day,
And I must hunt the whole night through
To feed my hungry owlets, till
At dawn we sleep, Tu-whit, Tu-whoo!"

Song—The Owl

Alfred, Lord Tennyson

When cats run home and light is come,
And dew is cold upon the ground,
And the far-off stream is dumb,
And the whirring sail goes round,
And the whirring sail goes round;
Alone and warming his five wits,
The white owl in the belfry sits.

When merry milkmaids click the latch,
And rarely smells the new-mown hay,
And the cock hath sung beneath the thatch
Twice or thrice his roundelay,
Twice or thrice his roundelay;
Alone and warming his five wits,
The white owl in the belfry sits.

The Cow

Roy Wilkinson

Heavily, wearily, moves the cow
In the peaceful country scene,
Sleepily nodding towards the ground
As she grazes the pastures green.

Her big, bulky mass of a body
Flops on the earth and she seems,
Chewing and chewing and chewing,
Lost in her own world of dreams.

The Horse

Roy Wilkinson

Dancing on tip-toes,
This is the horse,
Scarcely touching the ground.
Tossing his mane,
Flicking his tail,
Rearing and jumping around.

See him prancing
Over the field,
Kicking his hooves in the air,
Bucking, rolling,
Galloping swiftly,
Unburdened of every care.

The Cat and the Moon

William Butler Yeats

The cat went here and there
And the moon spun round like a top,
And the nearest kin of the moon,
The creeping cat, looked up.

Black Minnaloushe stared at the moon,
For, wander and wail as he would,
The pure cold light in the sky
Troubled his animal blood.

Minnaloushe runs in the grass
Lifting his delicate feet.
Do you dance, Minnaloushe, do you dance?
When two close kindred meet,

What better than call a dance?
Maybe the moon may learn,
Tired of that courtly fashion,
A new dance turn.

Minnaloushe creeps through the grass
From moonlit place to place,
The sacred moon overhead
Has taken a new phase.

Does Minnaloushe know that his pupils
Will pass from change to change,
And that from round to crescent,
From crescent to round they range?

Minnaloushe creeps through the grass
Alone, important and wise,
And lifts to the changing moon
His changing eyes.

Five Eyes

Walter de la Mare

In Hans' old Mill his three black cats
Watch the bins for the thieving rats.
Whisker and claw, they crouch in the night,
Their five eyes smouldering green and bright:
Squeaks from the flour sacks, squeaks from where
The cold wind stirs on the empty stair,
Squeaking and scampering, everywhere.
Then down they pounce, now in, now out,
At whisking tail, and sniffing snout;
While lean old Hans he snores away
Till peep of light at break of day;
Then up he climbs to his creaking mill,
Out come his cats all grey with meal—
Jekkel, and Jessup, and one-eyed Jill.

The Eagle

Alfred, Lord Tennyson

He clasps the crag with crooked hands;
Close to the sun in lonely lands,
Ring'd with the azure world, he stands.

The wrinkled sea beneath him crawls;
He watches from his mountain walls,
And like a thunderbolt he falls.

Mighty Eagle

Percy Bysshe Shelley

Mighty eagle! thou that soarest
O'er the misty mountain forest,
    And amid the light of morning
Like a cloud of glory highest,
And when night descends defiest
    The embattled tempests' warning!

The Plaint of the Camel

Charles Edward Carryl

"Canary-birds feed on sugar and seed,
Parrots have crackers to crunch;
And, as for the poodles, they tell me the noodles
Have chickens and cream for their lunch.
But there's never a question
About my digestion—
Anything does for me!

"Cats, you're aware, can repose in a chair,
Chickens can roost upon rails;
Puppies are able to sleep in a stable,
And oysters can slumber in pails.
But no one supposes
A poor Camel dozes—
Any place does for me!

"Lambs are enclosed where it's never exposed,
Coops are constructed for hens;
Kittens are treated to houses well heated,
And pigs are protected by pens.
But a Camel comes handy
Wherever it's sandy—
Anywhere does for me!

"People would laugh if you rode a giraffe,
Or mounted the back of an ox;
It's nobody's habit to ride on a rabbit,
Or try to bestraddle a fox.
But as for a Camel, he's
Ridden by families—
Any load does for me!

"A snake is as round as a hole in the ground,
And weasels are wavy and sleek;
And no alligator could ever be straighter
Than lizards that live in a creek,
But a Camel's all lumpy
And bumpy and humpy—
Any shape does for me!"

Fishes

Roy Wilkinson

In the ever flowing water
Up and down I love to roam,
Whether it be lake or river
Water, water is my home.

Perhaps a glimpse of me you saw,
In the water something shone.
You looked again, what did you see?
Nothing, I had gone.

Nicholas Nye

Walter de la Mare

Thistle and darnell and dock grew there,
    And a bush, in the corner, of may,
On the orchard wall I used to sprawl
    In the blazing heat of the day;
Half asleep and half awake,
    While the birds went twittering by,
And nobody there my lone to share
    But Nicholas Nye.

Nicholas Nye was lean and gray,
    Lame of leg and old,
More than a score of donkey's years
    He had been since he was foaled;
He munched the thistles, purple and spiked,
    Would sometimes stoop and sigh,
And turn to his head, as if he said,
    "Poor Nicholas Nye!"

Alone with his shadow he'd drowse in the meadow,
    Lazily swinging his tail,
At break of day he used to bray,—
    Not much too hearty and hale;
But a wonderful gumption was under his skin,
    And a clean calm light in his eye,
And once in a while, he'd smile:
    Would Nicholas Nye.

Seem to be smiling at me, he would,
From his bush in the corner, of may,—
Bony and ownerless, widowed and worn,
Knobble-kneed, lonely and gray;
And over the grass would seem to pass
'Neath the deep dark blue of the sky,
Something much better than words between me
And Nicholas Nye.

But dusk would come in the apple boughs,
The green of the glow-worm shine,
The birds in nest would crouch to rest,
And home I'd trudge to mine;
And there, in the moonlight, dark with dew,
Asking not wherefore nor why,
Would brood like a ghost, and as still as a post,
Old Nicholas Nye.

The Wolf

Georgia R. Durston

When the pale moon hides and the wild wind wails,
And over the treetops the nighthawk sails,
The gray wolf sits on the world's far rim
And howls, and it seems to comfort him.

The wolf is a lonely soul, you see,
No beast in the wood, nor bird in the tree,
But shuns his path; in the windy gloom
They give him plenty, and plenty of room.

So he sits with his long, lean face to the sky
Watching the ragged clouds go by.
There in the night, alone, apart,
Singing the song of his lone, wild heart.

Far away, on the world's dark rim
He howls, and it seems to comfort him.

The Shrewmouse

Fiona Macleod

The creatures with the shining eyes
That live among the tender grass
See great stars falling down the skies
And mighty comets pass.

Torches of thought within the mind
Wave fire upon the dancing streams
Of souls that shake upon them wind
In rain of falling dreams.

The shrewmouse builds her windy nest
And laughs amid the corn:
She hath no dreams within her breast:
God smiled when she was born.

The Fieldmouse

Cecil Frances Alexander

Where the acorn tumbles down,
Where the ash tree sheds its berry,
With your fur so soft and brown,
With your eye so round and merry,
Scarcely moving the long grass,
Fieldmouse, I can see you pass.

Little thing, in what dark den,
Lie you all the winter sleeping?
Till warm weather comes again,
Then once more I see you peeping
Round about the tall tree roots,
Nibbling at their fallen fruits.

Fieldmouse, fieldmouse, do not go,
Where the farmer stacks his treasure,
Find the nut that falls below,
Eat the acorn at your pleasure,
But you must not steal the grain
He has stacked with so much pain.

Make your hole where mosses spring,
Underneath the tall oak's shadow,
Pretty, quiet harmless thing,
Play about the sunny meadow.
Keep away from corn and house,
None will harm you, little mouse.

The Donkey

Gilbert Chesterton

When fishes flew and forests walked
And figs grew upon thorn,
Some moment when the moon was blood
Then surely I was born;

With monstrous head and sickening cry
And ears like errant wings,
The devil's walking parody
On all four-footed things.

The tattered outlaw of the earth,
Of ancient crooked will;
Starve, scourge, deride me: I am dumb,
I keep my secret still.

Fools! For I also had my hour;
One far fierce hour and sweet:
There was a shout about my ears,
And palms before my feet.

Cows

Pelham Moffat

Now the gentle cows are standing
Knee-deep in the dewy grass.
Dawn has found them, patient shadows,
Watching hours that softly pass.

Moving slowly over meadows,
Munching quiet unhurried ways,
They have nought to do but wander
Down the rich unheeded days.

Seal

William Jay Smith

See how he dives
From the rocks with a zoom!
See how he darts
Through his watery room
Past crabs and eels
And green seaweed,
Past fluffs of sandy
Minnow feed!
See how he swims
With a swerve and a twist,
A flip of the flipper,
A flick of the wrist!
Quicksilver-quick,
Softer than spray,
Down he plunges
And sweeps away;
Before you can think,
Before you can utter
Words like "Dill pickle"
Or "Apple butter,"
Back up he swims
Past Sting Ray and Shark,
Out with a zoom,
A whoop, a bark;
Before you can say
Whatever you wish,
He plops at your side
With a mouthful of fish!

The Tyger

William Blake

Tyger, tyger, burning bright
In the forests of the night,
What immortal hand or eye
Could frame thy fearful symmetry?

In what distant deeps or skies
Burnt the fire of thine eyes?
On what wings dare he aspire?
What the hand dare seize the fire?

And what shoulder and what art
Could twist the sinews of thy heart?
And when thy heart began to beat,
What dread hand and what dread feet?

What the hammer? what the chain?
In what furnace was thy brain?
What the anvil? What dread grasp
Dare its deadly terrors clasp?

When the stars threw down their spears,
And water'd heaven with their tears,
Did He smile His work to see?
Did He who made the lamb make thee?

Tyger, tyger, burning bright
In the forests of the night,
What immortal hand or eye
Dare frame thy fearful symmetry?

from The Blind Men and the Elephant

A Hindoo Fable

John Godfrey Saxe

It was six men of Indostan
  To learning much inclined,
Who went to see the Elephant
  (Though all of them were blind),
That each by observation
  Might satisfy the mind.

The *First* approached the Elephant,
  And happening to fall
Against his broad and sturdy side
  At once began to bawl:
"God bless me! but the Elephant
  Is very like a wall!"

The *Second*, feeling of his tusk,
  Cried, "Ho! What have we here
So very round and smooth and sharp?
  To me 'tis mighty clear
This wonder of an Elephant
  Is very like a spear".

The *Third* approached the animal,
    And happening to take
The squirming trunk within his hands,
    Then boldly up and spake:
"I see," quoth he, "the Elephant
    Is very like a snake!"

The *Fourth* reached out his eager hand,
    And felt about the knee.
"What most this wondrous beast is like
    Is mighty plain," quoth he;
"'T is clear enough the Elephant
    Is very like a tree!"

The *Fifth*, who chanced to touch the ear,
    Said: "E'en the blindest man
Can tell what this resembles most;
    Deny the fact who can,
This marvel of an Elephant
    Is very like a fan!"

The *Sixth* no sooner had begun
    About the beast to grope,
Than, seizing on the swinging tail
    That fell within his scope,
"I see," quoth he, "the Elephant
    Is very like a rope!"

And so these men of Indostan
    Disputed loud and long,
Each in his own opinion
    Exceeding stiff and strong,
Though each was partly in the right,
    And all were in the wrong!

Unstooping

Walter de la Mare

Low on his fours the Lion
Treads with the surly Bear;
But Men straight upward from the dust
Walk with their heads in air;

The free sweet winds of heaven,
The sunlight from on high
Beat on their clear bright cheeks and brows
As they go striding by;
The doors of all their houses
They arch so they may go,
Uplifted o'er the four-foot beasts,
Unstooping, to and fro.

Ant, Bee and Butterfly

Eugene Schwartz

Have you ever watched the humble ants
Cast up hillocks of dirt?
And carve out catacomb-like halls
Sequestered in the earth?
Within they form a little world,
So perfect in itself,
Where each the other serves and so
Ensouls the common wealth.
Rotting wood they turn to good,
Dead carrion make living,
While on her eggs their calm Queen broods;
Prime Mother, ever giving.

The busy bee asks not the aim
Nor purpose of his labor,
For in it he such sweetness finds
That the task itself he savors.
The bloom and bee, the bee and hive
Form a sweet trinity;
For through the bee the seed shall thrive,
And through the blossom lives the bee.

When the chrysalis seems most asleep
Or deathlike, she is weaving
On the warp and woof of her living loom
And her primal form receiving.
Then, as a golden butterfly,
Casting off the gray and cold,
She awakens, self-created,
Reborn, renewed and whole.

The Leap of Roushan Beg

Henry Wadsworth Longfellow

Mounted on Kyrat strong and fleet,
His chestnut steed with four white feet,
 Roushan Beg, called Kurroglou,
Son of the road and bandit chief,
Seeking refuge and relief,
 Up the mountain pathway flew.

Such was Kyrat's wondrous speed,
Never yet could any steed
 Reach the dust-cloud in his course.
More than maiden, more than wife,
More than gold and next to life
 Roushan the Robber loved his horse.

In the land that lies beyond
Erzeroum and Trebizond,
 Garden-girt his fortress stood;
Plundered khan, or caravan
Journeying north from Koordistan,
 Gave him wealth and wine and food.

Seven hundred and fourscore
Men at arms his livery wore,
 Did his bidding night and day;
Now, through regions all unknown,
He was wandering, lost, alone,
 Seeking without guide his way.

Suddenly the pathway ends,
Sheer the precipice descends,
 Loud the torrent roars unseen;
Thirty feet from side to side
Yawns the chasm; on air must ride
 He who crosses this ravine.

Following close in his pursuit,
At the precipice's foot
 Reyhan the Arab of Orfah
Halted with his hundred men,
Shouting upward from the glen,
 "La Illáh illa Alláh!"

Gently Roushan Beg caressed
Kyrat's forehead, neck, and breast;
Kissed him upon both his eyes;
Sang to him in his wild way,
As upon the topmost spray
Sings a bird before it flies.

"O my Kyrat, O my steed,
Round and slender as a reed,
Carry me this peril through!
Satin housings shall be thine,
Shoes of gold, O Kyrat mine!
O thou soul of Kurroglou!

"Soft thy skin as silken skein,
Soft as woman's hair thy mane,
Tender are thine eyes and true;
All thy hoofs like ivory shine,
Polished bright; O life of mine,
Leap, and rescue Kurroglou!"

Kyrat, then, the strong and fleet,
Drew together his four white feet,
Paused a moment on the verge,
Measured with his eye the space,
And into the air's embrace
Leaped as leaps the ocean surge.

As the ocean surge o'er sand
Bears a swimmer safe to land,
Kyrat safe his rider bore;
Rattling down the deep abyss,
Fragments of the precipice
Rolled like pebbles on a shore.

Roushan's tasselled cap of red
Trembled not upon his head;
Careless sat he and upright;
Neither hand nor bridle shook,
Nor his head he turned to look,
As he galloped out of sight.

Flash of harness in the air,
Seen a moment like the glare
    Of a sword drawn from its sheath;
Thus the phantom horseman passed,
And the shadow that he cast
    Leaped the cataract underneath.

Reyhan the Arab held his breath
While this vision of life and death
    Passed above him. "Allahhu!"
Cried he. "In all Koordistan
Lives there not so brave a man
    As this robber Kurroglou!"

"The Leap of Roushan Beg" is based on a Persian legend. Trapped by Reyhan the Arab of Orfah after losing his way, Rousan Beg relies on his chestnut steed to save him. In his greatest moment of need, Roushan Beg places all his faith and trust in Kyrat, who leaps thirty feet across the chasm to save his master from a cruel fate at the hands of Reyhan.

The Chambered Nautilus

Oliver Wendell Holmes

This is the ship of pearl, which, poets feign,
    Sails the unshadowed main,
    The venturous bark that flings
On the sweet summer wind its purpled wings
In gulfs enchanted, where the Siren sings,
    And coral reefs lie bare,
Where the cold sea-maids rise to sun their streaming hair.

Its webs of living gauze no more unfurl;
    Wrecked is the ship of pearl!
    And every chambered cell,
Where its dim dreaming life was wont to dwell,
As the frail tenant shaped his growing shell,
    Before thee lies revealed,
Its irised ceiling rent, its sunless crypt unsealed!

Year after year beheld the silent toil
    That spread his lustrous coil;
    Still, as the spiral grew,
He left the past year's dwelling for the new,
Stole with soft step its shining archway through,
    Built up its idle door,
Stretched in his last-found home, and knew the old no more.

Thanks for the heavenly message brought by thee,
    Child of the wandering sea,
    Cast from her lap, forlorn!
From thy dead lips a clearer note is born
Than ever Triton blew from wreathéd horn!
    While on mine ear it rings,
Through the deep caves of thought I hear a voice that sings:

Build thee more stately mansions, O my soul,
    As the swift seasons roll!
    Leave thy low-vaulted past!
Let each new temple, nobler than the last,
Shut thee from heaven with a dome more vast,
    Till thou at length art free,
Leaving thine outgrown shell by life's unresting sea!

History

FROM The Kalevala

TRANSLATED BY W. F. KIRBY

I am driven by my longing,
And my understanding urges
That I should commence my singing,
And begin my recitation.
I will sing the people's legends,
And the ballads of the nation.
To my mouth the words are flowing,
And the words are gently falling,
Quickly as my tongue can shape them,
And between my teeth emerging...

Let us clasp our hands together,
Let us interlock our fingers;
Let us sing a cheerful measure,
Let us use our best endeavours,
While our dear ones hearken to us,
And our loved ones are instructed,
While the young ones are standing round us,
Of the rising generation,
Let them learn the words of magic,
And recall our songs and legends,
Of the belt of Väinämöinen,
Of the forge of Ilmarinen,
And of Kaukomieli's swordpoint,
And of Joukahainen's crossbow:
Of the utmost bounds of Pohja,
And of Kalevala's wide heathlands.

Then the aged Väinämöinen
Went upon his journey singing,
Sailing in his boat of copper,
In his vessel made of copper,

Sailed away to loftier regions,
To the land beneath the heavens.
There he rested with his vessel,
Rested weary, with his vessel,
But his kantele he left us,
Left his charming harp in Suomi,
For his people's lasting pleasure,
Mighty songs for Suomi's children.

The Challenge of Thor

Henry Wadsworth Longfellow

I am the God Thor,
I am the War God,
I am the Thunderer!
Here in my Northland,
My fastness and fortress,
Reign I forever!

Here amid icebergs
Rule I the nations;
This is my hammer,
Miölner the mighty;
Giants and sorcerers
Cannot withstand it!

These are the gauntlets
Wherewith I wield it,
And hurl it afar off;
This is my girdle;
Whenever I brace it,
Strength is redoubled!

The light thou beholdest
Stream through the heavens,
In flashes of crimson,
Is but my red beard
Blown by the night-wind,
Affrighting the nations!

Jove is my brother;
Mine eyes are the lightning;
The wheels of my chariot
Roll in the thunder,
The blows of my hammer
Ring in the earthquake!

Force rules the world still,
Has ruled it, shall rule it;
Meekness is weakness,
Strength is triumphant,
Over the whole earth
Still is it Thor's Day!

Thou art a God too,
O Galilean!
And thus singled-handed
Unto the combat,
Gauntlet or Gospel,
Here I defy thee!

The Forging of Thor's Hammer

S. M. Ryan

Blow bellows, blow,
Set the sparks a-glow!
For Sindri of Swartheim,
The shaper of swords,
Is molding and making
Gifts for the Gods.

Blow bellows, blow,
Set the sparks a-glow!
A ring of red gold
For the master of men;
A boar with bright bristles
For Frey and his friends,
But Thunderer Thor
Needs weapons of war!

Blow bellows, blow,
Set the sparks a-glow!
Fierce and fiery
Flames the furnace,
Molten metals gleam like gold;
Clash and clang of hefty hammers
In the hands of sweltering smiths.
Hard and heavy, strong as steel,
Mighty Miolnir's forged and fashioned.
Blow bellows, blow,
Set the sparks a-glow.

The Siegfried Song

from "Ring of the Nibelungen"
Richard Wagner

Needful, needful, masterful sword
What blow was that that broke thee?
To shreds I've shattered
Thy shining steel,
Now flames the fire around thy fragments.
Ho-ho!
Ho-hey!
Bellows blow
Brighten the blaze.

Wild in the woodlands
Waxed a tree,
That I in forest felled;
The good brown ash
To charcoal I charred
On hearth in heaps it now lies.
Ho-ho!
Ho-hey!
Bellows blow
Brighten the blaze.

The charcoal I charred me
How bravely it burns,
How fiercely it flames and glows
In showers of sparks,
It scatters its fire
And fuses the shreds of the steel.
Ho-ho!
Ho-hey!
Bellows blow
Brighten the blaze.

Hymn of Creation
from The Rig Veda

nasad asin, no sad asit tadanim;
nasid rajo no vioma paro yat.
kim avarivah? kuha? kasya sarmann?
ambhah kim asid, gahanam gabhiram?

na mrytur asid, amrtam na tarhi.
na ratria ahna asit praketah.
anid avatam svadhaya tad ekam.
tasmad dhanyan na parah kim canasa.

tama asit tamasa gulham agre;
apraketam salilam sarvam a idam.
tuchyenabhu apihitam yad asit,
tapasas tan mahinajayataikam.

There was not non-existent nor existent:
There was no realm of air, no sky beyond it.
What covered in and where? And what gave shelter?
Was water there, unfathomed depth of water?

Death was not then, nor was there aught immortal:
No sign was there, the day's and the night's divider.
That One Thing, breathless, breathed by its own nature,
Apart from it was nothing whatsoever.

Darkness there was: at first concealed in darkness
This All was indiscriminated chaos.
All that existed then was void and formless:
By the great power of Warmth was born that One.

The Gayatri Mantra

from The Rig Veda

Om Bhur Buvaha Suvaha
Thath Savithur Varenyam
Bhargo Devasya Dheemahi
Dhiyo Yonaha Prachodayath

The Gayatri Mantra is revered by both Buddhists and Hindus worldwide. It is considered to be a supreme vehicle for gaining spiritual enlightenment. It is based on a Vedic Sanskrit verse from a hymn of the Rigveda, attributed to the rishi Viśvāmitra.

It is addressed to the Immanent and Transcendent Divine, which has been given the name "Savitha," meaning "that from which all this is born." Gayatri is Annapurna, the Mother, the sustaining Force that animates all life. The Gayatri is considered as Vedasara, "the essence of the Vedas." Veda means knowledge, and this prayer fosters and sharpens the knowledge-yielding faculty.

Its recitation is traditionally preceded by om and the phrase bhūr bhuvah svah, known as the mahāvyāhrti ("great utterance").

Meaning of the individual words:

Om:	*The primeval sound*
Bhur:	*The physical world*
Bhuvah:	*The mental world*
Suvah:	*The celestial, spiritual world*
Thath:	*That; God; transcendental Paramatma*
Savithur:	*The Sun, Creator, Preserver*
Varenyam:	*Most adorable, enchanting*
Bhargo:	*Luster, effulgence*
Devasya:	*Resplendent,supreme Lord*
Dheemahi:	*We meditate upon*
Dhiyo:	*The intellect,understanding*
Yo:	*May this light*
Nah:	*Our*
Prachodayath:	*Enlighten,guide,inspire*

Ancient India

Every moment the voice of love comes from left and right,
But here on earth is darkness,—grant us eternal light.
We have lived in heaven, the angels were our friends.
Thither let us go, for there our suffering ends.

The Words of Krishna

from The Bhagavad Gita

Life cannot slay. Life is not slain!
Never the spirit was born; the spirit shall cease to be never;
Never was time it was not; End and Beginning are dreams!
Birthless and deathless and changeless remaineth the spirit for ever;
Death hath not touched it at all, dead though the house of it seems!

Nay, but as when one layeth
His worn-out robes away,
And, taking new ones, sayeth,

"These will I wear to-day!"

So putteth by the spirit
Lightly its garb of flesh,
And passeth to inherit,
A residence afresh.

from Brahma

Ralph Waldo Emerson

If the red slayer think he slays,
Or if the slain think he is slain,
They know not well the subtle ways
I keep, and pass, and turn again.

Far or forgot to me is near,
Shadow and sunlight are the same,
The vanish'd gods to me appear,
And one to me are shame and fame

They reckon ill who leave me out;
When me they fly, I am the wings;
I am the doubter and the doubt,
And I the hymn the Brahmin sings.

Indra and the Dragon

from The Rig Veda

The manly deeds of Indra shall be sung.
The first was when the thunderstone he flung
And smote the dragon.
He released the fountains.
He opened the channels of the breasted mountains.
With magic weapon he rode out to meet the foe,
He killed the dragon Vritri with one blow,
And, like to bellowing cattle rushing free
The gladsome waters then descended to the sea.
Around the monster torrents surged,
Nor paused, nor stayed, but ever onward urged.
They covered Vritri by a joyful wave,
And bore him to a darksome ocean grave.

Epic of Gilgamesh

from the Prologue

His name was called Gilgamesh.
From the very day of his birth,
He was two-thirds god, one third man.
The Great Goddess Aruru designed him,
Planned his body, prepared his form.
A perfect body the gods gave
For the creation of Gilgamesh.
Shamash the Sun gave beauty;
Adad the Storm gave courage,
And so he surpassed all others.
He was two-thirds god, one third man,
The form of his body no one can match.
Eleven cubits high he is; nine spans his chest
As he turns to see the lands all around him.
But he comes to the city of Uruk.
Long was his journey.
Weary, worn down by his labours
He inscribed upon a stone
When he returned
This story…

The Importance of Agriculture

from The Zend Avesta, holy book of the Zorastrians

Zarathustra: "O Maker of the World, what is the first thing which gives most pleasure to the earth?"

Ahura Mazdao: *"When a pure man walks over the earth."*

Zarathustra: "O Maker of the World, what is the second thing which gives most pleasure to the earth?"

Ahura Mazdao: *"When a pure man builds a house."*

Zarathustra: "O Maker of the World, what is the third thing which gives most pleasure to the earth?"

Ahura Mazdao: *"When there is fire and women and children."*

Zarathustra: "O Maker of the World, what is the fourth thing which gives most pleasure to the earth?"

Ahura Mazdao: *"When there are fine cattle and good flocks."*

Zarathustra: "O Maker of the World, what is the fifth thing which gives most pleasure to the earth?"

Ahura Mazdao: *"When there is growing good corn and fine fruits."*

To Ahura Mazdao

from The Zend Avesta

We revere thee, O Ahura Mazdao
We praise thee
O God of Wisdom, Lord of Life!
We come to thee
With our pure thoughts
With our pure words
With our pure deeds
We dedicate to Thee
The noblest sheath of our bodies,
O Lord of Wisdom, Lord of Life
Thou the day's light
Thou the highest of the high
Thou who we call the sun.

Ancient Persia

Dorothy Harrer

In the flaming fire we worship thee,
    Master of Wisdom,
    Lord of Light,
    AHURA-MAZDA,
O Spirit speak to us
    In the glory of the Sun,
    O Lord of Life.

From the regions of the North,
From the regions of the South,
Forth rushed Ahriman the deadly,
And the demons of darkness, the evil-doers;

Thus spake Ahriman, the deadly Deceiver:
    "Kill him, destroy him, Hated Zarathustra."

Thus spake Zarathustra:
    "The word of AHURA-MAZDA is my weapon,
    With his sword will I strike
    The holy word of the Lord of Light,
    The living word of Creation."
    Forth fled Ahriman, the Deceiver,
    And the wicked evil-doing Demons
    Into the depths of outer darkness.

Ancient Persia

Bear the sun to the earth!
You, O human being
Are set between light and darkness.
Be a warrior of the light!
Love the earth!
Into a radiant diamond
Transform the plants,
Transform the animals,
Transform yourself.

Coming Forth into the Day

Homage to thee, O Ra, at thy tremendous rising!
Thou risest! Thou shinest! the heavens are rolled aside!
Thou art the King of Gods, thou art the All-comprising,
From thee we come, in thee are deified.

Thy rays are on all faces; Thou art inscrutable.
Age after age thy life renews its eager prime.
Time whirls its dust beneath thee; thou art immutable,
Maker of Time, thyself beyond all Time.

Thou passest through the portals that close behind the night,
Gladdening the souls of them that lay in sorrow.
The True of Word, the Quiet Heart, arise to drink thy light;
Thou art Today and Yesterday; Thou art Tomorrow!

Homage to thee, O Ra, who wakest life from slumber!
Thou risest! Thou shinest! Thy radiant face appears!
Millions of years have passed—we cannot count their number—
Millions of years shall come. Thou art above the years!

Prayer to Isis

Nehes, nehes, nehes,	Awake, awake, awake,
Nehes em hotep,	Awake in peace,
Nehes em neferu,	Awake in beauty,
Nebet hotepet,	Rest thou in peace,
Weben em hotep,	Rise thou in peace,
Weben em neferu,	Rise thou in beauty,
Nutjert en Ankh,	Goddess of Life,
Nefer em Pet!	Beautiful in Heaven!
Pet em hotep,	Heaven is in peace,
Ta em hotep,	Earth is in peace,
Nutjert sat Nut,	Daughter of Nut,
Sat Geb,	Daughter of Geb,
Merit Auser,	Beloved of Osiris,
Nutjert Asha-renu!	Goddess rich in names!
Anekh hrak,	All praise to You,
Anekh hrak,	All praise to You,
Tua atu,	I adore You,
Tua atu,	I adore You,
Nebet Aset!	Lady Isis!

Egyptian Hymn to the Sun

Hail to thee, O Ra, O perfect and eternal One,
Great Hawk that fliest with the rising Sun;
Between the turquoise sycamores thou risest young forever,
Thine image flashing on the bright celestial river.

Thou passest through the portals that close behind the night,
Gladdening the souls of them that lie in sorrow,
The True of Word, the Quiet Heart arise to drink thy light;
Thou are Today and Yesterday, Thou art Tomorrow.

Thou Art in My Heart

from Akhnaton's Longer Hymn to the Aton

When Thou risest in the eastern horizon of heaven,
Thou fillest every land with thy beauty.

When Thou settest in the western horizon of heaven,
The world is in darkness like the dead.

Bright is the earth when Thou risest,
When Thou shinest as Aton by day.
The darkness is banished when Thou sendest forth thy rays.

How manifold are all Thy works.
They are hidden from before us.
O Thou sole God, whose powers no other possesseth,
Thou didst create the earth according to Thy desire
While Thou wast alone.

The world is in Thy hand,
Even as Thou hast made them.
When Thou hast risen they live.
When Thou settest they die.
For Thou art duration beyond Thy mere limbs.
By Thee man liveth
And their eyes look upon Thy beauty
Until Thou settest.

Thou makest the beauty of form.
Thou art in my heart.

The Creation

Genesis 1:1-5

Hebrew transliteration

B'resheet bara Elohim et hashamayim ve'et ha'arets.	In the beginning God created the heaven and the earth.
Veha'arets hayetah tohu vavohu vechoshech al-penay tehom veruach Elohim merachefet al-penay hamayim.	And the earth was without form, and void; and darkness was upon the face of the deep. And the Spirit of God moved upon the face of the waters.
Vayomer Elohim yehi-or vayehi-or.	And God said, Let there be light: and there was light.
Vayar Elohim et-ha'or ki-tov vayavdel Elohim beyn ha'or uveyn hachoshech.	And God saw the light, that it was good: and God divided the light from the darkness.
Vayikra Elohim la-or yom velachoshech kara laylah vayehi-erev vayehi-boker yom echad.	And God called the light Day, and the darkness he called Night. And the evening and the morning were the first day.

The Ten Commandents

Exodus 20:2-17

I. Have thou no other gods but me,
II. And to no image bow thy knee.
III. Take not the name of God in vain:
IV. The Sabbath day do not profane.
V. Honor thy father and mother too;
VI. And see that thou no murder do.
VII. Abstain from words and deeds unclean;
VIII. Nor steal, though thou art poor and mean.
IX. Bear not false witness, shun that blot;
X. What is thy neighbor's covet not.

These laws, O Lord, write in my heart, that I,
May in thy faithful service live and die.

David and Goliath

Hannah Flagg Gould

Young David was a ruddy lad
With silken, sunny locks,
The youngest son that Jesse had:
He kept his father's flocks.

Goliath was a Philistine,
A giant, huge and high;
He lifted, like a towering pine,
His head towards the sky.

He was the foe of Israel's race,
A mighty warrior, too;
And on he strode from place to place,
And many a man he slew.

So Saul, the king of Israel then,
Proclaimed it to and fro,
That most he'd favor of his men
The one, who'd kill the foe.

Yet all, who saw this foe draw near,
Would feel their courage fail;
For not an arrow, sword, or spear,
Could pierce the giant's mail.

But Jesse's son conceived a way,
That would deliverance bring;
Whereby he might Goliath slay,
And thus relieve the king.

Then quick he laid his shepherd's crook
Upon a grassy bank;
And off he waded in the brook
From which the lambkins drank.

He culled and fitted to his sling
Five pebbles, smooth and round;
And one of these he meant should bring
The giant to the ground.

"I've killed a lion and a bear,"
Said he, "and now I'll slay
The Philistine, and by the hair
I'll bring his head away!"

Then onward to the battle-field
The youthful hero sped;
He knew Goliath by his shield,
And by his towering head.

But when, with only sling and staff,
The giant saw him come,
In triumph he began to laugh;
Yet David struck him dumb.

He fell! ‘Twas David’s puny hand
That caused his overthrow!
Though long the terror of the land,
A pebble laid him low.

The blood from out his forehead gushed,
He rolled, and writhed, and roared.
The little hero on him rushed,
And drew his ponderous sword.

Before its owner’s dying eye
He held the gleaming point
Upon his throbbing neck to try;
Then severed cord and joint.

He took the head, and carried it
And laid it down by Saul,
And showed him where the pebble hit
That caused the giant’s fall.

The boy, who had Goliath slain
With pebbles and a sling,
Was raised, in after years, to reign
As Israel’s second king!

‘Twas not the courage, skill, or might,
Which David had, alone,
That helped him Israel’s foe to fight
And conquer, with a stone.

But, when the shepherd stripling went
Goliath thus to kill,
God used him as an instrument,
His purpose to fulfill!

The 23rd Psalm

A Psalm of David

The Lord is my Shepherd; I shall not want.
He maketh me to lie down in green pastures;
He leadeth me beside the still waters.
He restoreth my soul;
He leadeth me in the paths of righteousness for His name' sake.

Yea, though I walk through the valley of the shadow of death,
I will fear no evil: For thou art with me;
Thy rod and thy staff, they comfort me.
Thou preparest a table before me in the presence of mine enemies;
Thou annointest my head with oil; My cup runneth over.

Surely goodness and mercy shall follow me all the days of my life,
and I will dwell in the House of the Lord forever.

To Every Thing There Is a Season

Ecclesiastes 3:1-8

To every thing there is a season,
and a time to every purpose under the heaven:
A time to be born, a time to die;
a time to plant, and a time to pluck up that which is planted;
A time to kill, and a time to heal;
a time to break down, and a time to build up;
A time to weep, and a time to laugh;
a time to mourn, and a time to dance;
A time to cast away stones, and a time to gather stones together;
a time to embrace, and a time to refrain from embracing;
A time to get, and a time to lose;
a time to keep, and a time to cast away;
A time to rend, and a time to sew;
a time to keep silence, and a time to speak;
A time to love, and a time to hate;
a time of war, and a time of peace.

The Destruction of Sennacherib

George Gordon, Lord Byron

The Assyrian came down like the wolf on the fold,
And his cohorts were gleaming in purple and gold;
And the sheen of their spears was like stars on the sea,
When the blue wave rolls nightly on deep Galilee.

Like the leaves of the forest when Summer is green,
That host with their banners at sunset were seen:
Like the leaves of the forest when Autumn hath blown,
That host on the morrow lay withered and strown.

For the Angel of Death spread his wings on the blast,
And breathed in the face of the foe as he passed;
And the eyes of the sleepers waxed deadly and chill,
And their hearts but once heaved, and for ever grew still!

And there lay the steed with his nostril all wide,
But through it there rolled not the breath of his pride;
And the foam of his gasping lay white on the turf,
And cold as the spray of the rock-beating surf.

And there lay the rider distorted and pale,
With the dew on his brow, and the rust on his mail:
And the tents were all silent, the banners alone,
The lances unlifted, the trumpet unblown.

And the widows of Ashur are loud in their wail,
And the idols are broke in the temple of Baal;
And the might of the Gentile, unsmote by the sword,
Hath melted like snow in the glance of the Lord!

The Destruction of Sennacherib was first published in 1815 in Lord Byron's Hebrew Melodies. It is based on an event described in the Bible (2 Kings 18-19) during the campaign by Assyrian king Sennacherib to capture Jerusalem in 701 BC.

Sennacherib sacked scores of cities and towns in Judah and carrried off over 200,000 people. These ten northern tribes became known as the Ten Lost Tribes. King Hezekiah of Judah realized the error of his rebellion against Assyria which had caused the invasion and sent a great tribute of gold, silver and other treasures to Sennacherib.

The Assyrian army besieged Jerusalem nevertheless. Sennacherib left his supreme commander in charge of the siege while he himself went to fight the Egyptians. The Assyrian commander repeatedly blasphemed Judah and their god Yahweh. Hezekiah tore off his clothes in deep anguish and prayed to Yahweh in the Temple. That night the angel of Yahweh killed 185,000 Assyrian troops and Sennacherib returned to Nineveh in disgrace.

The rhythm of the poem, an anapestic tetrameter, has a feel of the beat of a galloping horse's hooves as the Assyrian rides into battle.

Vision of Belshazzar

George Gordon, Lord Byron

The King was on his throne,
The Satraps throng'd the hall;
A thousand bright lights shone
O'er that high festival.
A thousand cups of gold,
In Judah deem'd divine—
Jehovah's vessels hold
The godless Heathen's wine.

In that same hour and hall,
The fingers of a hand
Came forth against the wall,
And wrote as if on sand:
The fingers of a man;
A solitary hand
Along the letters ran,
And traced them like a wand.

The monarch saw, and shook,
And bade no more rejoice;
All bloodless wax'd his look,
And tremulous his voice.
"Let the men of lore appear,
The wisest of the earth,
And expound the words of fear,
Which mar our royal mirth."

Chaldea's seers are good,
But here they have no skill;
And the unknown letters stood
Untold and awful still.
And Babel's men of age
Are wise and deep in lore;
But now they were not sage,
They saw—but knew no more.

A captive in the land.
A stranger and a youth,
He heard the king's command,
He saw the writing's truth;
The lamps around were bright,
The prophecy in view;
He read it on that night,
The morrow proved it true.

"Belshazzar's grave is made,
His kingdom pass'd away,
He, in the balance weigh'd,
Is light and worthless clay;
The shroud, his robe of state,
His canopy the stone;
The Mede is at his gate!
The Persian on his throne!"

Hymn to Prometheus

Roy Wilkinson

Hail to Prometheus, the Titan,
    The helper of man and creator.
Clay was the substance he used
    And in likeness of gods then he shaped it.
Goodness and evil from hearts
    Of the beasts in man's breast he enfolded.
Fire he brought down from the realms
    Of the skies to perfect his creation.
Movement of stars he explained
    To the wondering earth dwelling people.

Numbers he taught them to use
  And the plants which heal sickness he showed them.
Symbols he taught them to write,
  Representing the sounds of their speaking.
Building of ships he did teach
  And the training of beasts to man's service.
Into the depths of the earth
  Did he guide men to find precious metals.
Zeus he defied and brought fire
  Down again when the god would deny men.
Torment and anguish he suffered
  For harsh was the fate decreed for him.
Bound to a cliff overhanging
  A sinister cleft was Prometheus.
Bravely the Titan endured
  And at length one arrived to release him.

FROM ANDROMEDA

CHARLES KINGSLEY

Then on the brows of the maiden a veil bound Pallas Athené;
Ample it fell to her feet, deep-fringed, a wonder of weaving.
Ages and ages agone it was wrought on the heights of Olympus,
Wrought in the gold-strung loom, by the finger of cunning Athené.

In it she wove all creatures that teem in the womb of the ocean;
Nereid, siren, and triton, and dolphin, and arrowy fishes
Glittering round, many-hued, on the flame-red folds of the mantle.

In it she wove, too, a town where gray-haired kings sat in judgment;
Sceptre in hand in the market they sat, doing right by the people,
Wise: while above watched Justice, and near, far-seeing Apollo.

Round it she wove for a fringe all herbs of the earth and the water,
Violet, asphodel, ivy, and vine-leaves, roses and lilies,
Coral and sea-fan and tangle, the blooms and the palms of the ocean:
Now from Olympus she bore it, a dower to the bride of a hero.

from The Iliad, Book I

Homer, translated by C. S. Calverley

Sing, O daughter of heaven,
    of Peleus' son, of Achilles,
Him whose terrible wrath
    brought thousand woes on Achaia,
Many a stalwart soul
    did it hurl untimely to Hades,
Souls of the heroes of old:
    and their bones lay strown on the sea-sands,
Prey to the vulture and dog.
    Yet was Zeus fulfilling a purpose;
Since that far-off day,
    when in hot strife parted asunder
Atreus' sceptered son,
    and the chos'n of heaven, Achilles.
Say then, which of the Gods
    Bid arise up battle between them?

The Odyssey

Andrew Lang

As one that for a weary space has lain
    Lull'd by the song of Circe and her wine
    In gardens near the pale of Proserpine,
Where that Ææan isle forgets the main,
    And only the low lutes of love complain,
    And only shadows of wan lovers pine—
As such an one were glad to know the brine
Salt on his lips, and the large air again—
So gladly from the songs of modern speech
    Men turn, and see the stars, and feel the free
        Shrill wind beyond the close of heavy flowers,
        And through the music of the languid hours
They hear like Ocean on a western beach
    The surge and thunder of the Odyssey.

from The Odyssey, Book I

Homer, Translated by Samuel Butler

ἄνδρα μοι ἔννεπε, μοῦσα, πολύτροπον, ὃς μάλα πολλὰ
πλάγχθη, ἐπεὶ Τροίης ἱερὸν πτολίεθρον ἔπερσεν
πολλῶν δ᾽ ἀνθρώπων ἴδεν ἄστεα καὶ νόον ἔγνω,
πολλὰ δ᾽ ὅ γ᾽ ἐν πόντῳ πάθεν ἄλγεα ὃν κατὰ θυμόν,
ἀρνύμενος ἥν τε ψυχὴν καὶ νόστον ἑταίρων.
ἀλλ᾽ οὐδ᾽ ὧς ἑτάρους ἐρρύσατο, ἱέμενός περ·
αὐτῶν γὰρ σφετέρῃσιν ἀτασθαλίῃσιν ὄλοντο,
νήπιοι, οἳ κατὰ βοῦς Ὑπερίονος Ἠελίοιο
ἤσθιον· αὐτὰρ ὁ τοῖσιν ἀφείλετο νόστιμον ἦμαρ.
τῶν ἁμόθεν γε, θεά, θύγατερ Διός, εἰπὲ καὶ ἡμῖν.

Greek transliteration

andra moi ennepe, mousa, polutropon, hos mala polla
plagchthê, epei Troiês hieron ptoliethron epersen;
pollôn d' anthrôpôn iden astea kai noon egnô,
polla d' ho g' en pontô pathen algea hon kata thumon,
arnumenos hên te psuchên kai noston hetairôn.
all' oud' hôs hetarous errusato, hiemenos per;
autôn gar spheterêsin atasthaliêsin olonto,
nêpioi, hoi kata Bous Huperionos Êelioio
êsthion; autar ho toisin apheileto nostimon hêmar.
tôn hamothen ge, Thea, Thugater Dios, eipe kai hêmin.

English translation

*Tell me, O Muse, of that ingenious hero who travelled far
and wide after he had sacked the famous town of Troy.
Many cities did he visit, and many were the nations
with whose manners and customs he was acquainted;
moreover he suffered much by sea while trying to save
his own life and bring his men safely home; but do what
he might he could not save his men, for they perished
through their own sheer folly in eating the cattle of the
Sun-god Hyperion; so the god prevented them from ever
reaching home. Tell me, too, about all these things, oh
daughter of Jove, from whatsoever source you may know
them.*

Ancient Greek pronunciation guide: See page 199.

To a Buddha Seated on a Lotus

Sarojini Naidu

Lord Buddha, on thy Lotus-throne,
With praying eyes and hands elate,
What mystic rapture dost thou own,
Immutable and ultimate?
What peace, unravished of our ken,
Annihilate from the world of men?

The wind of change for ever blows
Across the tumult of our way,
To-morrow's unborn griefs depose
The sorrows of our yesterday.
Dream yields to dream, strife follows strife,
And Death unweaves the webs of Life.

For us the travail and the heat,
The broken secrets of our pride,
The strenuous lessons of defeat,
The flower deferred, the fruit denied;
But not the peace, supremely won,
Lord Buddha, of thy Lotus-throne.

With futile hands we seek to gain
Our inaccessible desire,
Diviner summits to attain,
With faith that sinks and feet that tire;
But nought shall conquer or control
The heavenward hunger of our soul.

The end, elusive and afar,
Still lures us with its beckoning flight,
And all our mortal moments are
A session of the Infinite.
How shall we reach the great, unknown
Nirvana of thy Lotus-throne?

Hercules

Eileen Hutchins

Who is this who cometh as in conquest?
  Strong he strides and free.
Light of glory gleams around his temples,
  More than man is he.

Dark has been the danger of his daring,
  Fierce the first and fell;
None can know the fashion of his faring
  Hither out of hell.

Who is this who cometh as in conquest?
  Strong he strides and free.
Light of glory gleams around his temples,
  Man and god is he.

Zeus

Homer

He whose all-conscious eyes the world behold,
The eternal Thunderer sat, enthroned in gold;
High heaven the footstool of his feet he makes,
And wide beneath him all Olympus shakes.

Roma

O Roma nobilis,	O noble Rome,
Orbis et domina.	The circle and mistress.
Omnium urbium,	Of all cities,
Excellentissima.	Most excellent.
Salutem dicimus	We give greetings
Tibi per omnia;	To you among all
Te benedicimus,	To you we give blessing,
Salve per saecula.	Salute through the year.

from Horatius at the Bridge

Lord Thomas Babington Macaulay

Lars Porsena of Clusium,
By the Nine Gods he swore
That the great house of Tarquin
Should suffer wrong no more.
By the Nine Gods he swore it,
And named a trysting day,
And bade his messengers ride forth,
East and west and south and north,
To summon his array.

To eastward and to westward
Have spread the Tuscan bands;
Nor house, nor fence, nor dovecot
In Crustumerium stands.
Verbenna down to Ostia
Hath wasted all the plain;
Astur hath stormed Janiculum,
And the stout guards are slain.

They held a council standing
Before the River-Gate;
Short time was there, ye well may guess,
For musing or debate.
Out spake the Consul roundly:
"The bridge must straight go down;
For since Janiculum is lost,
Naught else can save the town."

Just then, a scout came flying,
All wild with haste and fear:
"To arms! To arms! Sir Consul:
Lars Porsena is here."
On the low hills to westward
The Consul fixed his eye,
And saw the swarthy storm of dust
Rise fast along the sky.

And nearer fast and nearer
    Doth the red whirlwind come;
And louder still and still more loud,
From underneath that rolling cloud,
Is heard the trumpet's war-note proud,
    The trampling, and the hum.
And plainly and more plainly
    Now through the gloom appears,
Far to left and far to right,
In broken gleams of dark-blue light,
The long array of helmets bright,
    The long array of spears.

Then out spoke brave Horatius,
    The Captain of the Gate:
"To every man upon this earth,
    Death cometh soon or late.
And how can man die better
    Than facing fearful odds,
For the ashes of his fathers,
    And the temples of his Gods,

"And for the tender mother
    Who dandled him to rest,
And for the wife who nurses
    His baby at her breast,
And for the holy maidens
    Who feed the eternal flame,
To save them from false Sextus,
    That wrought the deed of shame?

"Hew down the bridge, Sir Consul,
    With all the speed ye may;
I, with two more to help me,
    Will hold the foe in play.
In yon strait path a thousand
    May well be stopped by three.
Now who will stand on either hand,
    And keep the bridge with me?"

Then out spake Spurius Lartius;
A Ramnian proud was he:
"Lo, I will stand at thy right hand,
And keep the bridge with thee."
And out spake strong Herminius;
Of Titian blood was he:
"I will abide on thy left side,
And keep the bridge with thee."

"Horatius," quoth the Consul,
"As thou sayest, so let it be."
And straight against that great array
Forth went the dauntless Three.
For Romans in Rome's quarrel
Spared neither land nor gold,
Nor son nor wife, nor limb nor life,
In the brave days of old.

Then none was for a party;
Then all were for the state;
Then the great man helped the poor,
And the poor man loved the great:
Then lands were fairly portioned;
Then spoils were fairly sold:
The Romans were like brothers
In the brave days of old.

Now Roman is to Roman
More hateful than a foe,
And the Tribunes beard the high,
And the Fathers grind the low.
As we wax hot in faction,
In battle we wax cold:
Wherefore men fight not as they fought
In the brave days of old.

Now while the Three were tightening
Their harness on their backs,
The Consul was the foremost man
To take in hand an axe:
And Fathers mixed with Commons
Seized hatchet, bar and crow,
And smote upon the planks above,
And loosed the props below.

Meanwhile the Tuscan army,
 Right glorious to behold,
Came flashing back the noonday light,
Rank behind rank, like surges bright
 Of a broad sea of gold.
Four hundred trumpets sounded
 A peal of warlike glee,
As that great host, with measured tread,
And spears advanced, with ensigns spread,
Rolled slowly towards the bridge's head,
 Where stood the dauntless Three.

The Three stood calm and silent,
 And looked upon the foes,
And a great shout of laughter
 From all the vanguard rose:
And forth three chiefs came spurring
 Before that deep array;
To earth they sprang, their swords they drew,
 And lifted high their shields, and flew
To win the narrow way:

Aunus from green Tifernum,
 Lord of the Hill of Vines;
And Seius, whose eight hundred slaves
 Sicken in Ilva's mines;
And Picus, long to Clusium
 Vassal in peace and war,
Who led to fight his Umbrian powers
From that grey crag where, girt with towers,
The fortress of Nequinum lowers
 O'er the pale waves of Nar.

Stout Lartius hurled down Aunus
 Into the stream beneath:
Herminius struck at Seius,
 And clove him to the teeth:
At Picus brave Horatius
 Darted one fiery thrust;
And the proud Umbrian's guilded arms
 Clashed in the bloody dust.

But now no sound of laughter
    Was heard among the foes.
A wild and wrathful clamour
    From all the vanguard rose.
Six spears' lengths from the entrance
    Halted that deep array,
And for a space no man came forth
    To win the narrow way.

But all Etruria's noblest
    Felt their hearts sink to see
On the earth the bloody corpses,
    In their path the dauntless Three:
And, from the ghastly entrance
    Where those bold Romans stood,
All shrank, like boys who unaware,
Ranging the woods to start a hare,
Come to the mouth of the dark lair
Where, growling low, a fierce old bear
    Lies amidst bones and blood.

Was none who would be foremost
    To lead such dire attack:
But those behind cried "Forward!"
    And those before cried "Back!"
And backward now and forward
    Wavers the deep array;
And on the tossing sea of steel,
To and fro the standards reel;
And the victorious trumpet-peal
    Dies fitfully away.

Yet one man for one moment
    Strode out before the crowd;
Well known was he to all the Three,
    And they gave him greeting loud.
"Now welcome, welcome, Sextus!
    Now welcome to thy home!
Why dost thou stay, and turn away?
    Here lies the road to Rome."

But meanwhile axe and lever
    Have manfully been plied;
And now the bridge hangs tottering
    Above the boiling tide.
"Come back, come back, Horatius!"
    Loud cried the Fathers all.
"Back, Lartius! Back, Herminius!
    Back, ere the ruin fall!"

Back darted Spurius Lartius;
    Herminius darted back:
And, as they passed, beneath their feet
    They felt the timbers crack.
But when they turned their faces,
    And on the further shore
Saw brave Horatius stand alone,
    They would have crossed once more.

But with a crash like thunder
    Fell every loosened beam,
And, like a dam, the mighty wreck
    Lay right athwart the stream:
And a loud shout of triumph
    Rose from the walls of Rome,
As to the highest turret-tops
    Was splashed the yellow foam.

And, like a horse unbroken
    When first he feels the rein,
The furious river struggled hard,
    And tossed his tawny mane,
And burst the curb and bounded,
    Rejoicing to be free,
And whirling down, in fierce career,
Battlement, and plank, and pier
    Rushed headlong to the sea.

Alone stood brave Horatius,
    But constant still in mind;
Thrice thirty thousand foes before,
    And the broad flood behind.
"Down with him!" cried false Sextus,
    With a smile on his pale face.
"Now yield thee", cried Lars Porsena,
    "Now yield thee to our grace!"

Round turned he, as not deigning
 Those craven ranks to see;
Nought spake he to Lars Porsena,
 To Sextus nought spake he;
But he saw on Palatinus
 The white porch of his home;
And he spake to the noble river
 That rolls by the towers of Rome.

"Oh Tiber! father Tiber!
 To whom the Romans pray,
A Roman's life, a Roman's arms,
 Take thou in charge this day!"
So he spake and, speaking sheathed
 The good sword by his side,
And with his harness on his back,
 Plunged headlong in the tide.

No sound of joy or sorrow
 Was heard from either bank;
But friends and foes in dumb surprise,
With parted lips and straining eyes,
 Stood gazing where he sank;
And when above the surges
 They saw his crest appear,
All Rome sent forth a rapturous cry,
And even the ranks of Tuscany
 Could scarce forbear to cheer.

But fiercely ran the current,
 Swollen high by months of rain:
And fast his blood was flowing;
 And he was sore in pain,
And heavy with his armour,
 And spent with changing blows:
And oft they thought him sinking,
 But still again he rose.

Never, I ween, did swimmer,
 In such an evil case,
Struggle through such a raging flood
 Safe to the landing place:
But his limbs were borne up bravely
 By the brave heart within,
And our good father Tiber
 Bare bravely up his chin.

"Curse on him!" quoth false Sextus;
"Will not the villain drown?
But for this stay, ere close of day,
We would have sacked the town!"
"Heaven help him!" quoth Lars Porsena,
"And bring him safe to shore;
For such a gallant feat of arms
Was never seen before."

And now he feels the bottom:
Now on dry earth he stands;
Now round him throng the Fathers;
To press his gory hands;
And now, with shouts and clapping,
And noise of weeping loud,
He enters through the River-Gate,
Borne by the joyous crowd.

They gave him of the corn-land,
That was of public right,
As much as two strong oxen
Could plough from morn till night;
And they made a molten image,
And set it up on high,
And there it stands unto this day
To witness if I lie.

It stands in the Comitium,
Plain for all folk to see;
Horatius in his harness,
Halting upon one knee:
And underneath is written,
In letters all of gold,
How valiantly he kept the bridge
In the brave days of old.

And still his name sounds stirring
Unto the men of Rome,
As the trumpet-blast that calls to them
To charge the Volscian home;
And wives still pray to Juno
For boys with hearts as bold
As his who kept the bridge so well
In the brave days of old.

And in the nights of winter,
  When the cold north winds blow,
And the long howling of the wolves
  Is heard amidst the snow;
When round the lonely cottage
  Roars loud the tempest's din,
And the good logs of Algidus
  Roar louder yet within;

When the oldest cask is opened,
  And the largest lamp is lit;
When the chestnuts glow in the embers,
  And the kid turns on the spit;
When young and old in circle
  Around the firebrands close;
When the girls are weaving baskets
  And the lads are shaping bows;

When the goodman mends his armour,
  And trims his helmet's plume;
And the goodwife's shuttle merrily
  Goes flashing through the loom;
With weeping and with laughter
  Still is the story told,
How well Horatius kept the bridge
  In the brave days of old.

Rider at the Gate

John Masefield

A windy night was blowing on Rome,
The cressets guttered on Caesar's home,
The fish-boats, moored at the bridge, were breaking
The rush of the river to yellow foam.

The hinges whined to the shutters shaking,
When clip-clop-clep came a horse-hoofs raking
The stones of the road at Caesar's gate;
The spear-butts jarred at the guard's awaking.

"Who goes there?" said the guard at the gate.
"What is the news, that you ride so late?"
"News most pressing, that must be spoken
To Caesar alone, and that cannot wait."

"The Caesar sleeps; you must show a token
That the news suffice that he be awoken.
What is the news, and whence do you come?
For no light cause may his sleep be broken."

"Out of the dark of the sands I come,
From the dark of death, with news for Rome,
A word so fell that it must be uttered
Though it strike the soul of the Caesar dumb."

Caesar turned in his bed and muttered,
With a struggle for breath the lamp-flame guttered;
Calpurnia heard her husband moan:
"The house is falling,
The beaten men come into their own."

"Speak your word," said the guard at the gate;
"Yes, but bear it to Caesar straight,
Say, 'Your murderers' knives are honing,
Your killers' gang is lying in wait.'

"Out of the wind that is blowing and moaning,
Through the city palace and the country loaning,
I cry, 'For the world's sake, Caesar, beware,
And take this warning as my atoning.

"'Beware of the Court, of the palace stair,
Of the downcast friend, who speaks so fair,
Keep from the Senate, for Death is going
On many men's feet to meet you there.'

"I, who am dead, have ways of knowing
Of the crop of death that the quick are sowing.
I, who was Pompey, cry it aloud
From the dark of death, from the wind blowing.

"I, who was Pompey, once was proud,
Now I lie in the sand without a shroud;
I cry to Caesar out of my pain,
'Caesar beware, your death is vowed.'"

The light grew grey on the window-pane,
The windcocks swung in a burst of rain,
The window of Caesar flung unshuttered,
The horse-hoofs died into wind again.

Caesar turned in his bed and muttered,
With a struggle for breath the lamp-flame guttered;
Calpurnia heard her husband moan:
"The house is falling,
The beaten men come into their own."

The Gladiator

from Childe Harold's Pilgrimage
George Gordon, Lord Byron

I see before me the Gladiator lie:
He leans upon his hand—his manly brow
Consents to death, but conquers agony,
And his droop'd head sinks gradually low—
And through his side the last drops, ebbing slow
From the red gash, fall heavy, one by one,
Like the first of a thunder-shower; and now
The arena swims around him—he is gone,
Ere ceased the inhuman shout which hail'd the
wretch who won.

He heard it, but he heeded not—his eyes
Were with his heart, and that was far away;
He reck'd not of the life he lost nor prize,
But where his rude hut by the Danube lay,
There where his young barbarians all at play,
There was their Dacian mother—he, their sire,
Butcher'd to make a Roman holiday—
All this rush'd with his blood—Shall he expire
And unavenged?—Arise! ye Goths, and glut your ire!

The Prologue

from The New Testament, John 1:1-5

Greek

Ἐν ἀρχῇ ἦν ὁ Λόγος, καὶ ὁ Λόγος ἦν πρὸς τὸν Θεόν, καὶ Θεὸς ἦν ὁ Λόγος.

Οὗτος ἦν ἐν ἀρχῇ πρὸς τὸν Θεόν.

πάντα δι' αὐτοῦ ἐγένετο, καὶ χωρὶς αὐτοῦ ἐγένετο οὐδὲ ἕν ὃ γέγονεν.

ἐν αὐτῷ ζωὴ ἦν, καὶ ἡ ζωὴ ἦν τὸ φῶς τῶν ἀνθρώπων.

καὶ τὸ φῶς ἐν τῇ σκοτίᾳ φαίνει, καὶ ἡ σκοτία αὐτὸ οὐ κατέλαβεν.

Greek transliteration

en archê ên ho logos, kai ho logos ên pros ton theon, kai theos ên ho logos.

houtos ên en archê pros ton theon.

panta di autou egeneto kai chôris autou egeneto oude hen ho gegonen.

en autô zôe ên kai hê zôê ên to phôs tôn anthrôpôn.

kai to phôs en tê skotia phainei kai hê skotia autô ou katelaben.

In the beginning was the Word, and the Word was with God, and the Word was God.

The same was in the beginning with God.

All things were made by him; and without him was not any thing made that was made.

In him was life; and the life was the light of men.

And the light shineth in darkness; and the darkness comprehended it not.

Ancient Greek pronunciation guide:

A, α, (a) Alpha, as a in father
E, ε, (e) Epsilon, as e in get
H, ή, (ê) Eta, as long a in day
I, i, (ι) Iota, as i (short i) in sit, as ee (long i) as in keen
O,o (o) Omicron, as o in got
U,u (u) Upsilon, as a German u with an umlaut: ü
W,ω (ô) Omega, as o in coat, but held longer

ai, as the long i sound in high
au, as in cow
ei, as the long a sound in they
eu, as a regular e and u, but in one quick syllable. Sounds similar to doe (thus zeus, not ze+us)
hu, as a regular h and u, but in one syllable. Sounds like grew
ou, as in mood
ui, as a regular u and i, but in one syllable. Pronounced quickly, as in the French word oui

Treasures in Heaven

from The New Testament, Matthew 6:19-21

Lay not up for yourselves treasures upon earth, where moth and rust doth corrupt, and where thieves break through and steal:

But lay up for yourselves treasures in heaven, where neither moth nor rust doth corrupt, and where thieves do not break through nor steal:

For where your treasure is, there will your heart be also.

The Lilies of the Field

from The New Testament, Matthew 6:28-30

And why take ye thought for raiment? Consider the lilies of the field, how they grow; they toil not, neither do they spin:

And yet I say unto you, That even Solomon in all his glory was not arrayed like one of these.

Wherefore, if God so clothe the grass of the field, which to day is, and to morrow is cast into the oven, shall he not much more clothe you, O ye of little faith?

Ask and Ye Shall Receive

from The New Testament, Luke 11:9-10

And I say unto you, Ask, and it shall be given you; seek, and ye shall find; knock, and it shall be opened unto you.

For every one that asketh receiveth; and he that seeketh findeth; and to him that knocketh it shall be opened.

Charity

from The New Testament, 1 Corinthians 13

Though I speak with the tongues of men and of angels, and have not charity, I am become as sounding brass, or a tinkling cymbal.

And though I have the gift of prophecy, and understand all mysteries, and all knowledge; and though I have all faith, so that I could remove mountains, and have not charity, I am nothing.

And though I bestow all my goods to feed the poor, and though I give my body to be burned, and have not charity, it profiteth me nothing.

The Lord's Prayer

FROM *THE NEW TESTAMENT*, MATTHEW 6:9-13

Greek

Πάτερ ἡμῶν ὁ
    ἐν τοῖς οὐρανοῖς
ἁγιασθήτω τὸ ὄνομά σου
ἐλθέτω ἡ βασιλεία σου
γενηθήτω τὸ θέλημά σου,
ὡς ἐν οὐρανῷ καὶ ἐπὶ τῆς γῆς
τὸν ἄρτον ἡμῶν τὸν ἐπιούσιον
    δὸς ἡμῖν σήμερον
καὶ ἄφες ἡμῖν
    τὰ ὀφειλήματα ἡμῶν,
ὡς καὶ ἡμεῖς ἀφίεμεν
    τοῖς ὀφειλέταις ἡμῶν
καὶ μὴ εἰσενέγκῃς
    ἡμᾶς εἰς πειρασμόν,
ἀλλὰ ῥῦσαι ἡμᾶς
    ἀπὸ τοῦ πονηροῦ.
Αμήν.

Greek transliteration

Pater hêmôn ho
    en tois ouranois
hagiasthêtô to onoma sou:
elthetô hê basileia sou:
genêthêtô to thelêma sou,
hôs en ouranô kai epi tês gês:
ton arton hêmôn ton epiousion
    dos hêmin sêmeron
kai aphes hêmin
    ta opheilêmata hêmôn,
hôs kai hêmeis aphiemen
    tois opheiletais hêmôn:
kai mê eisenegkês
    hêmas eis peirasmon,
alla rusai hêmas
    apo tou ponêrou.
Amên.

Latin

Pater noster, qui es in caelis:
sanctificetur Nomen Tuum;
adveniat Regnum Tuum;
fiat voluntas Tua,
sicut in caelo, et in terra.
Panem nostrum cotidianum
    da nobis hodie;
et dimitte nobis debita nostra,
Sicut et nos dimittimus
    debitoribus nostris;
et ne nos inducas in tentationem;
sed libera nos a Malo.
Amen.

Our Father, which art in heaven,
hallowed be thy name;
thy kingdom come;
thy will be done,
in earth as it is in heaven.
Give us this day
    our daily bread.
And forgive us our trespasses,
as we forgive them that
    trespass against us.
And lead us not into temptation;
but deliver us from evil.
(For thine is the kingdom,
the power, and the glory,
for ever and ever.)
Amen.

Ancient Greek pronunciation guide: See page 199.

The Armour of God

from The New Testament, Ephesians 6:11-17

Put on the whole armour of God, that ye may be able to stand against the wiles of the devil.

For we wrestle not against flesh and blood, but against principalities, against powers, against the rulers of the darkness of this world, against spiritual wickedness in high places.

Wherefore take unto you the whole armour of God, that ye may be able to withstand in the evil day, and having done all, to stand.

Stand therefore, having your loins girt about with truth, and having on the breastplate of righteousness;

And your feet shod with the preparation of the gospel of peace;

Above all, taking the shield of faith, wherewith ye shall be able to quench all the fiery darts of the wicked.

And take the helmet of salvation, and the sword of the Spirit, which is the word of God.

from The Meditations of Marcus Aurelius

No more talk about the kind of man that a good man ought to be, but be such.

Men despise one another and flatter one another; and men wish to raise themselves above one another and crouch before one another.

How ridiculous and what a stranger he is who is surprised at anything which happens in life.

If it is not right, do not do it: if it is not true, do not say it.

Do nothing inconsiderately, nor without a purpose.

If you are able, correct by teaching those who do wrong; but if you cannot, remember that indulgence is given you for this purpose.

He who does wrong does wrong against himself. He who acts unjustly acts unjustly to himself, because he makes himself bad.

He often acts unjustly who does not do a certain thing; not only he who does a certain thing.

Receive wealth or prosperity without arrogance; and be ready to let it go.

Consider that men will do the same things nevertheless, even if you should burst.

The perfection of moral character consists in this, in passing every day as the last, and in being neither violently excited, nor torpid, nor playing the hypocrite.

Look within. Within is the fountain of good, and it will ever bubble up if you will ever dig.

The art of life is more like the wrestler's art than the dancer's in respect of this, that it should stand ready and firm to meet onsets which are sudden and unexpected.

Consider yourself to be dead, and to have completed your life up to the present time; and live according to nature the remainder which is allowed you.

The War Song of the Vikings

Fiona Macleod

Let loose the hounds of war,
    The whirling swords!
Send them leaping afar,
Red in their thirst for war;
Odin laughs in his car
    At the screaming of the swords!

Far let the white-ones fly,
    The whirling swords!
Afar off the ravens spy
Death-shadows cloud the sky.
Let the wolves of the Gael die
    'Neath the screaming swords!

The Shining Ones yonder
    High in Valhalla
Shout now, with thunder:
Drive the Gaels under,
Cleave them asunder—
    Swords of Valhalla!

The Norwegian Rune Poem

Fé vældr frænda róge;
føðesk ulfr í skóge.

Úr er af illu jarne;
opt lypr ræinn á hjarne.

Þurs vældr kvinna kvillu;
kátr værðr fár af illu.

Óss er flæstra færða för;
en skalpr er sværða.

Ræið kveða rossom væsta;
Reginn sló sværðet bæzta.

Kaun er barna bölvan;
böl görver nán fölvan.

Hagall er kaldastr korna;
Kristr skóp hæimenn forna.

Nauðr gerer næppa koste;
nöktan kælr í froste.

Ís köllum brú bræiða;
blindan þarf at læiða.

Ár er gumna góðe;
get ek at örr var Fróðe.

Sól er landa ljóme;
lúti ek helgum dóme.

Týr er æinendr ása;
opt værðr smiðr blása.

Bjarkan er laufgroenstr líma;
Loki bar flærða tíma.

Maðr er moldar auki;
mikil er græip á hauki.

Lögr er, fællr ór fjalle foss;
en gull ero nosser.

Ýr er vetrgroenstr viða;
vænt er, er brennr, at sviða.

Old Norse pronunciation guide:
This Norwegian version has both alliterative Fornyrðislag meter and end rhyme.

a - as in "law" | *á - as in "father"*
e - as i in "gin" | *é - as ay in "day"*
i - as in "is" | *í - ee as in "speed"*
o - as in "omit" | *ó - as in "owe"*
Ø, ö - as in "not"
u - oo, as in "soot" | *ú - oo, as in "droop"*
y - u, as in French tu | *ý - u, as in German Tür*
ae - e as in "get" | *au - ou as in "house"*
ei - ay as in "day" | *ey - as in ei*
(ð) dh - a soft th as in "leather"
f - pronounced as English f initially, as English v in medial and final positions.
g - hard as in "give"
h - may be heavily aspirated, almost as a ch
j - always as English y
ng - as in "sing"
r - trilled; r on the end of the word is not given an extra syllabe.
s - always voiceless, as in "blast"
(Þ) th - as in "thorn"
z - pronounced as ts (as in German)

Translation:
Wealth is a source of discord among kinsmen;
the wolf lives in the forest.
Dross comes from bad iron;
the reindeer often races over the frozen snow.
Giant causes anguish to women;
misfortune makes few men cheerful.
Estuary is the way of most journeys;
but a scabbard is of swords.
Riding is said to be the worst thing for horses;
Reginn forged the finest sword.
Ulcer is fatal to children;
death makes a corpse pale.
Hail is the coldest of grain;
Christ created the world of old.
Constraint gives scant choice;
a naked man is chilled by the frost.
Ice we call the broad bridge;
the blind man must be led.
Plenty is a boon to men;
I say that Frothi was generous.
Sun is the light of the world;
I bow to the divine decree.
Tyr is a one-handed God;
often has the smith to blow.
Birch has the greenest leaves of any shrub;
Loki was fortunate in his deceit.
Man is an augmentation of the dust;
great is the talon-span of the hawk.
A waterfall is a river falling from a mountain;
but ornaments are of gold.
Yew is the greenest of trees in winter;
it is wont to crackle when it burns.

The Anchor

An Anglo-Saxon Riddle

I war with the wind, with the waves I wrestle;
I must battle with both when the bottom I seek,
My strange habitation by surges o'er-roofed.
I am strong in the strife, while still I remain;
As soon as I stir, they are stronger than I.
They wrench and they wrest, till I run from my foes;
What was put in my keeping they carry away.
If my back be not broken, I baffle them still.
The rocks are my helpers, when hard I am pressed;
Grimly I grip them. Guess what I'm called.

The Plough

An Anglo-Saxon Riddle

My beak is below, I burrow and nose
Under the ground. I go as I'm guided
By my master the farmer, old foe of the forest;
Bent and bowed, at my back he walks,
As he forces me forward over the field.
I gnash at the ground and tear with my teeth
When my master is strong and can steer me with skill.
If my master steer me with skill from behind.

The Home of Grendel

from Beowulf

A land of wolf slopes and windy headlands
Wildered fenways; there the fierce torrent
Shadowed by misty mountain shoulders
Dashes downward dark under earth.

Thence a mile's measure lies the mere
Fast overhung by frost-rimed forests,
Ringed is the water with roots of trees.

There may a watcher spy a night wonder:
Fire on the flood. No grey grandfather,
None nurtured by woman knows the place.

The Funeral Pyre

from Beowulf

The Geat folk fashioned — a peerless pyre
Hung 'round with helmets — and battle-boards,
With gleaming byrnies — as Beowulf bade.
In sorrow of soul — they laid on the pyre
Their mighty leader, — their well-loved lord.
The warriors kindled — the bale on the barrow
Wakened the greatest — of funeral fires.
Dark o'er the blaze — the wood-smoke mounted;
The winds were still, — and the sound of weeping
Rose with the roar — of the surging flame
Till the heat of the fire — had broken the body
With hearts that were heavy — they chanted their sorrow,
Singing a dirge — for the death of their lord;
And an aged woman — with upbound locks
Lamented for Beowulf, — wailing in woe.
Over and over — she uttered her dread
Of sorrow to come, — and bondage and shame.
The smoke of the bale-fire — rose to the sky!

The Knight's Prayer

from the Sarum Primer

God be in my head
And in my understanding;

God be in mine eyes
And in my looking;

God be in my mouth
And in my speaking;

God be in my heart
And in my thinking;

God be at my end
And at my departing.

Sir Galahad

Alfred, Lord Tennyson

My good blade carves the casques of men,
My tough lance thrusteth sure,
My strength is as the strength of ten,
Because my heart is pure.
The shattering trumpet shrilleth high,
The hard brands shiver on the steel,
The splinter'd spear-shafts crack and fly,
The horse and rider reel:
They reel, they roll in clanging lists,
And when the tide of combat stands,
Perfume and flowers fall in showers
That lightly rain from ladies' hands.

How sweet are looks that ladies bend
On whom their favours fall!
For them I battle till the end,
To save from shame and thrall:
But all my heart is drawn above,
My knees are bow'd in crypt and shrine:
I never felt the kiss of love,
Nor maiden's hand in mine.
More bounteous aspects on me beam,
Me mightier transports move and thrill;
So keep I fair thro' faith and prayer
A virgin heart in work and will.

When down the stormy crescent goes,
A light before me swims,
Between dark stems the forest glows,
I hear a noise of hymns:
Then by some secret shrine I ride;
I hear a voice, but none are there;
The stalls are void, the doors are wide,
The tapers burning fair.
Fair gleams the snowy altar-cloth,
The silver vessels sparkle clean,
The shrill bell rings, the censer swings,
And solemn chaunts resound between.

Sometimes on lonely mountain-meres
I find a magic bark;
I leap on board: no helmsman steers
I float till all is dark.
A gentle sound, an awful light!
Three angels bear the Holy Grail:
With folded feet, in stoles of white,
On sleeping wings they sail.
Ah, blessed vision! blood of God!
My spirit beats her mortal bars,
As down dark tides the glory slides,
And star-like mingles with the stars.

When on my goodly charger borne
Thro' dreaming towns I go,
The cock crows ere the Christmas morn,
The streets are dumb with snow.
The tempest crackles on the leads,
And, ringing, spins from brand and mail;
But o'er the dark a glory spreads,
And gilds the driving hail.
I leave the plain, I climb the height;
No branchy thicket shelter yields;
But blessed forms in whistling storms
Fly o'er waste fens and windy fields.

A maiden knight—to me is given
Such hope, I know not fear,
I yearn to breathe the airs of heaven
That often meet me here.
I muse on joy that will not cease,
Pure spaces clothed in living beams,
Pure lilies of eternal peace,
Whose odours haunt my dreams;
And, stricken by an angel's hand,
This mortal armour that I wear,
This weight and size, this heart and eyes,
Are touch'd, are turn'd to finest air.

The clouds are broken in the sky,
And thro' the mountain-walls
A rolling organ-harmony
Swells up, and shakes and falls.
Then move the trees, the copses nod,
Wings flutter, voices hover clear:
"O just and faithful knight of God!
Ride on! the prize is near."
So pass I hostel, hall, and grange;
By bridge and ford, by park and pale,
All-arm'd I ride, whate'er betide,
Until I find the Holy Grail.

A Song of King Arthur's Castle

A. C. Harwood

King Arthur's walls are strong and steep
By Western seas they stand;
Three sides sheer down upon the deep,
And one upon the strand.

And cliff and tower and crag resound
To hail or farewell shout,
As on that adamantine ground,
The knights ride in and out.

White waves on Arthur's castle wall,
And sun-gold in the spray;
And knights like stars in Arthur's hall
And he like Sun of Day.

In Arthur's hall with bread and wine
The feasting board is laid;
And they who at that table dine,
With spirit strength are stayed.

While music like the cleansing sea
Does so renew the heart,
That who sits down in misery
In steadfast joy shall part.

White waves on Arthur's castle wall,
And sun-gold in the spray;
And knights like stars in Arthur's hall
And he like Sun of Day.

The knight that rides from Arthur's court
Rests not save in the field,
Till friend or foe be all downfought
Or sorest quarrel healed.

And wild men see the armor gleam,
As through the wood they range,
And stand and gaze as in a dream
And feel a blessing strange.

White waves on Arthur's castle wall,
And sun-gold in the spray;
And knights like stars in Arthur's hall
And he like Sun of Day.

Or when he wrestles, fiend beset,
At midnight hour malign,
He feels the splendor o'er him yet
Of Arthur's seven-starred sign.

Then round him shines that castle tower,
And in its might he stands;
And all King Arthur's men with power
Strike battling in his hands.

White waves on Arthur's castle wall,
And sun-gold in the spray;
And knights like stars in Arthur's hall
And he like Sun of Day.

Arthur the King

Jehanne Mehta

Brave Arthur was buried, so legends they tell it
Deep under the mountains in days long ago,
With twelve faithful knights decked in armor like silver
With their long swords beside them in scabbards of gold.
"But dying is only a new kind of waking
Or a new kind of sleeping resplendent with dream...
And if times they are hard you have only to call me
And you'll not catch me napping," said Arthur the King.

So we'll kindle a beacon on every high mountain
To the sound of our music the valleys shall ring
To waken the sleepers of long vanished ages
To waken the knights and brave Arthur the King.

Well the dragon may prowl in the streets of the city
And the world may turn out to be not what it seems,
And many a job may be axed by tomorrow
And we may be obliged to abandon our dreams...
"But bring out the fool in his motley and bells
And remember the minstrels who taught you to sing,
And the quest it begins with the steps of the dance.
Won't you please find your partners," said Arthur the King.

So we'll kindle a beacon on every high mountain
To the sound of our music the valleys shall ring
To waken the sleepers of long vanished ages
To waken the knights and brave Arthur the King.

There's no need to seek far to find news of disaster
Of wars and of rumours of gathering gloom...
And it's hard to escape the dead weight of inertia
As we hear the fraught words of the prophets of doom.
"But each knight is equal around my round table
And each has a note and a rhythm to bring
And the quest it begins with the jig and the reel.
Won't you take out your fiddles," said Arthur the King.

So we'll kindle a beacon on every high mountain
To the sound of our music the valleys shall ring
To waken the sleepers of long vanished ages
To waken the knights and brave Arthur the King.

There are times when the fog is so thick on the hills
Fell enchantments have settled on river and lake
And the poisons have sunk so far into the earth
That we ask, "Is there anything left there to wake?"
"But bring in the morris, the sword dance and step dance
The music is there and you know how to sing
For the quest it begins with the song from the heart
Won't you join in the chorus," said Arthur the King.

So we'll kindle a beacon on every high mountain
To the sound of our music the valleys shall ring
To waken the sleepers of long vanished ages
To waken the knights and brave Arthur the King.

FROM A POET'S COMPLAINT OF THE BLACKSMITHS

FOURTEENTH CENTURY ENGLISH POEM

Swart smirched smiths, smattered with smoke
Drive me to death with din of their dents,
Such noise on nights one ne'er heard man never,
Such clashing of cries and clattering of knocks.
The craftsmen clamour for coal, coal, coal!
And blow their bellows their brains to burst.

They jostle and jangle, they jape and they jest.
They groove and they grind and they grumble together,
Hot with the heaving of heated hammers.
Of thick bull's hide are their branded aprons,
Their shanks are shod 'gainst shooting sparks.

Huge hammers they have and hard to handle,
Stark strokes strike they on the steeled stock.
"Well wrought, well wrought, well wrought,"
Might daunt the devil
Such life they lead,
All armourers, founders, forgemen,
Christ save them!

FROM THE GENERAL PROLOGUE

THE CANTERBURY TALES

GEOFFREY CHAUCER

Whan that Aprill, with his shoures soote
The droghte of March hath perced to the roote
And bathed every veyne in swich licour,
Of which vertu engendred is the flour;
Whan Zephirus eek with his sweete breeth
Inspired hath in every holt and heeth
The tendre croppes, and the yonge sonne
Hath in the Ram his halfe cours yronne,
And smale foweles maken melodye,
That slepen al the nyght with open eye—
(So priketh hem Nature in hir corages);
Thanne longen folk to goon on pilgrimages
And palmeres for to seken straunge strondes
To ferne halwes, kowthe in sondry londes;
And specially from every shires ende
Of Engelond, to Caunterbury they wende,
The hooly blisful martir for to seke
That hem hath holpen, whan that they were seeke.

Pronunciation notes for Chaucer's English:

The Canterbury Tales was written in Middle English, specifically in a dialect associated with London and spellings associated with the then emergent chancery standard. Chaucer's generation of English-speakers was among the last to pronounce <e> at the end of words.

The pronunciation of Chaucer's writing otherwise differs most prominently from Modern English in that his language had not undergone the Great Vowel Shift: pronouncing Chaucer's vowels as they would be pronounced today in European languages like Italian, Spanish or German generally produces pronunciations more like Chaucer's own than Modern English.

Generally, all letters in Middle English words were pronounced. (Silent letters in Modern English come from pronunciation shifts, which means that pronunciation is no longer closely reflected by the written form because of fixed spelling constraints imposed by the invention of dictionaries and printing.) Therefore 'knight' was pronounced [kniçt] (with a pronounced <k> and the <gh> as the <ch> in German 'Knecht'), not as in Modern English.

In earlier Middle English all written vowels were pronounced. By Chaucer's time, however, the final <e> had become silent in normal speech, but could optionally be pronounced in verse as the meter required (but was normally silent when the next word began with a vowel). Chaucer followed these conventions: -e is silent in 'kowthe' and 'Thanne', but is pronounced in 'straunge', 'ferne', 'ende', etc. (Presumably, the final <y> is partly or completely dropped in 'Caunterbury', so as to make the meter flow.)

An additional rule in speech, and often in poetry as well, was that a non-final unstressed <e> was dropped when adjacent to only a single consonant on either side if there was another short 'e' in an adjoining syllable. Thus, 'every' sounds like "evry" and 'palmeres' like "palmers".

The Moon Is Up

Alfred Noyes

The moon is up, the stars are bright.
The wind is fresh and free!
We're out to seek the gold tonight
Across the silver sea!
The world is growing grey and old:
Break out the sails again!
We're out to see a Realm of Gold
Beyond the Spanish Main.

We're sick of all the cringing knees,
The courtly smiles and lies
God, let Thy singing channel breeze
Lighten our hearts and eyes!
Let love no more be bought and sold
For earthly loss or gain;
We're out to seek an Age of Gold
Beyond the Spanish Main.

Beyond the light of far Cathay,
Beyond all mortal dreams,
Beyond the reach of night and day
Our El Dorado gleams,
Revealing—as the skies unfold—
A star without a stain,
The Glory of the Gates of Gold
Beyond the Spanish Main.

In the days of the Spanish New World Empire, the mainland of the American continent enclosing the Caribbean Sea and the Gulf of Mexico was referred to as the Spanish Main. It included present-day Florida, the east shore of the Gulf of Mexico in Texas, Mexico, Central America and the north coast of South America. In particular, the term is most strongly associated with that stretch of the Caribbean coastline that runs from the ports of Porto Bello on the Isthmus of Darien, through Cartagena de Indias in New Granada, and Maracaibo to the Orinoco delta.

Columbus

Joaquin Miller

Behind him lay the gray Azores,
    Behind the Gates of Hercules;
Before him not the ghost of shores,
    Before him only shoreless seas.
The good mate said: "Now must we pray,
    For lo! the very stars are gone.
Brave Admiral, speak, what shall I say?"
    "Why, say, 'Sail on! sail on! and on!'"

"My men grow mutinous day by day;
    My men grow ghastly wan and weak."
The stout mate thought of home; a spray
    Of salt wave washed his swarthy cheek.
"What shall I say, brave Admiral, say,
    If we sight naught but seas at dawn?"
"Why, you shall say at break of day,
    'Sail on! sail on! sail on! and on!'"

They sailed and sailed, as winds might blow,
    Until at last the blanched mate said:
"Why, now not even God would know
    Should I and all my men fall dead.
These very winds forget their way,
    For God from these dread seas is gone.
Now speak, brave Admiral, speak and say"—
    He said: "Sail on! sail on! and on!"

They sailed. They sailed. Then spake the mate:
    "This mad sea shows his teeth to-night.
He curls his lip, he lies in wait,
    With lifted teeth, as if to bite!
Brave Admiral, say but one good word:
    What shall we do when hope is gone?"
The words leapt like a leaping sword:
    "Sail on! sail on! sail on! and on!"

Then, pale and worn, he kept his deck,
    And peered through darkness. Ah, that night
Of all dark nights! And then a speck—
    A light! A light! A light! A light!
It grew, a starlit flag unfurled!
    It grew to be Time's burst of dawn.
He gained a world; he gave that world
    Its grandest lesson: "On! sail on!"

Poor Richard's Maxims

Sverre Elsmo

You've heard of Benjamin Franklin,
Of his work, his joys and whims,
As you read this poem you'll find, I'm sure
The truth in "Poor Richard's" maxims.

"Wealth is not his that has it"
'Cause money's not everything,
"But wealth is his that enjoys it"
Whether beggar, pauper or king.

"If a man could have half his wishes
He would certainly double his trouble,
So better a little with content
Than much with contention and grumble.

"Experience keeps a dear school
Yet fools will learn no other,
And he that cannot obey
Cannot command another.

"Don't go to the Doctor with each distemper,
Nor to the pot for every thirst,
Or to the lawyer for every quarrel,"
Just think a little first.

"Early to bed, and early to rise
Makes a man healthy, wealthy and wise,"
And should you sometimes tempted be,
Speak only truth, there's nothing in lies.

Now if I've changed a word or two
Or added here and there,
I simply meant to rhyme the lines,
Yet, with utmost care.

Benjamin Franklin was one of the Founding Fathers of the United States, a leading author and printer, political theorist, politician, postmaster, scientist, inventor, civic activist, statesman, and diplomat.

As a scientist, he was a major figure in the American Enlightenment and the history of physics for his discoveries and theories regarding electricity. He invented the lightning rod, bifocals, the Franklin stove, a carriage odometer, and the glass 'armonica'. He formed both the first public lending library in America and the first fire department in Pennsylvania.

Poor Richard's Almanack was a yearly almanac published by Franklin, who adopted the pseudonym of "Poor Richard" or "Richard Saunders". The publication appeared continually from 1732 to 1758 and was a best seller for a pamphlet published in the American colonies; print runs reached 10,000 per year.

Give Me Liberty, or Give Me Death!

From His Speech to The Virginia Convention

Patrick Henry

They tell us, sir, that we are weak—unable to cope with so formidable an adversary. But when shall we be stronger? Will it be the next week, or the next year? Will it be when we are totally disarmed, and when a British guard shall be stationed in every house? Shall we gather strength by irresolution and inaction? Shall we acquire the means of effectual resistance, by lying supinely on our backs, and hugging the delusive phantom of hope, until our enemies shall have bound us hand and foot?

Sir, we are not weak, if we make a proper use of the means which the God of nature hath placed in our power. Three millions of people, armed in the holy cause of liberty, and in such a country as that which we possess, are invincible by any force which our enemy can send against us. Besides, sir, we shall not fight our battles alone. There is a just God who presides over the destinies of nations, and who will raise up friends to fight our battles for us.

The battle, sir, is not to the strong alone; it is to the vigilant, the active, the brave. Besides, sir, we have no election. If we were base enough to desire it, it is now too late to retire from the contest. There is no retreat but in submission and slavery! Our chains are forged! Their clanking may be heard on the plains of Boston! The war is inevitable—and let it come! I repeat it, sir, let it come!

It is in vain, sir, to extenuate the matter. Gentlemen may cry, "Peace! Peace!"—but there is no peace. The war is actually begun! The next gale that sweeps from the north will bring to our ears the clash of resounding arms! Our brethren are already in the field! Why stand we here idle? What is it that gentlemen wish? What would they have? Is life so dear, or peace so sweet, as to be purchased at the price of chains and slavery? Forbid it, Almighty God! I know not what course others may take; but as for me, give me liberty, or give me death!

Only a few weeks before Paul Revere's midnight ride, Patrick Henry spoke to the Virginia Convention. Realizing that they might vote against sending troops, Henry spoke passionately and without notes. His speech is credited with having swung the balance in convincing the Virginia House of Burgesses to pass a resolution delivering the Virginia troops to the Revolutionary War.

Among the delegates to the convention were future Presidents Thomas Jefferson and George Washington. Reportedly, those in attendance, upon hearing the speech, shouted, "Give me liberty or give me death!"

Paul Revere's Ride

Henry Wadsworth Longfellow

Listen my children and you shall hear
Of the midnight ride of Paul Revere,
On the eighteenth of April, in Seventy-five;
Hardly a man is now alive
Who remembers that famous day and year.

He said to his friend, "If the British march
By land or sea from the town to-night,
Hang a lantern aloft in the belfry arch
Of the North Church tower as a signal light,—
One if by land, and two if by sea;
And I on the opposite shore will be,
Ready to ride and spread the alarm
Through every Middlesex village and farm,
For the country folk to be up and to arm."

Then he said "Good-night!" and with muffled oar
Silently rowed to the Charlestown shore,
Just as the moon rose over the bay,
Where swinging wide at her moorings lay
The Somerset, British man-of-war;
A phantom ship, with each mast and spar
Across the moon like a prison bar,
And a huge black hulk, that was magnified
By its own reflection in the tide.

Meanwhile, his friend through alley and street
Wanders and watches, with eager ears,
Till in the silence around him he hears
The muster of men at the barrack door,
The sound of arms, and the tramp of feet,
And the measured tread of the grenadiers,
Marching down to their boats on the shore.

Then he climbed the tower of the Old North Church,
By the wooden stairs, with stealthy tread,
To the belfry chamber overhead,
And startled the pigeons from their perch
On the sombre rafters, that round him made
Masses and moving shapes of shade,—
By the trembling ladder, steep and tall,
To the highest window in the wall,
Where he paused to listen and look down
A moment on the roofs of the town
And the moonlight flowing over all.

Beneath, in the churchyard, lay the dead,
In their night encampment on the hill,
Wrapped in silence so deep and still
That he could hear, like a sentinel's tread,
The watchful night-wind, as it went
Creeping along from tent to tent,
And seeming to whisper, "All is well!"
A moment only he feels the spell
Of the place and the hour, and the secret dread
Of the lonely belfry and the dead;
For suddenly all his thoughts are bent
On a shadowy something far away,
Where the river widens to meet the bay,—
A line of black that bends and floats
On the rising tide like a bridge of boats.

Meanwhile, impatient to mount and ride,
Booted and spurred, with a heavy stride
On the opposite shore walked Paul Revere.
Now he patted his horse's side,
Now he gazed at the landscape far and near,
Then, impetuous, stamped the earth,
And turned and tightened his saddle girth;
But mostly he watched with eager search
The belfry tower of the Old North Church,
As it rose above the graves on the hill,
Lonely and spectral and sombre and still.
And lo! as he looks, on the belfry's height
A glimmer, and then a gleam of light!
He springs to the saddle, the bridle he turns,
But lingers and gazes, till full on his sight
A second lamp in the belfry burns.

A hurry of hoofs in a village street,
A shape in the moonlight, a bulk in the dark,
And beneath, from the pebbles, in passing, a spark
Struck out by a steed flying fearless and fleet;
That was all! And yet, through the gloom and the light,
The fate of a nation was riding that night;
And the spark struck out by that steed, in his flight,
Kindled the land into flame with its heat.

He has left the village and mounted the steep,
And beneath him, tranquil and broad and deep,
Is the Mystic, meeting the ocean tides;
And under the alders that skirt its edge,
Now soft on the sand, now loud on the ledge,
Is heard the tramp of his steed as he rides.

It was twelve by the village clock
When he crossed the bridge into Medford town.
He heard the crowing of the cock,
And the barking of the farmer's dog,
And felt the damp of the river fog,
That rises after the sun goes down.

It was one by the village clock,
When he galloped into Lexington.
He saw the gilded weathercock
Swim in the moonlight as he passed,
And the meeting-house windows, black and bare,
Gaze at him with a spectral glare,
As if they already stood aghast
At the bloody work they would look upon.

It was two by the village clock,
When he came to the bridge in Concord town.
He heard the bleating of the flock,
And the twitter of birds among the trees,
And felt the breath of the morning breeze
Blowing over the meadow brown.
And one was safe and asleep in his bed
Who at the bridge would be first to fall,
Who that day would be lying dead,
Pierced by a British musket-ball.

You know the rest. In the books you have read
How the British Regulars fired and fled,—
How the farmers gave them ball for ball,
From behind each fence and farmyard wall,
Chasing the redcoats down the lane,
Then crossing the fields to emerge again
Under the trees at the turn of the road,
And only pausing to fire and load.

So through the night rode Paul Revere;
And so through the night went his cry of alarm
To every Middlesex village and farm,—
A cry of defiance, and not of fear,
A voice in the darkness, a knock at the door,
And a word that shall echo for evermore!
For, borne on the night-wind of the Past,
Through all our history, to the last,
In the hour of darkness and peril and need,
The people will waken and listen to hear
The hurrying hoof-beats of that steed,
And the midnight message of Paul Revere.

The Little Black-Eyed Rebel

Will Carleton

A boy drove into the city, his wagon loaded down
With food to feed the people of the British-governed town;
And the little black-eyed rebel, so innocent and sly,
Was watching for his coming from the corner of her eye.

His face looked broad and honest, his hands were brown and tough,
The clothes he wore upon him were homespun, coarse, and rough;
But one there was who watched him, who long time lingered nigh,
And cast at him sweet glances from the corner of her eye.

He drove up to the market, he waited in the line;
His apples and potatoes were fresh and fair and fine;
But long and long he waited, and no one came to buy,
Save the black-eyed rebel, answering from the corner of her eye.

"Now who will buy my apples?" he shouted, long and loud;
And "Who wants my potatoes?" he repeated to the crowd;
But from all the people round him came no word of a reply,
Save the black-eyed rebel, answering from the corner of her eye.

For she knew that 'neath the lining of the coat he wore that day,
Were long letters from the husbands and the fathers far away,
Who were fighting for the freedom that they meant to gain or die;
And a tear like silver glistened in the corner of her eye.

But the treasures—how to get them? crept the question through her mind,
Since keen enemies were watching for what prizes they might find:
And she paused a while and pondered, with a pretty little sigh;
Then resolve crept through her features, and a shrewdness fired her eye.

So she resolutely walked up to the wagon old and red;
"May I have a dozen apples for a kiss?" she sweetly said:
And the brown face flushed to scarlet; for the boy was somewhat shy,
And he saw her laughing at him from the corner of her eye.

"You may have them all for nothing, and more, if you want," quoth he.
"I will have them, my good fellow, but can pay for them," said she;
And she clambered on the wagon, minding not who all were by,
With a laugh of reckless romping in the corner of her eye.

Clinging round his brawny neck, she clasped her fingers white and small,
And then whispered, "Quick! the letters! thrust them underneath my shawl!
Carry back again this package, and be sure that you are spry!"
And she sweetly smiled upon him from the corner of her eye.

Loud the motley crowd were laughing at the strange, ungirlish freak,
And the boy was scared and panting, and so dashed he could not speak;
And, "Miss, I have good apples," a bolder lad did cry;
But she answered, "No, I thank you," from the corner of her eye.

With the news of loved ones absent to the dear friends they would greet,
Searching them who hungered for them, swift she glided through the street.
"There is nothing worth the doing that it does not pay to try,"
Thought the little black-eyed rebel, with a twinkle in her eye.

Mary Redmond was called "The Little Black-Eyed Rebel" and lived in Philadelphia. During the occupation by the British she was ever ready to assist in the secret delivery of letters to women from husbands who were fighting in the Continental Army.

The despatches were usually sent by a boy, who carried them stitched in the back of his coat when he came into the city bringing provisions to market. One morning, when there was some reason to fear he was suspected, and his movements watched by the enemy, Mary undertook to get the papers in safety from him. She went, as usual, to the market, and, in a pretended game of romps threw her shawl over the boy's head, and thus secured the prize letters for the women of Philadelphia. She hastened with the papers to her anxious friends, who read them by stealth, after the windows had been carefully closed.

Yankee Doodle

Yankee Doodle went to town
A-riding on a pony,
Stuck a feather in his cap
And called it macaroni.

Yankee Doodle keep it up,
Yankee Doodle dandy,
Mind the music and the step,
And with the girls be handy.

Father and I went down to camp,
Along with Captain Gooding,
And there we see the men and boys,
As thick as hasty pudding.

And there we see a thousand men
As rich as Squire David;
And what they wasted every day,
I wish it could be savèd.

And there we see a swamping gun
Large as a log of maple,
Upon a deucèd little cart,
A load for father's cattle.

And every time they shoot it off,
It takes a horn of powder,
And makes a noise like father's gun,
Only a nation louder.

We saw a little barrel too,
The heads were made of leather;
They knocked on it with little clubs
And called the folks together.

And there was Captain Washington,
And gentle folks about him;
They say he's grown so 'tarnal proud
He will not ride without 'em.

He got him on his meeting clothes,
Upon a slapping stallion;
He sat the world along in rows,
In hundreds and in millions.

In CONGRESS, July 4, 1776
The unanimous Declaration of the thirteen united States of America

from the Preamble and Text

When in the Course of human events,
it becomes necessary for one people
to dissolve the political bands
which have connected them with another,
and to assume among the powers of the earth,
the separate and equal station
to which the Laws of Nature
and of Nature's God entitle them,
a decent respect
to the opinions of mankind
requires that they should declare
the causes which impel them
to the separation.

We hold these truths to be self-evident,
that all men are created equal,
that they are endowed by their Creator
with certain unalienable Rights,
that among these are Life, Liberty
and the pursuit of Happiness.
That to secure these rights,
Governments are instituted among Men,
deriving their just powers
from the consent of the governed,
That whenever any Form of Government
becomes destructive of these ends,
it is the Right of the People
to alter or to abolish it,
and to institute new Government,
laying its foundation on such principles
and organizing its powers in such form,
as to them shall seem most likely
to effect their Safety and Happiness.

We, therefore,
the Representatives of the united States of America,
in General Congress, Assembled,
appealing to the Supreme Judge of the world
for the rectitude of our intentions,
do, in the Name,
and by Authority of the good People of these Colonies,
solemnly publish and declare,
That these United Colonies are,
and of Right ought to be Free and Independent States;
that they are Absolved from all Allegiance to the British Crown,
and that all political connection between them
and the State of Great Britain,
is and ought to be totally dissolved;
and that as Free and Independent States,
they have full Power to levy War,
conclude Peace,
contract Alliances,
establish Commerce,
and to do all other Acts and Things
which Independent States may of right do.

And for the support of this Declaration,
with a firm reliance on the protection of divine Providence,
we mutually pledge to each other
our Lives, our Fortunes and our sacred Honor.

The Ten Amendments in Rhyme (The Bill of Rights)

Carl Bridgman

Amendment #1

Religion is a special right I give to everyone,
But not a right for Congress to establish only one.
I give to all the right to speak and even to assemble,
And you can even send complaints and make our congress tremble.

Amendment #2

To many, it's a real cool thing to keep and own a gun,
To others, it's a tool for evil, when the evil's done.
And still today, I give this right for good, that's understood;
Protection, hunting, shooting sports, all these are very good.

Amendment #3
My right's a bit unusual and not too often seen,
But here I give it anyway in case there is a need.
Whenever there is peace or war in our great country fair,
Your homes shall be protected from a soldier living there.

Amendment #4
Now here's a right that makes us feel secure with many features:
We have the right to be secure from search or even seizures.
Search warrants are required as well as having real good cause,
Without them even cops can be accused of breaking laws.

Amendment #5
In this amendment you're assured that you are fairly tried
Of any major crime to which you may be clearly tied;
And if you own some land for which the public has a need,
Just compensation must be paid to you to own your deed.

Amendment #6
About a crime for which you're held it must be understood;
You have the right to speedy trial; this is for your own good.
You have the right to counsel who will stand up for your side.
Accusers, they must be there too, to look you in the eye.

Amendment #7
At common law sometimes you're sued for things of little cost,
And often it is best for us to take that little loss.
But value more than twenty dollars triggers something new;
'Cause now the right to trial by jury can be used by you.

Amendment #8
Some things in laws and judgments leave a lot to be desired,
'Cause some opinions vary as the judgments they require.
For instance, now you have a right to bail, but not excessive,
But ideas of excessive for some Judges are impressive.

Amendment #9
Within this Bill, so wonderful, with lawful rights displayed,
There's one more thing that's needed here, and this one thing I say;
You must not think that this is all our rights herein fulfilled;
There's right of life and liberty and happiness as well.

Amendment #10
The constitution makes it clear, the powers of the Fed.
All others are now delegated to our states instead.
The last four words are critical to this great Bill of Rights,
"Or to the people," when they're read, makes everything alright.

Napoleon's Farewell

George Gordon, Lord Byron

Farewell to the Land where the gloom of my Glory
Arose and o'ershadow'd the earth with her name—
She abandons me now—but the page of her story,
The brightest or blackest, is fill'd with my fame.
I have warr'd with a world which vanquish'd me only
When the meteor of Conquest allured me too far;
I have coped with the nations which dread me thus lonely,
The last single Captive to millions in war.

Farewell to thee, France! when thy diadem crown'd me,
I made thee the gem and the wonder of earth,
But thy weakness decrees I should leave as I found thee,
Decay'd in thy glory, and sunk in thy worth.
Oh! for the veteran hearts that were wasted
In strife with the storm, when their battles were won
Then the Eagle, whose gaze in that moment was lasted,
Had still soar'd with eyes fix'd on victory's sun!

Farewell to thee, France!—but when Liberty rallies
Once more in thy regions, remember me then,
The violet still grows in the depth of thy valleys;
Though wither'd, thy tear will unfold it
Yet, yet, I may baffle the hosts that surround us,
And yet may thy heart leap awake to my voice
There are links which must break in the chain that has bound us,
Then turn thee and call on the Chief of thy choice!

And Did Those Feet in Ancient Time

William Blake

And did those feet in ancient time
Walk upon England's mountains green:
And was the holy Lamb of God
On England's pleasant pastures seen!

And did the Countenance Divine
Shine forth upon our clouded hills?
And was Jerusalem builded here
Among those dark Satanic mills?

Bring me my bow of burning gold:
Bring me my arrows of desire:
Bring me my spear: O clouds, unfold!
Bring me my chariot of fire!

I will not cease from mental fight,
Nor shall my sword sleep in my hand
Till we have built Jerusalem
In England's green and pleasant land.

Song to the Men of England

Percy Bysshe Shelley

Men of England, wherefore plough
For the lords who lay ye low?
Wherefore weave with toil and care
The rich robes your tyrants wear?

Wherefore feed, and clothe, and save,
From the cradle to the grave,
Those ungrateful drones who would
Drain your sweat—nay, drink your blood?

Wherefore, Bees of England, forge
Many a weapon, chain, and scourge,
That these stingless drones may spoil
The forced produce of your toil?

Have ye leisure, comfort, calm,
Shelter, food, love's gentle balm?
Or what is it ye buy so dear
With your pain and with your fear?

The seed ye sow, another reaps;
The wealth ye find, another keeps;
The robes ye weave, another wears;
The arms ye forge, another bears.

Sow seed,—but let no tyrant reap;
Find wealth,—let no imposter heap;
Weave robes,—let not the idle wear;
Forge arms,—in your defence to bear.

Shrink to your cellars, holes, and cells;
In halls ye deck another dwells.
Why shake the chains ye wrought? Ye see
The steel ye tempered glance on ye.

With plough and spade, and hoe and loom,
Trace your grave, and build your tomb,
And weave your winding-sheet, till fair
England be your sepulchre!

The Charge of the Light Brigade

Alfred, Lord Tennyson

Half a league, half a league,
Half a league onward,
All in the valley of Death
Rode the six hundred.
"Forward the Light Brigade!
Charge for the guns!" he said.
Into the valley of Death
Rode the six hundred.

Forward, the Light Brigade!
"Was there a man dismay'd?
Not tho' the soldier knew
Some one had blunder'd.
Theirs not to make reply,
Theirs not to reason why,
Theirs but to do and die.
Into the valley of Death
Rode the six hundred.

Cannon to right of them,
Cannon to left of them,
Cannon in front of them
Volley'd and thunder'd;
Storm'd at with shot and shell,
Boldly they rode and well,
Into the jaws of Death,
Into the mouth of hell
Rode the six hundred.

Flash'd all their sabres bare,
Flash'd as they turn'd in air
Sabring the gunners there,
Charging an army, while
All the world wonder'd.
Plunged in the battery-smoke
Right thro' the line they broke;
Cossack and Russian
Reel'd from the sabre-stroke
Shatter'd and sunder'd.
Then they rode back, but not,
Not the six hundred.

Cannon to right of them,
Cannon to left of them,
Cannon behind them
    Volley'd and thunder'd;
Storm'd at with shot and shell,
While horse and hero fell,
They that had fought so well
Came thro' the jaws of Death,
Back from the mouth of hell,
All that was left of them,
    Left of six hundred.

When can their glory fade?
O the wild charge they made!
    All the world wonder'd.
Honor the charge they made!
Honor the Light Brigade,
    Noble six hundred!

The Charge of the Light Brigade was a charge of British cavalry led by Lord Cardigan against Russian forces during the Battle of Balaclava in the Crimean War on October 25, 1854. A final Allied cavalry charge, stemming from a misinterpreted order from Lord Raglan, led to one of the most famous and ill-fated events in British military history.

The order, scribbled in pencil by General Richard Airey, was misunderstood: "Lord Raglan wishes the Cavalry to advance rapidly to the front, follow the enemy, and try to prevent the enemy carrying away the guns. Troop Horse Artillery may accompany. French Cavalry is on your left. Immediate."

Of the 673 soldiers of the Light Brigade who charged into the North Valley above Balaclava, 118 were killed, 127 were wounded, and 60 taken prisoner.

The futility of the action and its reckless bravery prompted the French Marshal Pierre Bosquet to state "C'est magnifique, mais ce n'est pas la guerre." ("It is magnificent, but it is not war.") He continued, in a rarely quoted phrase: "C'est de la folie." ("It is madness.")

I Hear America Singing

Walt Whitman

I hear America singing, the varied carols I hear;
Those of mechanics—each one singing his,
        as it should be, blithe and strong;
The carpenter singing his, as he measures his plank or beam,
The mason singing his, as he makes ready for work,
        or leaves off work;
The boatman singing what belongs to him in his boat—
        the deckhand singing on the steamboat deck;
The shoemaker singing as he sits on his bench—
        the hatter singing as he stands;
The wood-cutter's song—the ploughboy's,
        on his way in the morning,
            or at the noon intermission,
                or at sundown;
The delicious singing of the mother—
        or of the young wife at work—
            or of the girl sewing or washing—
Each singing what belongs to her, and to none else;
The day what belongs to the day—
At night, the party of young fellows, robust, friendly,
Singing, with open mouths, their strong melodious songs.

Battle Hymn of the Republic

Julia Ward Howe

Mine eyes have seen the glory of the coming of the Lord:
He is trampling out the vintage where the grapes of wrath are stored;
He hath loosed the fatal lightning of his terrible swift sword:
    His truth is marching on.

I have seen Him in the watch-fires of a hundred circling camps;
They have builded Him an altar in the evening dews and damps;
I can read His righteous sentence by the dim and flaring lamps.
    His Day is marching on.

I have read a fiery gospel, writ in burnished rows of steel:
"As ye deal with my contemners, so with you my grace shall deal;
Let the Hero, born of woman, crush the serpent with his heel,
    Since God is marching on."

He has sounded forth the trumpet that shall never call retreat;
He is sifting out the hearts of men before his judgment-seat:
Oh! be swift, my soul, to answer Him! be jubilant, my feet!
    Our God is marching on.

In the beauty of the lilies Christ was born across the sea,
With a glory in his bosom that transfigures you and me:
As he died to make men holy, let us die to make men free,
    While God is marching on.

The Gettysburg Address

Abraham Lincoln, at the Dedication of the National Cemetery in Gettysburg

Four score and seven years ago
our fathers brought forth on this continent
a new nation,
conceived in liberty,
and dedicated to the proposition
that all men are created equal.

Now we are engaged in a great civil war,
testing whether that nation,
or any nation, so conceived and so dedicated,
can long endure.

We are met on a great battle-field of that war.

We have come to dedicate
a portion of that field,
as a final resting place
for those who here gave their lives
that that nation might live.

It is altogether fitting and proper
that we should do this.
But, in a larger sense,
we can not dedicate,
we can not consecrate,
we can not hallow this ground.

The brave men, living and dead,
who struggled here,
have consecrated it,
far above our poor power to add or detract.

The world will little note,
nor long remember
what we say here,
but it can never forget
what they did here.

It is for us the living,
rather, to be dedicated here
to the unfinished work
which they who fought here
have thus far so nobly advanced.

It is rather for us to be here dedicated
to the great task remaining before us—
that from these honored dead
we take increased devotion
to that cause for which they gave
the last full measure of devotion—
that we here highly resolve
that these dead shall not have died in vain—
that this nation, under God,
shall have a new birth of freedom—
and that government
of the people, by the people, for the people,
shall not perish from the earth.

The Second Inaugural Address

Abraham Lincoln, 1865

...With malice toward none,
with charity for all,
with firmness in the right,
as God gives us to see the right,
let us strive on to finish the work we are in,
to bind up the nation's wounds,
to care for him who shall have borne the battle,
and for his widow,
and his orphan—
to do all which may achieve and cherish
a just and lasting peace
among ourselves
and with all nations.

O Captain! My Captain!

Walt Whitman

O Captain! my Captain! our fearful trip is done,
The ship has weathered every rack, the prize we sought is won,
The port is near, the bells I hear, the people all exulting,
While follow eyes the steady keel, the vessel grim and daring;
But O heart! heart! heart!
O the bleeding drops of red,
Where on the deck my Captain lies,
Fallen cold and dead.

O Captain! my Captain! rise up and hear the bells;
Rise up—for you the flag is flung—for you the bugle trills,
For you bouquets and ribboned wreaths—for you the shores a-crowding,
For you they call, the swaying mass, their eager faces turning;
Here Captain! dear father!
This arm beneath your head!
It is some dream that on the deck
You've fallen cold and dead.

My Captain does not answer, his lips are pale and still,
My father does not feel my arm, he has no pulse nor will.
The ship is anchored safe and sound, its voyage closed and done,
From fearful trip the victor ship comes in with object won;
Exult O shores, and ring O bells!
But I, with mournful tread,
Walk the deck my Captain lies,
Fallen cold and dead.

Alabama

Khé-tha-á-hi (Eagle Wing)

My brethren,
among the legends of my people
it is told how a chief,
leading the remnant of his people,
crossed a great river,
and striking his tipi-stake upon the ground,
exclaimed, "A-la-bá-ma!"
This in our language means
"Here we may rest!"

But he saw not the future.
The white man came:
he and his people could not rest there;
they were driven out,
and in a dark swamp
they were thrust down into the slime and killed.
The word he so sadly spoke
has given a name to one of the white man's states.
There is no spot under those stars
that now begin to smile upon us,
where the Indian can plant his foot
and sigh "A-la-bá-ma."

FROM INDIAN NAMES

LYDIA HUNTLEY SIGOURNEY

Ye say they all have passed away,
That noble race and brave,
That their light canoes have vanished
From off the crested wave;
That 'mid the forests where they roamed,
There rings no hunter shout;
But their name is on your waters,
Ye may not wash it out.

'Tis where Ontario's billow
Like ocean's surge is curled,
Where strong Niagara's thunders wake
The echo of the world,
Where red Missouri bringeth
Rich tribute from the West,
And Rappahannock sweetly sleeps
On green Virginia's breast.

Ye say their conelike cabins,
That clustered o'er the vale,
Have fled away like withered leaves
Before the autumn gale,
But their memory liveth on your hills,
Their baptism on your shore,
Your everlasting rivers speak
Their dialect of yore.

Old Massachusetts wears it,
Within her lordly crown,
And broad Ohio bears it
Amid his young renown;
Connecticut hath wreathed it
Where her quiet foliage waves;
And bold Kentucky breathed it hoarse
Through all her ancient caves.

Wachuset hides its lingering voice
Within his rocky heart,
And Allegheny graves its tone
Throughout his lofty chart;
Monadnock, on his forehead hoar,
Doth seal the sacred trust;
Your mountains build their monument,
Though ye destroy their dust.

The New Colossus

Emma Lazarus

Not like the brazen giant of Greek fame,
With conquering limbs astride from land to land;
Here at our sea-washed, sunset gates shall stand
A mighty woman with a torch, whose flame
Is the imprisoned lightning, and her name
Mother of Exiles. From her beacon-hand
Glows world-wide welcome; her mild eyes command
The air-bridged harbor that twin cities frame.

"Keep, ancient lands, your storied pomp!" cries she
With silent lips. "Give me your tired, your poor,
Your huddled masses yearning to breathe free,
The wretched refuse of your teeming shore.
Send these, the homeless, tempest-tost to me,
I lift my lamp beside the golden door!"

In 1882 Emma Lazarus was asked to donate an original poem to the fundraising effort to build a pedestal for the Statue of Liberty. She initially declined, stating she could not write a poem about a statue. At the time, she was involved in aiding refugees to New York. These refugees lived in conditions that the wealthy Lazarus had never experienced. She saw a way to express her empathy for these refugees in terms of the statue. "The New Colossus", was written in 1883. A bronze tablet that bears the text of her most famous poem is in the Statue of Liberty Museum in the base below the pedestal.

Casey at the Bat

A Ballad of the Republic, Sung in the Year 1888

Ernest Lawrence Thayer

The outlook wasn't brilliant for the Mudville nine that day;
The score stood four to two, with but one inning more to play,
And then when Cooney died at first, and Barrows did the same,
A pall-like silence fell upon the patrons of the game.

A straggling few got up to go in deep despair. The rest
Clung to that hope which springs eternal in the human breast;
They thought, "If only Casey could but get a whack at that—
We'd put up even money now, with Casey at the bat."

But Flynn preceded Casey, as did also Jimmy Blake,
And the former was a hoodoo, while the latter was a cake;
So upon that stricken multitude grim melancholy sat;
For there seemed but little chance of Casey getting to the bat.

But Flynn let drive a single, to the wonderment of all,
And Blake, the much despised, tore the cover off the ball;
And when the dust had lifted, and men saw what had occurred,
There was Jimmy safe at second and Flynn a-hugging third.

Then from five thousand throats and more there rose a lusty yell;
It rumbled through the valley, it rattled in the dell;
It pounded on the mountain and recoiled upon the flat,
For Casey, mighty Casey, was advancing to the bat.

There was ease in Casey's manner as he stepped into his place;
There was pride in Casey's bearing and a smile lit Casey's face.
And when, responding to the cheers, he lightly doffed his hat,
No stranger in the crowd could doubt 'twas Casey at the bat.

Ten thousand eyes were on him as he rubbed his hands with dirt.
Five thousand tongues applauded when he wiped them on his shirt.
Then while the writhing pitcher ground the ball into his hip,
Defiance flashed in Casey's eye, a sneer curled Casey's lip.

And now the leather-covered sphere came hurtling through the air,
And Casey stood a-watching it in haughty grandeur there.
Close by the sturdy batsman the ball unheeded sped—
"That ain't my style," said Casey. "Strike one!" the umpire said.

From the benches, black with people, there went up a muffled roar,
Like the beating of the storm-waves on a stern and distant shore;
"Kill him! Kill the umpire!" shouted some one on the stand;
And it's likely they'd have killed him had not Casey raised his hand.

With a smile of Christian charity great Casey's visage shone;
He stilled the rising tumult; he bade the game go on;
He signaled to the pitcher, and once more the dun sphere flew;
But Casey still ignored it, and the umpire said "Strike two!"

"Fraud!" cried the maddened thousands, and echo answered "Fraud!"
But one scornful look from Casey and the audience was awed.
They saw his face grow stern and cold, they saw his muscles strain,
And they knew that Casey wouldn't let that ball go by again.

The sneer has fled from Casey's lip, the teeth are clenched in hate;
He pounds with cruel violence his bat upon the plate.
And now the pitcher holds the ball, and now he lets it go,
And now the air is shattered by the force of Casey's blow.

Oh, somewhere in this favored land the sun is shining bright,
The band is playing somewhere, and somewhere hearts are light,
And somewhere men are laughing, and little children shout;
But there is no joy in Mudville—mighty Casey has struck out.

In the Bazaars of Hyderabad

Sarojini Naidu

What do you sell, O ye merchants?
Richly your wares are displayed.
Turbans of crimson and silver,
Tunics of purple brocade,
Mirror with panels of amber,
Daggers with handles of jade.

What do you weigh, O ye vendors?
Saffron and lentil and rice.
What do you grind, O ye maidens?
Sandalwood, henna, and spice.
What do you call , O ye pedlars?
Chessman and ivory dice.

What do you make, O ye goldsmiths?
Wristlet and anklet and ring,
Bells for the feet of blue pigeons
Frail as a dragonfly's wing,
Girdles of gold for dancers,
Scabbards of gold for the king.

What do you cry, O ye fruitmen?
Citron, pomegranate, and plum.
What do you play, O musicians?
Cither, sarangi, and drum.
What do you chant, O magicians?
Spells for aeons to come.

What do you weave, O ye flowergirls
With tassels of azure and red?
Crowns for the brow of a bridegroom,
Chaplets to garland his bed,
Sheets of white blossoms new-garnered
To perfume the sleep of the dead.

Sarojini Naidu, also known as The Nightingale of India, was a child prodigy, freedom fighter, and poet. She graduated top of her class from Madras University at the age of twelve and went on to study at King's College in Cambridge. Naidu was the first woman to become the President of the Indian National Congress. She was active in the Indian Independence Movement, joining Mahatma Gandhi in the Salt March to Dandi.

Buffalo Dusk

Carl Sandburg

The buffaloes are gone.

And those who saw the buffaloes are gone.

Those who saw the buffaloes by thousands and how they pawed the prairie sod into dust with their hoofs, their great heads down pawing on in a great pageant of dusk,

Those who saw the buffaloes are gone.

And the buffaloes are gone.

The American bison once roamed the grasslands of North America in massive herds and were the most numerous single species of large wild mammal on Earth. Bison were hunted almost to extinction in the late 19th century, primarily by market hunters. The U.S. government promoted bison hunting to weaken the North American Indian population by removing their main food source.

"Buffalo Bill" Cody, himself a former hunter, spoke in favor of protecting the bison. Such proposals were discouraged since the Plains Indians, often at war with the U.S., depended on bison for their life.

In 1874, President Grant vetoed a bill to protect the dwindling bison herds, and General Sheridan pleaded to Congress to slaughter the herds, to deprive the Indians of their food.

Sympathy

Paul Laurence Dunbar

I know what the caged bird feels, alas!
    When the sun is bright on the upland slopes;
When the wind stirs soft through the springing grass,
And the river flows like a stream of glass;
    When the first bird sings and the first bud opes,
And the faint perfume from its chalice steals—
I know what the caged bird feels!

I know why the caged bird beats his wing
    Till its blood is red on the cruel bars;
For he must fly back to his perch and cling
When he fain would be on the bough a-swing;
    And a pain still throbs in the old, old scars
And they pulse again with a keener sting—
I know why he beats his wing!

I know why the caged bird sings, ah me,
    When his wing is bruised and his bosom sore,—
When he beats his bars and he would be free;
It is not a carol of joy or glee,
    But a prayer that he sends from his heart's deep core,
But a plea, that upward to Heaven he flings—
I know why the caged bird sings!

Paul Laurence Dunbar, the son of former slaves from Ohio, wrote his first poem at age six and gave his first public recital at nine. Dunbar's first published work came in a newspaper put out by his high school acquaintances Wilbur and Orville Wright, who owned a printing press. The Wright brothers later invested in the Dayton Tattler, a newspaper aimed at the black community, edited and published by Dunbar.

Oak and Ivy, his first collection, was published in 1892. Though his book was received well locally, Dunbar still had to work as an elevator operator to help pay off his debt to his publisher. He sold his book for a dollar to people who rode the elevator.

As more people came in contact with his work, however, his reputation spread. In 1893, he was invited to recite at the World's Fair, where he met Frederick Douglass, the renowned abolitionist who rose from slavery to political and literary prominence in America. Douglass praised Dunbar as one of the most promising young men in America.

Chicago

Carl Sandburg

Hog Butcher for the World,
Tool Maker, Stacker of Wheat,
Player with Railroads and the Nation's Freight Handler;
Stormy, husky, brawling,
City of the Big Shoulders:

They tell me you are wicked and I believe them, for I have seen your painted women under the gas lamps luring the farm boys.
And they tell me you are crooked and I answer: Yes, it is true I have seen the gunman kill and go free to kill again.
And they tell me you are brutal and my reply is: On the faces of women and children I have seen the marks of wanton hunger.
And having answered so I turn once more to those who sneer at this my city, and I give them back the sneer and say to them:
Come and show me another city with lifted head singing so proud to be alive and coarse and strong and cunning.
Flinging magnetic curses amid the toil of piling job on job, here is a tall bold slugger set vivid against the little soft cities;
Fierce as a dog with tongue lapping for action, cunning as a savage pitted against the wilderness,
Bareheaded,
Shoveling,
Wrecking,
Planning,
Building, breaking, rebuilding,
Under the smoke, dust all over his mouth, laughing with white teeth,
Under the terrible burden of destiny laughing as a young man laughs,
Laughing even as an ignorant fighter laughs who has never lost a battle,
Bragging and laughing that under his wrist is the pulse. and under his ribs the heart of the people,
Laughing!
Laughing the stormy, husky, brawling laughter of
Youth, half-naked, sweating, proud to be Hog
Butcher, Tool Maker, Stacker of Wheat, Player with
Railroads and Freight Handler to the Nation.

The Soldier

Rupert Chawner Brooke

If I should die, think only this of me:
  That there's some corner of a foreign field
That is forever England. There shall be
  In that rich earth a richer dust concealed;
A dust whom England bore, shaped, made aware,
  Gave, once, her flowers to love, her ways to roam,
A body of England's, breathing English air,
  Washed by the rivers, blest by the suns of home.
And think, this heart, all evil shed away,
  A pulse in the eternal mind, no less
    Gives somewhere back the thoughts by England given;
Her sights and sounds; dreams happy as her day;
  And laughter, learnt of friends; and gentleness,
    In hearts at peace, under an English heaven.

Cargoes

John Masefield

Quinquireme of Nineveh from distant Ophir,
Rowing home to haven in sunny Palestine,
With a cargo of ivory,
And apes and peacocks,
Sandalwood, cedarwood, and sweet white wine.

Stately Spanish galleon coming from the Isthmus,
Dipping through the Tropics by the palm-green shores,
With a cargo of diamonds,
Emeralds, amythysts,
Topazes, and cinnamon, and gold moidores.

Dirty British coaster with a salt-caked smoke stack,
Butting through the Channel in the mad March days,
With a cargo of Tyne coal,
Road-rails, pig-lead,
Firewood, iron-ware, and cheap tin trays.

The Destroyer of Worlds

J. Robert Oppenheimer

We waited until the blast had passed,
  walked out of the shelter and then it was extremely solemn.
We knew the world would not be the same.
A few people laughed, a few people cried.
Most people were silent.
I remembered the line from the Hindu scripture, the Bhagavad-Gita:
Vishnu is trying to persuade the prince that he should do his duty,
  and to impress him he takes on his multi-armed form and says,

  "Now I am become Death, the destroyer of worlds."

I suppose we all thought that, one way or another.

In 1942, Oppenheimer became director of the Manhattan Project, the top-secret effort to develop an atomic bomb, located at Los Alamos, New Mexico. His words were spoken moments after the test detonation at Alamogordo on July 16, 1945.

Oppenheimer later grew concerned about the atomic bomb's destructive potential, and strongly advocated civilian control of atomic energy and opposed development of the hydrogen bomb. In 1954, he was suspended as a chief advisor from the U.S. Atomic Energy Commission during the Red Scare.

A decade later, President John F. Kennedy awarded (and Lyndon B. Johnson presented) Oppenheimer the Enrico Fermi Award as a gesture of political rehabilitation.

from The Inaugural Address

John F. Kennedy, 1961

The world is very different now. For man holds in his mortal hands the power to abolish all forms of human poverty and all forms of human life. And yet the same revolutionary beliefs for which our forebears fought are still at issue around the globe—the belief that the rights of man come not from the generosity of the state but from the hand of God.

We dare not forget today that we are the heirs of that first revolution. Let the word go forth from this time and place, to friend and foe alike, that the torch has been passed to a new generation of Americans—born in this century, tempered by war, disciplined by a hard and bitter peace, proud of our ancient heritage—and unwilling to witness or permit the slow undoing of those human rights to which this nation has always been committed, and to which we are committed today at home and around the world.

Let every nation know, whether it wishes us well or ill, that we shall pay any price, bear any burden, meet any hardship, support any friend, oppose any foe to assure the survival and the success of liberty.

This much we pledge—and more.

Now the trumpet summons us again—not as a call to bear arms, though arms we need—not as a call to battle, though embattled we are—but a call to bear the burden of a long twilight struggle, year in and year out, "rejoicing in hope, patient in tribulation"—a struggle against the common enemies of man: tyranny, poverty, disease and war itself.

Can we forge against these enemies a grand and global alliance, North and South, East and West, that can assure a more fruitful life for all mankind? Will you join in that historic effort?

In the long history of the world, only a few generations have been granted the role of defending freedom in its hour of maximum danger. I do not shrink from this responsibility—I welcome it. I do not believe that any of us would exchange places with any other people or any other generation. The energy, the faith, the devotion which we bring to this endeavor will light our country and all who serve it—and the glow from that fire can truly light the world.

And so, my fellow Americans: ask not what your country can do for you—ask what you can do for your country.

My fellow citizens of the world: ask not what America will do for you, but what together we can do for the freedom of man.

Inspiration

Salutation to the Dawn

Look to this day:
For it is life, the very life of life.
In its brief course
Lie all the verities and realities of your existence.
The bliss of growth,
The glory of action,
The splendor of achievement
Are but experiences of time.

For yesterday is but a dream
And tomorrow is only a vision;
And today well-lived, makes
Yesterday a dream of happiness
And every tomorrow a vision of hope.
Look well therefore to this day;
Such is the salutation to the ever-new dawn!

Hymn to Osiris

I have come home.

I have entered humanhood, bound to rocks and plants, men and women, rivers and sky.

I shall be with you in this and other worlds.

When the cat arches in the doorway, think of me.
I have sometimes been like that.

When two men meet each other in the street, I am there speaking to you.

When you look up, know I am there—sun and moon—pouring my love around you.

All these things I am; portents, images, signs.

Though apart, I am part of you.

One of the million things in the universe, I am the universe, too.

You think I disguise myself as rivers and trees simply to confuse you?

Whatever I am, woman, cat or lotus, the same god breathes in every body.

You and I together are a single creation.

Neither death nor spite nor fear nor ignorance stops my love for you...

from The Holy Longing

Johann Wolfgang von Goethe

Distance does not make you falter now,
arriving in magic,
flying,
and finally,
insane for the light,
you are the butterfly and you are gone.

And so long as you haven't experienced this:
to die and so to grow,
you are only a troubled guest on the dark earth.

Our Birth Is But a Sleep and a Forgetting

from Ode: Intimations of Immortality

William Wordsworth

Our birth is but a sleep and a forgetting:
The Soul that rises with us, our life's Star,
 Hath had elsewhere its setting,
  And cometh from afar:
 Not in entire forgetfulness,
 And not in utter nakedness,
But trailing clouds of glory do we come
 From God, who is our home:
Heaven lies about us in our infancy!
Shades of the prison-house begin to close
 Upon the growing Boy,
But He beholds the light, and whence it flows,
 He sees it in his joy;
The Youth, who daily farther from the east
 Must travel, still is Nature's Priest,
 And by the vision splendid
 Is on his way attended;
At length the Man perceives it die away,
And fade into the light of common day.

No Man Is an Island

John Donne

No man is an island entire of itself;
every man is a piece of the continent,
a part of the main;
if a clod be washed away by the sea,
Europe is the less,
as well as if a promontory were,
as well as any manner of thy friends or of thine own were;
any man's death diminishes me,
because I am involved in mankind.
And therefore never send to know for whom the bell tolls;
it tolls for thee.

The Conclusion

Johann Wolfgang von Goethe

I have come to the frightening conclusion that I am the decisive element.

It is my personal approach that creates the climate.

It is my daily mood that makes the weather.

I possess tremendous power to make a life miserable or joyous.

I can be a tool of torture, or an instrument of inspiration.

I can humiliate or humor, hurt or heal.

In all situations, it is my response that decides whether a crisis will be escalated or de-escalated, and a person humanized or dehumanized.

If we treat people as they are, we make them worse.

If we treat people as they ought to be, we help them become what they are capable of becoming.

from Wilhelm Meister's Apprenticeship

Johann Wolfgang von Goethe

The world is so empty if one thinks only of mountains, rivers and cities; but to know someone here and there who thinks and feels with us, and though distant, is close to us in spirit—this makes the earth for us an inhabited garden.

from Life

Emily Dickinson

If I can stop one heart from breaking,
I shall not live in vain;
If I can ease one life the aching,
Or cool one pain,
Or help one fainting robin
Unto his nest again,
I shall not live in vain.

I Never Saw a Moor

Emily Dickinson

I never saw a moor,
I never saw the sea;
Yet know I how the heather looks,
And what a wave must be.

I never spoke with God,
Nor visited in heaven;
Yet certain am I of the spot
As if the chart were given.

Be Strong

Maltbie Davenport Babcock

Be strong!
We are not here to play, to dream, to drift.
We have hard work to do, and loads to lift.
Shun not the struggle; face it. 'Tis God's gift.

Be strong!
Say not the days are evil,— Who's to blame?
And fold the hands and acquiesce,—O shame!
Stand up, speak out, and bravely, in God's name.

Be strong!
It matters not how deep entrenched the wrong,
How hard the battle goes, the day, how long.
Faint not, fight on! To-morrow comes the song.

The Snowdrops

Annie Matheson

"Where are all the snowdrops?" asked the sun
"Dead" said the frost "and buried every one."
"A foolish answer," said the sun,
"They did not die, asleep they lie
And I will wake them, I, the sun
Into the night, all clad in white
They shall grow every one."

Determination

Ella Wheeler Wilcox

There is no chance, no destiny, no fate,
Can circumvent or hinder or control
The firm resolve of a determined soul.
Gifts count for nothing; will alone is great;
All things give way before it, soon or late.
What obstacle can stay the mighty force
Of the sea-seeking river in its course,
Or cause the ascending orb of day to wait?
Each well-born soul must win what it deserves.
Let the fool prate of luck.
The fortunate is he whose earnest purpose never swerves,
Whose slightest action or inaction serves
The one great aim. Why, even Death stands still,
And waits an hour sometimes for such a will.

Up-Hill

Christina Rossetti

Does the road wind up-hill all the way?
  Yes, to the very end.
Will the day's journey take the whole long day?
  From morn to night, my friend.

But is there for the night a resting-place?
  A roof for when the slow dark hours begin.
May not the darkness hide it from my face?
  You cannot miss that inn.

Shall I meet other wayfarers at night?
  Those who have gone before.
Then must I knock, or call when just in sight?
  They will not keep you standing at that door.

Shall I find comfort, travel-sore and weak?
  Of labour you shall find the sum.
Will there be beds for me and all who seek?
  Yea, beds for all who come.

If

Rudyard Kipling

If you can keep your head when all about you
Are losing theirs and blaming it on you;
If you can trust yourself when all men doubt you,
But make allowance for their doubting too;

If you can wait and not be tired by waiting,
Or, being lied about, don't deal in lies,
Or, being hated, don't give way to hating,
And yet don't look too good, nor talk too wise;

If you can dream—and not make dreams your master;
If you can think—and not make thoughts your aim;
If you can meet with triumph and disaster
And treat those two imposters just the same;

If you can bear to hear the truth you've spoken
Twisted by knaves to make a trap for fools,
Or watch the things you gave your life to broken,
And stoop and build 'em up with wornout tools;

If you can make one heap of all your winnings
And risk it on one turn of pitch-and-toss,
And lose, and start again at your beginnings
And never breath a word about your loss;

If you can force your heart and nerve and sinew
To serve your turn long after they are gone,
And so hold on when there is nothing in you
Except the Will which says to them: "Hold on";

If you can talk with crowds and keep your virtue,
Or walk with kings—nor lose the common touch;
If neither foes nor loving friends can hurt you;
If all men count with you, but none too much;

If you can fill the unforgiving minute
With sixty seconds' worth of distance run -
Yours is the Earth and everything that's in it,
And—which is more—you'll be a Man, my son!

from Song of the Open Road

Walt Whitman

Afoot and light-hearted, I take to the open road,
Healthy, free, the world before me,
The long brown path before me, leading wherever I choose.

Henceforth I ask not good-fortune—I myself am good fortune;
Henceforth I whimper no more, postpone no more, need nothing,
Strong and content, I travel the open road.

The earth—that is sufficient;
I do not want the constellations any nearer;
I know they are very well where they are;
I know they suffice for those who belong to them.

Invictus

William Ernest Henley

Out of the night that covers me,
Black as the pit from pole to pole,
I thank whatever gods may be
For my unconquerable soul.

In the fell clutch of circumstance
I have not winced nor cried aloud.
Under the bludgeonings of chance
My head is bloody, but unbowed.

Beyond this place of wrath and tears
Looms but the Horror of the shade,
And yet the menace of the years
Finds, and shall find, me unafraid.

It matters not how strait the gate,
How charged with punishments the scroll.
I am the master of my fate:
I am the captain of my soul.

Invictus is Latin for "undefeated." Henley fell victim to tuberculosis of the bone at the age of twelve and his left leg was amputated below the knee. A few years later, the disease progressed to his right foot, threatening his other leg. The pioneering surgeon Joseph Lister saved his foot and Henley wrote "Invictus" from a hospital bed while recovering.

While incarcerated on Robben Island prison, Nelson Mandela recited the poem to other prisoners and was empowered by its message of self mastery.

FROM ODE

A. W.E. O'SHAUGHNESSY

We are the music makers,
And we are the dreamers of dreams,
Wandering by lone sea-breakers,
And sitting by desolate streams;
World-losers and world-forsakers,
On whom the pale moon gleams:
Yet we are the movers and shakers
Of the world for ever, it seems.

With wonderful deathless ditties,
We build up the world's great cities,
And out of a fabulous story
We fashion an empire's glory:
One man with a dream, at pleasure,
Shall go forth and conquer a crown;
And three with a new song's measure
Can trample an empire down.

We, in the ages lying
In the buried past of earth,
Built Nineveh with our sighing,
And Babel itself with our mirth;
And o'erthrew them with prophesying
To the old of the new world's worth;
For each age is a dream that is dying,
Or one that is coming to birth.

HE WISHES FOR THE CLOTHS OF HEAVEN

WILLIAM BUTLER YEATS

Had I the heavens' embroidered cloths,
Enwrought with golden and silver light,
The blue and the dim and the dark cloths
Of night and light and the half light,
I would spread the cloths under your feet:
But I, being poor, have only my dreams;
I have spread my dreams under your feet;
Tread softly because you tread on my dreams.

The Bridge Builder

Will Allen Dromgoole

An old man, going a lone highway,
Came, at the evening, cold and gray,
To a chasm, vast, and deep, and wide,
Through which was flowing a sullen tide.

The old man crossed in the twilight dim;
The sullen stream had no fear for him;
But he turned, when safe on the other side,
And built a bridge to span the tide.

"Old man," said a fellow pilgrim, near,
"You are wasting strength with building here;
Your journey will end with the ending day;
You never again will pass this way;
You've crossed the chasm, deep and wide-
Why build you this bridge at the evening tide?"

The builder lifted his old gray head:
"Good friend, in the path I have come," he said,
"There followeth after me today,
A youth, whose feet must pass this way.

This chasm, that has been naught to me,
To that fair-haired youth may a pitfall be.
He, too, must cross in the twilight dim;
Good friend, I am building this bridge for him."

A Creed

John Masefield

I hold that when a person dies
    His soul returns again to earth;
Arrayed in some new flesh-disguise
    Another mother gives him birth.
With sturdier limbs and brighter brain
The old soul takes the road again.

Such is my own belief and trust;
    This hand, this hand that holds the pen,
Has many a hundred times been dust
    And turned, as dust, to dust again;
These eyes of mine have blinked and shown
In Thebes, in Troy, in Babylon.

All that I rightly think or do,
Or make, or spoil, or bless, or blast,
Is curse or blessing justly due
For sloth or effort in the past.
My life's a statement of the sum
Of vice indulged, or overcome.

I know that in my lives to be
My sorry heart will ache and burn,
And worship, unavailingly,
The woman whom I used to spurn,
And shake to see another have
The love I spurned, the love she gave.

And I shall know, in angry words,
In gibes, and mocks, and many a tear,
A carrion flock of homing-birds,
The gibes and scorns I uttered here.
The brave word that I failed to speak
Will brand me dastard on the cheek.

And as I wander on the roads
I shall be helped and healed and blessed;
Dear words shall cheer and be as goads
To urge to heights before unguessed.
My road shall be the road I made;
All that I gave shall be repaid.

So shall I fight, so shall I tread,
In this long war beneath the stars;
So shall a glory wreathe my head,
So shall I faint and show the scars,
Until this case, this clogging mould,
Be smithied all to kingly gold.

A Helper of Mankind

Adolph Arenson

May wisdom shine through me,
May love glow within me,
May strength penetrate me,
That in me may arise
A helper of mankind,
A servant of holy things,
Selfless, and true.

At the Ringing of the Bells

Rudolf Steiner

To wonder at beauty,
Stand guard over truth,
Look up to the noble,
Resolve on the good:
This leadeth man truly
To purpose in living,
To right in his doing,
To peace in his feeling,
To light in his thinking,
And teaches him trust
In the working of God,
In all that there is,
In the width of the world,
In the depth of the soul.

Desiderata

Max Ehrmann

Go placidly amid the noise and the haste,
  and remember what peace there may be in silence.

As far as possible, without surrender,
  be on good terms with all persons.
Speak your truth quietly and clearly;
  and listen to others,
  even to the dull and the ignorant;
  they too have their story.
Avoid loud and aggressive persons;
  they are vexatious to the spirit.

If you compare yourself with others,
  you may become vain or bitter,
  for always there will be greater and lesser persons than yourself.
Enjoy your achievements as well as your plans.
Keep interested in your own career, however humble;
  it is a real possession in the changing fortunes of time.

Exercise caution in your business affairs,
 for the world is full of trickery.
But let this not blind you to what virtue there is;
 many persons strive for high ideals,
 and everywhere life is full of heroism.
Be yourself. Especially do not feign affection.
Neither be cynical about love,
 for in the face of all aridity and disenchantment,
 it is as perennial as the grass.

Take kindly the counsel of the years,
 gracefully surrendering the things of youth.
Nurture strength of spirit to shield you in sudden misfortune.
But do not distress yourself with dark imaginings.
Many fears are born of fatigue and loneliness.

Beyond a wholesome discipline,
 be gentle with yourself.
You are a child of the universe
 no less than the trees and the stars;
 you have a right to be here.
And whether or not it is clear to you,
 no doubt the universe is unfolding as it should.

Therefore be at peace with God,
 whatever you conceive Him to be.
And whatever your labors and aspirations,
 in the noisy confusion of life,
 keep peace in your soul.

With all its sham, drudgery, and broken dreams,
 it is still a beautiful world.
Be cheerful.
Strive to be happy.

The Road Not Taken

Robert Frost

Two roads diverged in a yellow wood,
And sorry I could not travel both
And be one traveler, long I stood
And looked down one as far as I could
To where it bent in the undergrowth;

Then took the other, as just as fair
And having perhaps the better claim,
Because it was grassy and wanted wear;
Though as for that, the passing there
Had worn them really about the same,

And both that morning equally lay
In leaves no step had trodden black.
Oh, I kept the first for another day!
Yet knowing how way leads on to way,
I doubted if I should ever come back.

I shall be telling this with a sigh
Somewhere ages and ages hence:
Two roads diverged in a wood, and I—
I took the one less traveled by,
And that has made all the difference.

Where the Rainbow Ends

Richard Rive

Where the rainbow ends
There's going to be a place, brother,
Where the world can sing all sorts of songs,
And we're going to sing together, brother,
You and I, though you're white, and I'm not.
It's going to be a sad song, brother,
Because we don't know the tune,
And it's a difficult tune to learn.
But we can learn, brother, you and I.
There's no such tune as a black tune.
There's no such tune as a white tune.
There's only music, brother,
And it's music we're going to sing
Where the rainbow ends.

The Knighthood of the Present Age

Karl Koenig

There is a knighthood of the present age whose members do not ride through the darkness of physical forests as of old, but through the forests of darkened minds.

They are armed with spiritual armor and an inner sun makes them radiant.

Out of them shines healing, healing that flows from a knowing of the Image of Man as a spiritual being.

They must create an inner order, inner justice, peace and conviction in the darkness of our time.

A Ripple of Hope

Robert Francis Kennedy

It is from numberless diverse acts
of courage and belief
that human history is shaped.

Each time a person stands up for an ideal
or strikes out against injustice,
he or she sends forth a tiny ripple of hope,
and crossing each other
from a million different centers
of energy and daring
those ripples build a current
which can sweep down the mightiest walls
of oppression and resistance.

Our Deepest Fear

Marianne Williamson

Our deepest fear is not that we are inadequate. Our deepest fear is that we are powerful beyond measure.

It is our light, not our darkness that most frightens us. We ask ourselves, Who am I to be brilliant, gorgeous, talented, fabulous?

Actually, who are you not to be? You are a child of God.

Your playing small does not serve the world. There is nothing enlightened about shrinking so that other people won't feel insecure around you. We are all meant to shine, as children do.

We were born to make manifest the glory of God that is within us. It's not just in some of us; it's in everyone.

And as we let our own light shine, we unconsciously give other people permission to do the same. As we are liberated from our own fear, our presence automatically liberates others.

The famous passage from Marianne Williamson's book 'A Return to Love: Reflections on the Principles of A Course in Miracles' is often erroneously attributed to the inaugural address of Nelson Mandela.

About the misattribution Williamson said, "Several years ago, this paragraph from A Return to Love began popping up everywhere, attributed to Nelson Mandela's 1994 inaugural address. As honored as I would be had President Mandela quoted my words, indeed he did not. I have no idea where that story came from, but I am gratified that the paragraph has come to mean so much to so many people."

Gifts

William Ward

On the day of your birth
You were given gifts,
The seeds of your own will,
To sow upon the earth,
That through your work
The seeds might grow
Into a fruitful garden
Protected by the Tree of Life
Whose branches hold up heaven.

Now your roots grip solid ground,
Glad to be alive.
Your head bears a golden crown
Like the sun that lights the sky.
Your breath weaves in and out
Like the ocean tides,
As the fountain of your heart
Sings the song of life.

You crossed the rainbow bridge,
You left your heavenly home
To walk the green, fruitful earth
Beneath the starry dome.
You know this is the place
To give all your gifts away,
Scattering them like golden seeds
Unfolding every day.
Seed-deeds ripen beneath the sun
Rooted in fertile will
To become the Bread of Life
When the seeds are milled.

Soul Cricket

Dennis Klocek

My soul, a cricket in a jar,
Too small to jump up to the rim,
Trapped by walls that look so clear,
But steadfast hold me stuck within.

The sight of freedom all around
Proves futile when I try to pass;
The walls give off a ringing sound
When I knock my head against the glass.

Striving, patient, I must grow,
Dependent on my keeper's grace,
Until the day that I leap free
And meet my keeper face to face.

In truth the cricket is the cage;
Each soul it's prison soon defines.
We labor on until old age,
But the jar lies open all the time.

To My Fellow Swimmers

Message from the Hopi Elders, September 2001

We have been telling the people that this is the Eleventh Hour. Now you must go back and tell the people that this is the Hour and there are things to be considered.

Where are you living? What are you doing? What are your relationships? Are you in the right relation? Where is your water? Know your garden.

It is time to speak your truth. Create your community. Be good to each other. And do not look outside yourself for the leader.

There is a river flowing now very fast. It is so great and swift that there are those who will be afraid. They will try to hold onto the shore. They will feel they are being torn apart and they will suffer greatly. Know the river has its destination.

The elders say we must let go of the shore, and push off and into the river, keep our eyes open, and our head above the water.

See who is in there with you and celebrate.

At this time in history, we are to take nothing personally, least of all ourselves, for the moment that we do, our spiritual growth and journey comes to a halt.

The time of the lone wolf is over.

Gather yourselves!

Banish the word struggle from your attitude and your vocabulary. All that you do now must be done in a sacred manner and in celebration.

We are the ones we have been waiting for.

Narrative Poems

This Is the Key of the Kingdom

This is the Key of the Kingdom;
In that Kingdom is a city;
In that city is a town;
In that town there is a street;
In that street there winds a lane;
In that lane there is a yard;
In that yard there is a house;
In that house there waits a room;
In that room an empty bed;
And on that bed a basket—
A Basket of Sweet Flowers,
    Of Flowers, of Flowers,
    A Basket of Sweet Flowers.

Flowers in a Basket,
Basket on the bed,
Bed in the chamber,
Chamber in the house,
House in the weedy yard,
Yard in the winding lane,
Lane in the broad street,
Street in the high town,
Town in the city,
City in the Kingdom—
This is the Key of the Kingdom,
    Of the Kingdom this is the Key.

This Is the House That Jack Built

Mother Goose

This is the house that Jack built.

This is the malt
That lay in the house that Jack built.

This is the rat,
That ate the malt
That lay in the house that Jack built.

This is the cat,
That killed the rat,
That ate the malt
That lay in the house that Jack built.

This is the dog,
That worried the cat,
That killed the rat,
That ate the malt
That lay in the house that Jack built.

This is the cow with the crumpled horn,
That tossed the dog,
That worried the cat,
That killed the rat,
That ate the malt
That lay in the house that Jack built.

This is the maiden all forlorn,
That milked the cow with the crumpled horn,
That tossed the dog,
That worried the cat,
That killed the rat,
That ate the malt
That lay in the house that Jack built.

This is the man all tattered and torn,
That kissed the maiden all forlorn,
That milked the cow with the crumpled horn,
That tossed the dog,
That worried the cat,
That killed the rat,
That ate the malt
That lay in the house that Jack built.

This is the priest all shaven and shorn,
That married the man all tattered and torn,
That kissed the maiden all forlorn,
That milked the cow with the crumpled horn,
That tossed the dog,
That worried the cat,
That killed the rat,
That ate the malt
That lay in the house that Jack built.

This is the cock that crowed in the morn,
That waked the priest all shaven and shorn,
That married the man all tattered and torn,
That kissed the maiden all forlorn,
That milked the cow with the crumpled horn,
That tossed the dog,
That worried the cat,
That killed the rat,
That ate the malt
That lay in the house that Jack built.

This is the farmer sowing his corn,
That kept the cock that crowed in the morn,
That waked the priest all shaven and shorn,
That married the man all tattered and torn,
That kissed the maiden all forlorn,
That milked the cow with the crumpled horn,
That tossed the dog,
That worried the cat,
That killed the rat,
That ate the malt
That lay in the house that Jack built.

I Had a Cat

I had a cat and the cat pleased me,
I fed my cat by yonder tree;
Cat goes fiddle-i-fee.

I had a hen and the hen pleased me,
I fed my hen by yonder tree;
Hen goes chimmy-chuck, chimmy-chuck,
Cat goes fiddle-i-fee.

I had a duck and the duck pleased me,
I fed my duck by yonder tree;
Duck goes quack, quack,
Hen goes chimmy-chuck, chimmy-chuck,
Cat goes fiddle-i-fee.

I had a goose and the goose pleased me,
I fed my goose by yonder tree;
Goose goes swishy, swashy,
Duck goes quack, quack,
Hen goes chimmy-chuck, chimmy-chuck,
Cat goes fiddle-i-fee.

I had a sheep and the sheep pleased me,
I fed my sheep by yonder tree;
Sheep goes baa, baa,
Goose goes swishy, swashy,
Duck goes quack, quack,
Hen goes chimmy-chuck, chimmy-chuck,
Cat goes fiddle-i-fee.

I had a pig and the pig pleased me,
I fed my pig by yonder tree;
Pig goes griffy, gruffy,
Sheep goes baa, baa,
Goose goes swishy, swashy,
Duck goes quack, quack,
Hen goes chimmy-chuck, chimmy-chuck,
Cat goes fiddle-i-fee.

I had a cow and the cow pleased me,
I fed my cow by yonder tree;
Cow goes moo, moo,
Pig goes griffy, gruffy,
Sheep goes baa, baa,
Goose goes swishy, swashy,
Duck goes quack, quack,
Hen goes chimmy-chuck, chimmy-chuck,
Cat goes fiddle-i-fee.

I had a horse and the horse pleased me,
I fed my horse by yonder tree;
Horse goes neigh, neigh,
Cow goes moo, moo,
Pig goes griffy, gruffy,
Sheep goes baa, baa,
Goose goes swishy, swashy,
Duck goes quack, quack,
Hen goes chimmy-chuck, chimmy-chuck,
Cat goes fiddle-i-fee.

I had a dog and the dog pleased me,
I fed my dog by yonder tree;
Dog goes bow-wow, bow-wow,
Horse goes neigh, neigh,
Cow goes moo, moo,
Pig goes griffy, gruffy,
Sheep goes baa, baa,
Goose goes swishy, swashy,
Duck goes quack, quack,
Hen goes chimmy-chuck, chimmy-chuck,
Cat goes fiddle-i-fee.

The Fisherman and the Flounder

John Godfrey Saxe

A fisherman, poor as poor can be,
Who lived in a hovel beside the sea,
Was fishing one day, when "Lo!" he cries,
"I've caught a flounder of wondrous size!
As fine a flounder as one could wish!"
"O no! you haven't!" exclaimed the fish;
"In spite of my scaly skin," he said,
"I am not a fish, but a Prince instead;
Condemned to suffer this watery woe;
So I beg, good man, you will let me go!"
The fisherman, frightened at what he heard,
Let the flounder go with never a word
Except "Good-by! I'd rather eschew
Than cook a flounder who talks like you!"

His hovel now the fisherman sought,
And told his wife of the fish he caught,
And how his luck was all in vain,
For he let the flounder off again!
"And did you ask for nothing?—alack!"
The woman cried: "Go presently back,
And tell the Prince our wretched lot,
And ask him to give us a finer cot!"
To mind his wife he was something loth,
But he feared the woman when she was wroth;

And so he went to the ocean-side,
And thus the fisherman loudly cried:

"O good flounder in the sea,
Hither quickly come to me;
For Pauline, my loving dame,
Wants queer things I fear to name."

Whereat the flounder, swimming near,
Said, "Why, O why, am I summoned here?"
And the trembling fisherman answered thus:
"My dame is always making a fuss;
A cosey hovel is hers and mine,
But she fain would have a cottage fine!"
"Go home," said the fish, "this very minute;
The cottage is hers; you'll find her in it!"

He hied him home in haste, and lo!
The fisherman found it even so.
"How happy," he cried, "we now shall be!"
But the woman answered, "We shall see!"
When a month was past, the woman sighed
For a larger house. "Now go," she cried,
"And tell the flounder ('tis my command)
I want a mansion large and grand!"
To mind the dame he was truly loth,
But he feared the woman when she was wroth;

So he went again to the ocean-side,
And loudly thus the fisherman cried:

> *"O good flounder in the sea,*
> *Hither quickly come to me;*
> *For Pauline, my loving dame,*
> *Wants queer things I fear to name."*

Whereat the flounder, swimming near,
Said, "Why again am I summoned here?"
And the trembling fisherman answered thus:
"My wife is always making a fuss;
She deems our cottage much too small;
She wants a mansion large and tall."
"Go home," said the fish, "this very minute;
The mansion is there—you'll find her in it!"

He hied him home in haste, and lo!
The fisherman found it even so!
And he cried, "How happy we shall be!"
But the woman answered, "We shall see!"
When a week was past, the woman sighed
For a castle grand. "Now go," she cried,
"And tell the flounder that he must give
Your wife a palace wherein to live."
To mind the dame he was greatly loth,
But he feared the woman when she was wroth;

So he went again to the ocean-side,
And softly thus the fisherman cried:

> *"O good flounder in the sea,*
> *Hither quickly come to me;*
> *For Pauline, my loving dame,*
> *Wants queer things I fear to name!"*

Whereat the flounder, swimming near,
Said, "Why again am I summoned here?"
And the trembling fisherman answered thus:
"My dame is always making a fuss;
She deems our mansion poorly planned;
She wants a palace great and grand!"
"Go home," said the fish, "this very minute;
The palace is there—you'll find her in it!"

He hied him home in haste, and, lo!
The fisherman found it even so,
And he cried, "How happy we shall be!"
But the woman answered, "We shall see!"
When a day was past, with growing pride,
For regal power the woman sighed;
And she bade the fisherman tell the fish
To reign as a king was now her wish.
To mind the dame he was sadly loth,
But he feared the woman when she was wroth,

So he went again to the ocean-side,
And softly thus the fisherman cried:

> *"O good flounder in the sea,*
> *Hither quickly come to me;*
> *For Pauline, my loving dame,*
> *Wants queer things I fear to name."*

Whereat the flounder, swimming near,
Said, "Why again am I summoned here?"
And the trembling fisherman answered thus:
"My dame is always making a fuss;
She has got a palace great and grand,
And now she asks for royal command!"
"Go home!" said the fish, "at the palace gate
You'll find her a king in royal state!"

He hied him home in haste, and, lo!
The fisherman found it even so.
"Good faith," said he, "'tis a charming thing
To be, like you, a sovereign king!
With a golden crown upon your brow,
I'm sure you'll be contented now!"

"Not I, indeed," the woman said,
"A triple crown would grace my head;
And I am worthy, I humbly hope—
Go tell the flounder to make me pope!"
"A pope? my dear—it cannot be done!
The Church, you know, allows but one!"
"Nay, none of your nonsense, man," said she,
"A pope—a pope I am bound to be!
The Prince will find it an easy thing
To make a pope as to make a king!"
To mind the dame he was sorely loth,
But he feared the woman when she was wroth,

So he went again to the ocean-side,
And thus the fisherman faintly cried:

> *"O good flounder in the sea,*
> *Hither quickly come to me,*
> *For Pauline, my loving dame,*
> *Wants queer things I fear to name!"*

Whereat the flounder, swimming near,
Said, "Why again am I summoned here?"
"Alack, alack!" the fisherman said,
"Whatever has turned the woman's head,
She is ill-content with royal scope,
And now, good luck! she would fain be pope!"
"Go home!" the flounder gruffly cried,
"And see the end of foolish pride;
You'll find her in her hovel again,
And there, till death, shall she remain!"

Saxe's poem is based on the Brothers Grimm fairy tale "The Fisherman and His Wife." There are many versions of the story in different cultures, each varying slightly in the wife's demands.

The Russian version "The Tale of the Fisherman and the Fish" is a fairy tale in verse by Alexander Pushkin which he wrote in 1833. The tale is about a fisherman who managed to catch a "Golden Fish" which promised to fulfill any wish of his in exchange for letting it go. In Pushkin's poem, an old man and woman have been living poorly for many years. They have a small hut, and every day the man goes out to fish.

One day, he throws in his net and pulls out seaweed two times in succession, but on the third time he pulls out a golden fish. The fish pleads for its life, promising any wish in return. However, the old man does not want anything, and lets the fish go. When he returns and tells his wife about the golden fish, she gets angry and tells her husband to go ask the fish for a new washboard, and the fish happily grants this small request.

Her requests become increasingly demanding until he asks that his wife be made the Ruler of the Sea. The fish cures her greed by putting her back in the old cottage and giving back the broken washboard.

Hiawatha's Childhood

Henry Wadsworth Longfellow

By the shores of Gitche Gumee,
By the shining Big-Sea-Water,
Stood the wigwam of Nokomis,
Daughter of the Moon, Nokomis.
Dark behind it rose the forest,
Rose the black and gloomy pine-trees,
Rose the firs with cones upon them;
Bright before it beat the water,
Beat the clear and sunny water,
Beat the shining Big-Sea-Water.

There the wrinkled, old Nokomis
Nursed the little Hiawatha;
Rocked him in his linden cradle,
Bedded soft in moss and rushes,
Safely bound with reindeer sinews;
Stilled his fretful wail by saying,
"Hush! The Naked Bear will get thee!"
Lulled him into slumber, singing,
"Ewa-yea! my little owlet!
Who is this that lights the wigwam,
With his great eyes lights the wigwam?
Ewa-yea! my little owlet!"

Many things Nokomis taught him
Of the stars that shine in heaven;
Showed the broad, white road in heaven,
Pathway of the ghosts, the shadows,
Running straight across the heavens,
Crowded with the ghosts, the shadows.

At the door on summer evenings
Sat the little Hiawatha;
Heard the whispering of the pine-trees,
Heard the lapping of the water,
Sounds of music, words of wonder;
"Minne-wawa!" said the pine-trees,
"Mudway-aushka! said the water.

Saw the firefly, Wah-wah-taysee,
Flitting through the dusk of evening,
With the twinkle of its candle
Lighting up the brakes and bushes;
And he sang the song of children,
Sang the song Nokomis taught him:

"Wah-wah-taysee, little firefly,
Little, flitting, white-fire insect,
Little, dancing, white-fire creature,
Light me with your little candle,
Ere upon my bed I lay me,
Ere in sleep I close my eyelids!"

Saw the moon rise from the water
Rippling, rounding from the water;
Saw the flecks and shadows on it;
Whispered, "What is that, Nokomis?"
And the good Nokomis answered
"Once a warrior, very angry,
Seized his grandmother, and threw her
Up into the sky at midnight;
Right against the moon he threw her;
Tis her body that you see there."

Saw the rainbow in the heaven,
In the eastern sky, the rainbow;
Whispered, "What is that, Nokomis?"
And the good Nokomis answered:
"'Tis the heaven of flowers you see there.
All the wild-flowers of the forest,
All the lilies of the prairie,
When on earth they fade and perish,
Blossom in that heaven above us."

When he heard the owls at midnight,
Hooting, laughing in the forest,
"What is that?" he cried in terror;
"What is that," he said, "Nokomis?"
And the good Nokomis answered:
"That is but the owl and owlet,
Talking in their native language,
Talking, scolding at each other."

Then the little Hiawatha
Learned of every bird its language,
Learned their names and all their secrets—
How they built their nests in summer,
Where they hid themselves in winter—
Talked with them whene'er he met them,
Called them "Hiawatha's Chickens."

Of all beasts he learned the language,
Learned their names and all their secrets—
How the beavers built their lodges,
Where the squirrels hid their acorns,
How the reindeer ran so swiftly,
Why the rabbit was so timid;
Talked with them whene'er he met then,
Called them "Hiawatha's Brothers."

The Peace Pipe

Henry Wadsworth Longfellow

Gitche Manito, the mighty,
The creator of the nations,
Looked upon them with compassion,
With paternal love and pity;
Looked upon their wrath and wrangling
But as quarrels among children,
But as feuds and fights of children!

Over them he stretched his right hand,
To subdue their stubborn natures,
To allay their thirst and fever,
By the shadow of his right hand;
Spake to them with voice majestic
As the sound of far-off waters,
Falling into deep abysses,
Warning, chiding, spake in this wise:

"O my children! my poor children!
Listen to the words of wisdom,
Listen to the words of warning,
From the lips of the Great Spirit,
From the Master of Life, who made you!

I have given you lands to hunt in,
I have given you streams to fish in,
I have given you bear and bison,
I have given you roe and reindeer,
I have given you brant and beaver,
Filled the marshes full of wild-fowl,
Filled the rivers full of fishes:
Why then are you not contented?
Why then will you hunt each other?

I am weary of your quarrels,
Weary of your wars and bloodshed,
Weary of your prayers for vengeance,
Of your wranglings and dissensions;
All your strength is in your union,
All your danger is in discord;
Therefore be at peace henceforward,
And as brothers live together."

Lochinvar

Sir Walter Scott

O young Lochinvar is come out of the west,
Through all the wide Border his steed was the best;
And save his good broadsword he weapons had none,
He rode all unarm'd, and he rode all alone.
So faithful in love, and so dauntless in war,
There never was knight like the young Lochinvar.

He staid not for brake, and he stopp'd not for stone,
He swam the Eske river where ford there was none;
But ere he alighted at Netherby gate,
The bride had consented, the gallant came late:
For a laggard in love, and a dastard in war,
Was to wed the fair Ellen of brave Lochinvar.

So boldly he enter'd the Netherby Hall,
Among bride's-men, and kinsmen, and brothers and all:
Then spoke the bride's father, his hand on his sword,
(For the poor craven bridegroom said never a word,)
"O come ye in peace here, or come ye in war,
Or to dance at our bridal, young Lord Lochinvar?"

"I long woo'd your daughter, my suit you denied;—
Love swells like the Solway, but ebbs like its tide—
And now I am come, with this lost love of mine,
To lead but one measure, drink one cup of wine.
There are maidens in Scotland more lovely by far,
That would gladly be bride to the young Lochinvar."

The bride kiss'd the goblet: the knight took it up,
He quaff'd off the wine, and he threw down the cup.
She look'd down to blush, and she look'd up to sigh,
With a smile on her lips and a tear in her eye.
He took her soft hand, ere her mother could bar,—
"Now tread we a measure!" said young Lochinvar.

So stately his form, and so lovely her face,
That never a hall such a gailiard did grace;
While her mother did fret, and her father did fume
And the bridegroom stood dangling his bonnet and plume:
And the bride-maidens whisper'd, "'Twere better by far
To have match'd our fair cousin with young Lochinvar."

One touch to her hand, and one word in her ear,
When they reach'd the hall-door, and the charger stood near;
So light to the croupe the fair lady he swung,
So light to the saddle before her he sprung!
"She is won! we are gone, over bank, bush, and scaur;
They'll have fleet steeds that follow," quoth young Lochinvar.

There was mounting 'mong Graemes of the Netherby clan;
Forsters, Fenwicks, and Musgraves, they rode and they ran:
There was racing and chasing on Cannobie Lee,
But the lost bride of Netherby ne'er did they see.
So daring in love, and so dauntless in war,
Have ye e'er heard of gallant like young Lochinvar?

The Sailor's Consolation

William Pitt

One night came on a hurricane,
    The sea was mountains rolling,
When Barney Buntline turned his quid,
    And said to Billy Bowling:

"A strong nor-wester's blowing, Bill;
    Hark! don't ye hear it roar, now?
Lord help 'em, how I pities them
    Unhappy folks on shore now!

"Foolhardy chaps who live in towns,
    What danger they are all in,
And now lie quaking in their beds,
    For fear the roof should fall in;

"Poor creatures! how they envies us,
    And wishes, I've a notion,
For our good luck, in such a storm,
    To be upon the ocean!

"And as for them who're out all day
    On business from their houses,
And late at night are coming home,
    To cheer their babes and spouses,—

"While you and I, Bill, on the deck
    Are comfortably lying,
My eyes! what tiles and chimney-pots
    About their heads are flying!

"And very often have we heard
    How men are killed and undone
By overturns of carriages,
    By thieves, and fires in London;

"We know what risks all landsmen run,
    From noblemen to tailors;
Then, Bill, let us thank Providence
    That you and I are sailors."

A Ballad of John Silver

John Masefield

We were schooner-rigged and rakish, with a long and lissome hull,
And we flew the pretty colours of the cross-bones and the skull;
We'd a big black Jolly Roger flapping grimly at the fore,
And we sailed the Spanish Water in the happy days of yore.

We'd a long brass gun amidships, like a well-conducted ship,
We had each a brace of pistols and a cutlass at the hip;
It's a point which tells against us, and a fact to be deplored,
But we chased the goodly merchant-men and laid their ships aboard.

Then the dead men fouled the scuppers and the wounded filled the chains,
And the paint-work all was spatter-dashed with other people's brains,
She was boarded, she was looted, she was scuttled till she sank,
And the pale survivors left us by the medium of the plank.

O! then it was (while standing by the taffrail on the poop)
We could hear the drowning folk lament the absent chicken-coop;
Then, having washed the blood away, we'd little else to do
Than to dance a quiet hornpipe as the old salts taught us to.

O! the fiddle on the fo'c's'le, and the slapping naked soles,
And the genial "Down the middle, Jake, and curtsey when she rolls!"
With the silver seas around us and the pale moon overhead,
And the look-out not a-looking and his pipe-bowl glowing red.

Ah! the pig-tailed, quidding pirates and the pretty pranks we played,
All have since been put a stop-to by the naughty Board of Trade;
The schooners and the merry crews are laid away to rest,
A little south the sunset in the Islands of the Blest.

Tubal Cain

Charles Mackay

Old Tubal Cain was a man of might
In the days when the Earth was young;
By the fierce red light of his furnace bright
The strokes of his hammer rung;
And he lifted high his brawny hand
On the iron glowing clear,
Till the sparks rushed out in scarlet showers,
As he fashioned the sword and spear.
And he sang—"Hurra for my handiwork!
Hurra for the spear and sword!
Hurra for the hand that shall wield them well,
For he shall be king and lord!"

To Tubal Cain came many a one,
As he wrought by his roaring fire,
And each one prayed for a strong steel blade
As the crown of his desire:
And he made them weapons sharp and strong,

Till they shouted loud for glee,
And gave him gifts of pearl and gold,
And spoils of the forest free.
And they sang—"Hurra for Tubal Cain,
Who hath given us strength anew!
Hurra for the smith, hurra for the fire,
And hurra for the metal true!"

But a sudden change came o'er his heart
Ere the setting of the sun,
And Tubal Cain was filled with pain
For the evil he had done;
He saw that men, with rage and hate,
Made war upon their kind,
That the land was red with the blood they shed
In their lust for carnage blind.
And he said—"Alas! that ever I made,
Or that skill of mine should plan,
The spear and the sword for men whose joy
Is to slay their fellow man"

And for many a day old Tubal Cain
Sat brooding o'er his woe;
And his hand forebore to smite the ore
And his furnace smouldered low.
But he rose at last with a cheerful face,
And a bright courageous eye,
And bared his strong right arm for work,
While the quick flames mounted high.
And he sang—"Hurra for my handicraft!"
And the red sparks lit the air;
"Not alone for the blade was the strong steel made;"
And he fashioned the first ploughshare.

And men, taught wisdom from the past,
In friendship joined their hands,
Hung the sword in the hall, the spear on the wall,
And ploughed the willing lands;
And sang—"Hurra for Tubal Cain!
Our staunch good friend is he;
And for the ploughshare and the plough
To him our praise shall be.
But while oppression lifts its head,
Or a tyrant would be lord,
Though we may thank him for the plough,
We'll not forget the sword!"

FROM THE PIED PIPER OF HAMELIN

ROBERT BROWNING

Rats!
They fought the dogs and killed the cats,
And bit the babies in the cradles,
And ate the cheeses out of the vats,
And licked the soup from the cooks' own ladle's,
Split open the kegs of salted sprats,
Made nests inside men's Sunday hats,
And even spoiled the women's chats
By drowning their speaking
With shrieking and squeaking
In fifty different sharps and flats.

Into the street the Piper stept,
Smiling first a little smile,
As if he knew what magic slept
In his quiet pipe the while;
Then, like a musical adept,
To blow the pipe his lips he wrinkled,
And green and blue his sharp eyes twinkled,
Like a candle-flame where salt is sprinkled;
And ere three shrill notes the pipe uttered,
You heard as if an army muttered;
And the muttering grew to a grumbling;
And the grumbling grew to a mighty rumbling;
And out of the houses the rats came tumbling.
Great rats, small rats, lean rats, brawny rats,
Brown rats, black rats, gray rats, tawny rats,
Grave old plodders, gay young friskers,
Fathers, mothers, uncles, cousins,
Cocking tails and pricking whiskers,
Families by tens and dozens,
Brothers, sisters, husbands, wives—
Followed the Piper for their lives.
From street to street he piped advancing,
And step for step they followed dancing.

Yussouf

James Russell Lowell

A stranger came one night to Yussouf's tent,
Saying, "Behold one outcast and in dread,
Against whose life the bow of power is bent,
Who flies, and hath not where to lay his head;
I come to thee for shelter and for food,
To Yussouf, called through all our tribes 'The Good.'"

"This tent is mine," said Yussouf, "but no more
Than it is God's; come in and be at peace;
Freely shallt thou partake of all my store
As I of His who buildeth over these
Our tents his glorious roof of night and day,
And at whose door none ever yet heard Nay."

So Yussouf entertained his guest that night,
And, waking him ere day, said: "Here is gold;
My swiftest horse is saddled for thy flight;
Depart before the prying day grow bold."
As one lamp lights another, nor grows less,
So nobleness enkindleth nobleness.

That inward light the stranger's face made grand,
Which shines from all self-conquest; kneeling low,
He bowed his forehead upon Yussouf's hand,
Sobbing: "O Sheik, I cannot leave thee so;
I will repay thee; all this thou hast done
Unto that Ibrahim who slew thy son!"

"Take thrice the gold," said Yussouf "for with thee
Into the desert, never to return,
My one black thought shall ride away from me;
First-born, for whom by day and night I yearn,
Balanced and just are all of God's decrees;
Thou art avenged, my first-born, sleep in peace!"

FROM THE LADY OF SHALOTT

ALFRED, LORD TENNYSON

On either side the river lie
Long fields of barley and of rye,
That clothe the wold and meet the sky;
And thro' the field the road runs by
    To many-tower'd Camelot;
And up and down the people go,
Gazing where the lilies blow
Round an island there below,
    The island of Shalott.

Willows whiten, aspens quiver,
Little breezes dusk and shiver
Through the wave that runs for ever
By the island in the river
    Flowing down to Camelot.
Four grey walls, and four grey towers,
Overlook a space of flowers,
And the silent isle imbowers
    The Lady of Shalott.

By the margin, willow veil'd,
Slide the heavy barges trail'd
By slow horses; and unhail'd
The shallop flitteth silken-sail'd
    Skimming down to Camelot:
But who hath seen her wave her hand?
Or at the casement seen her stand?
Or is she known in all the land,
    The Lady of Shalott?

Only reapers, reaping early,
In among the bearded barley
Hear a song that echoes cheerly
From the river winding clearly;
    Down to tower'd Camelot;
And by the moon the reaper weary,
Piling sheaves in uplands airy,
Listening, whispers, "'Tis the fairy
    Lady of Shalott."

from Evangeline, A Tale of Acadie

Henry Wadsworth Longfellow

This is the forest primeval. The murmuring pines and the hemlocks,
Bearded with moss, and in garments green, indistinct in the twilight,
Stand like Druids of eld, with voices sad and prophetic,
Stand like harpers hoar, with beards that rest on their bosoms.
Loud from its rocky caverns, the deep-voiced neighboring ocean
Speaks, and in accents disconsolate answers the wail of the forest.

This is the forest primeval; but where are the hearts that beneath it
Leaped like the roe, when he hears in the woodland the voice of the
huntsman?
Where is the thatch-roofed village, the home of Acadian farmers,—
Men whose lives glided on like rivers that water the woodlands,
Darkened by shadows of earth, but reflecting an image of heaven?
Waste are those pleasant farms, and the farmers forever departed!
Scattered like dust and leaves, when the mighty blasts of October
Seize them, and whirl them aloft, and sprinkle them far o'er the ocean.
Naught but tradition remains of the beautiful village of Grand-Pré.

Ye who believe in affection that hopes, and endures, and is patient,
Ye who believe in the beauty and strength of woman's devotion,
List to the mournful tradition still sung by the pines of the forest;
List to a Tale of Love in Acadie, home of the happy.

The Highwayman

Alfred Noyes

PART ONE

The wind was a torrent of darkness upon the gusty trees,
The moon was a ghostly galleon tossed upon cloudy seas,
The road was a ribbon of moonlight looping the purple moor,
And the highwayman came riding—
Riding—riding—
The highwayman came riding, up to the old inn door.

He'd a French cocked hat on his forehead, and a bunch of lace at his chin;
He'd a coat of the claret velvet, and breeches of fine doe-skin.
They fitted with never a wrinkle; his boots were up to his thigh!
And he rode with a jeweled twinkle—
His rapier hilt a-twinkle—
His pistol butts a-twinkle, under the jeweled sky.

Over the cobbles he clattered and clashed in the dark inn-yard,
He tapped with his whip on the shutters, but all was locked and barred,
He whistled a tune to the window, and who should be waiting there
But the landlord's black-eyed daughter—
        Bess, the landlord's daughter—
Plaiting a dark red love-knot into her long black hair.

Dark in the dark old inn-yard a stable-wicket creaked
Where Tim, the ostler listened—his face was white and peaked—
His eyes were hollows of madness, his hair like mouldy hay,
But he loved the landlord's daughter—
        The landlord's black-eyed daughter;
Dumb as a dog he listened, and he heard the robber say:

"One kiss, my bonny sweetheart; I'm after a prize tonight,
But I shall be back with the yellow gold before the morning light.
Yet if they press me sharply, and harry me through the day,
Then look for me by moonlight,
        Watch for me by moonlight,
I'll come to thee by moonlight, though hell should bar the way."

He stood upright in the stirrups; he scarce could reach her hand,
But she loosened her hair in the casement! His face burnt like a brand
As the sweet black waves of perfume came tumbling o'er his breast,
Then he kissed its waves in the moonlight
        (O sweet black waves in the moonlight!),
And he tugged at his reins in the moonlight, and galloped away to the west.

PART TWO

He did not come in the dawning; he did not come at noon.
And out of the tawny sunset, before the rise of the moon,
When the road was a gypsy's ribbon over the purple moor,
The redcoat troops came marching—
        Marching—marching—
King George's men came marching, up to the old inn-door.

They said no word to the landlord; they drank his ale instead,
But they gagged his daughter and bound her to the foot of her narrow bed.
Two of them knelt at her casement, with muskets by their side;
There was Death at every window,
        And Hell at one dark window,
For Bess could see, through her casement, the road that he would ride.

They had bound her up at attention, with many a sniggering jest!
They had tied a rifle beside her, with the barrel beneath her breast!
"Now keep good watch!" and they kissed her. She heard the dead man say,
"Look for me by moonlight,
Watch for me by moonlight,
I'll come to thee by moonlight, though Hell should bar the way."

She twisted her hands behind her, but all the knots held good!
She writhed her hands till her fingers were wet with sweat or blood!
They stretched and strained in the darkness, and the hours crawled by like years
Till, on the stroke of midnight,
Cold on the stroke of midnight,
The tip of one finger touched it! The trigger at least was hers!

The tip of one finger touched it, she strove no more for the rest;
Up, she stood up at attention, with the barrel beneath her breast.
She would not risk their hearing, she would not strive again,
For the road lay bare in the moonlight,
Blank and bare in the moonlight,
And the blood in her veins, in the moonlight, throbbed to her love's refrain.

Tlot tlot, tlot tlot! Had they heard it? The horse-hooves, ringing clear;
Tlot tlot, tlot tlot, in the distance! Were they deaf that they did not hear?
Down the ribbon of moonlight, over the brow of the hill,
The highwayman came riding—
Riding—riding—
The redcoats looked to their priming! She stood up straight and still.

Tlot tlot, in the frosty silence! Tlot tlot, in the echoing night!
Nearer he came and nearer! Her face was like a light!
Her eyes grew wide for a moment, she drew one last deep breath,
Then her finger moved in the moonlight—
Her musket shattered the moonlight—
Shattered her breast in the moonlight and warned him—with her death.

He turned, he spurred to the West; he did not know who stood
Bowed, with her head o'er the casement, drenched in her own red blood!
Not till the dawn did he hear it, and his face grew grey to hear
How Bess, the landlord's daughter,
The landlord's black-eyed daughter,
Had watched for her love in the moonlight, and died in the darkness there.

Back, he spurred like a madman, shrieking a curse to the sky,
With the white road smoking behind him and his rapier brandished high!
Blood-red were his spurs in the golden noon, wine-red was his velvet coat
When they shot him down in the highway,
        Down like a dog in the highway,
And he lay in his blood in the highway, with the bunch of lace at his throat.

And still on a winter's night, they say, when the wind is in the trees,
When the moon is a ghostly galleon tossed upon cloudy seas,
When the road is a gypsy's ribbon looping the purple moor,
The highwayman comes riding—
        Riding—riding—
The highwayman comes riding, up to the old inn-door.

Over the cobbles he clatters and clangs in the dark inn-yard,
He taps with his whip on the shutters, but all is locked and barred,
He whistles a tune to the window, and who should be waiting there
But the landlord's black-eyed daughter—
        Bess, the landlord's daughter—
Plaiting a dark red love-knot into her long black hair.

Lord Ullin's Daughter

Thomas Campbell

A chieftain, to the Highlands bound,
    Cries, "Boatman, do not tarry!
And I'll give thee a silver pound
    To row us o'er the ferry."

"Now who be ye, would cross Lochgyle,
    This dark and stormy water?"
"O, I'm the chief of Ulva's isle,
    And this Lord Ullin's daughter.

"And fast before her father's men
    Three days we've fled together,
For should he find us in the glen,
    My blood would stain the heather.

"His horsemen hard behind us ride;
    Should they our steps discover,
Then who will cheer my bonny bride
    When they have slain her lover?"

Outspoke the hardy Highland wight,
 "I'll go, my chief—I'm ready:
It is not for your silver bright;
 But for your winsome lady:

And by my word! the bonny bird
 In danger shall not tarry;
So though the waves are raging white,
 I'll row you o'er the ferry."

By this the storm grew loud apace,
 The water-wraith was shrieking;
And in the scowl of heaven each face
 Grew dark as they were speaking.

But still as wilder blew the wind,
 And as the night grew drearer,
Adown the glen rode armèd men,
 Their trampling sounded nearer.

"O haste thee, haste!" the lady cries,
 "Though tempests round us gather;
I'll meet the raging of the skies,
 But not an angry father."

The boat has left a stormy land,
 A stormy sea before her,
When, oh! too strong for human hand,
 The tempest gather'd o'er her.

And still they row'd amidst the roar
 Of waters fast prevailing:
Lord Ullin reach'd that fatal shore,
 His wrath was changed to wailing.

For, sore dismay'd, through storm and shade,
 His child he did discover:
One lovely hand she stretch'd for aid,
 And one was round her lover.

"Come back! come back!" he cried in grief
 "Across this stormy water:
And I'll forgive your Highland chief,
 My daughter!—oh my daughter!"

'Twas vain: the loud waves lash'd the shore,
 Return or aid preventing:
The waters wild went o'er his child,
 And he was left lamenting.

Numbers and Grammar

One Is the Sun

One is the Sun who shines above,
Two is the prince when he finds his love,
The king, the queen, and their child are three,
Four are the winds that blow to me,
Five am I with my limbs and head,
Six is the honeycomb sweetening bread,
Seven are the stars that cross the sky,
Eight are the hours asleep I lie.

Number Poem

The bright-eyed stars do in the number rest,
And every man is by the numbers blest:
By one when upright on the earth he stands,
By two when lovingly he lifts his hands,
By three when he awakes, or dreams, or sleeps,
By four when every year its seasons keeps,
By five when opens out the summer's rose,
By six when Gabriel's snow-white lily blows,
By seven when every week its days do bring,
Thus do the numbers through the great world ring.

One, Two, Buckle My Shoe

Traditional

One, two,
Buckle my shoe;
Three, four,
Knock at the door;
Five, six,
Pick up sticks;
Seven, eight,
Lay them straight:
Nine, ten,
A big fat hen;
Eleven, twelve,
Dig and delve;
Thirteen, fourteen,
Maids a-courting;
Fifteen, sixteen,
Maids in the kitchen;
Seventeen, eighteen,
Maids a-waiting;
Nineteen, twenty,
My plate's empty.

Five Little Brothers

Ella Wheeler Wilcox

Five little brothers set out together
  To journey the livelong day,
In a curious carriage made of leather
  They hurried away, away!
One big brother, and three quite small,
And one wee fellow, no size at all.

The carriage was dark and none too roomy,
  And they could not move about;
The five little brothers grew very gloomy,
  And the wee one began to pout;
Till the biggest one whispered, "What do you say?
Let's leave the carriage and run away!"

So out they scampered, the five together,
    And off and away they sped—
When somebody found the carriage of leather,
    Oh, my, how she shook her head!
'Twas her little boy's shoe, as everyone knows,
And the five little brothers were five little toes.

Dancing on the Shore

Traditional

Ten little children, dancing on the shore.
The queen waved a royal wand, and out went four.

Six little children, dancing merrily
The queen waved a royal wand, and out went three.

Three little children, danced as children do;
The queen waved a royal wand and out went two.

One little maiden, dancing just for fun;
The queen waved a royal wand, and out went one.

Number Rhyme

Joan Marcus

We dance around the fir tree
    in every kind of weather,
Twelve little gnomes dancing all together.
We dance around the fir tree
    in every kind of weather,
Twelve little gnomes dancing all together.

Two big groups of six are we,
Two big groups of six.
Two big groups of six are we,
Two big groups of six.

We dance around the fir tree...

Three little groups of four are we,
Three little groups of four.
Three little groups of four are we,
Three little groups of four.

We dance around the fir tree...

Four little groups of three are we,
Four little groups of three.
Four little groups of three are we,
Four little groups of three.

We dance around the fir tree...

Six little groups of two are we,
Six little groups of two.
Six little groups of two are we,
Six little groups of two.

We dance around the fir tree...

The Number Twelve

Twelve children together are we
Merry and bright as you can see,
Twelve children hand in hand
In one circle here we stand.

Each with a partner, hand in hand,
Six pairs now before us stand.
Twelve is six lots of two.

Into two rings now we run
Six in a ring, quickly done.
Twelve is two lots of six.

Into four rings now we run
Three in a ring, quickly done.
Twelve is four lots of three.

Wait and we will show you more:
Three rings now in each is four.
Twelve is three lots of four.

*(Then all the children dance back
into one circle.)*

Twelve children together are we
Merry and bright as you can see,
Twelve children hand in hand
In one circle here we stand.

Number Verse

Eugene Schwartz

One is the Sun that shines so bright,
One is the moon so high;
One is the day and one is the night,
One is the sheltering sky.
One is a head so still and tame,
Upon one body whole with health;
And I is the one and the special name
That only I can call myself!

Two are the eyes with which I see,
Two are the ears that hear;
Joy and sorrow both live in me,
And so do courage and fear.
Darkness and Light must together live,
Night and day are as sister and brother;
And two are the hands that receive and give,
To help myself or serve another.

Around me in the world I see
Beast and plant and stone.
Nature weaves her world as Three,
But I am three in one:
A head well-wrought for wisdom's work,
A heart hallowed by love;
Strong limbs to labor on the earth
As Angels do above.

Summer and Autumn, Winter and Spring,
Through Four seasons passes the year;
Fire and Air, Water and Earth—
Out of these four does our whole world appear.

Five are the fingers upon each hand,
Each foot has its five toes;
Five rays has the star shining high o'er the land,
Five petals has the rose.
And when with limbs outstretched I alight,
Like a five-pointed star
All the world I make bright!

The Snow Queen casts Six-pointed flakes
On stormy winds to ride;
The crystal with its six clear walls
In deepest earth abides;
When the busy bee builds honeycombs
He sculpts them with six sides.
Wherever Light would find a home,
In storm, or cave, or honeycomb,
Six is its chosen number and form.

Arithmetic Verses

There was a family strange indeed;
Each member had a peculiar speed.
They could walk for half a day
Counting footsteps all the way.
Here they come, number one.

One

I am proper, neat and prim;
My walk is straight, my clothes are trim.
So I count my steps and you will see
That every one's the same for me.
One, two, three, four, five, six,
seven, eight, nine, ten, eleven, twelve.

Two

But my two steps are not the same,
For I must lean upon my cane.
Although I'm bent and weak and old,
I can still count with numbers bold.
One, *two,*
three, *four,*
five, *six,*
seven, *eight,*
nine, *ten,*
eleven, *twelve.*

Three

I'm a lad, light and gay
And I'd much rather play.
I can run with my ball
While the numbers I call.

One, two, *three,*
four, five, *six,*
seven, eight, *nine,*
ten, eleven, *twelve.*

Four

My step is strong;
I'll go not wrong.
With all my might
I'll guard what's right.
I'll always know
How far to go.
One, two, three, *four,*
five, six, seven, *eight,*
nine, ten, eleven, *twelve.*

Five

Like a mouse I go
Fearfully tip-toe,
Looking to the left,
Looking to the right;
Watching to and fro
Danger's not in sight.
Lightly I arrive,
I am number five.
One, two, three, four, *five,*
six, seven, eight, nine, *ten.*

Six

One, two, three, four, five, six
I can do lots of tricks!
I've a friend—number three—
He's a helper to me.
He has taught me to play
But I have my own way.
One, two, three, four, five, *six,*
seven, eight, nine, ten, eleven, *twelve.*

Ten

A giant am I, just sauntering by
To numbers so high I quickly will fly.
Ten, twenty, thirty, forty, fifty,
sixty, seventy, eighty, ninety, a hundred.

How Many Seconds in a Minute?

Christina Rossetti

How many seconds in a minute?
Sixty, and no more in it.
How many minutes in an hour?
Sixty for sun and shower.
How many hours in a day?
Twenty-four for work and play.
How many days in a week?
Seven both to hear and speak.
How many weeks in a month?
Four, as the swift moon runn'th.
How many months in a year?
Twelve the almanack makes clear.
How many years in an age?
One hundred says the sage.
How many ages in time?
No one knows the rhyme.

Time Rhyme

Dorothy Harrer

Sixty seconds make a minute,
Put a lot of kindness in it.
Sixty minutes make an hour.
Work with all your might and power.
Twelve bright hours make a day,
Time enough for work and play.
Twelve dark hours through the night
Give us sleep till morning light.
Seven days a week will make.
This we'll learn if pains we take.
Four to five weeks make the months.
Remember this or be a dunce.
Twelve long months will make a year,
In one of them your birthday, dear.

A Mathematics Poem

Michael Motteram

A circle has lots of possibilities;
There are many directions to go.
But with a line that is straight
There can only be this way or that!
If you live from the center of a circle
you will find your life all about you.
But should you live on a railway track
you can only go forward or back!

Euclid

Vachel Lindsay

Old Euclid drew a circle
On a sand-beach long ago.
He bounded and enclosed it
With angles thus and so.
His set of solemn greybeards
Nodded and argued much
Of arc and circumference,
Diameter and such.
A silent child stood by them
From morning until noon
Because they drew such charming
Round pictures of the moon.

Unknown

Is it where the Geometer draws his base,
And elegant quadrices float through space,
Where the circular points are the open door,
And conics osculate ever more?

Alphabet

Margaret Morgan

A is for Angel with heavenly wings;
B is for Bird that beautifully sings;
C is for Cat, curled up by the fire;
D is for Dog Rose—sometimes called briar;
E is for Eagle that soars in the sky;
F is for Flag, fluttering on high;
G is for Giraffe who looks over the wall;
H is for Hamster, so furry and small;
I is for Iceberg that floats in the sea;
J is for Jungle where animals roam free;
K is for Kingfisher, seen by the lake;
L is for Lamp that in darkness we take;
M is for Moon to shine in the night;
N is for Note that we hastily write;
O is for Orange so juicy and sweet;
P is for Peacock—not seen in the street;
Q is for Queen with jewels and crown;
R is for Rabbit, all fluffy and brown;
S is for Sea and for Sun and for Sand;
T is for Trumpet that plays in the Band;
U is for Unicorn, seen long ago;
V is for Valley that dips deep and low;
W is for Well—where wishes are made;
X is for eXciting games that are played;
Y is for Yacht that sails on the sea;
Z is for Zoo—where Zebras may be.

This is the Alphabet A through to Z;
26 letters—and each has been said.

If you are puzzled by the rhyme, or lack of rhyme, in the last two lines, knowing that the poem was written in Britain will help. In the United Kingdom, the last letter of the alphabet is pronounced "zed", reflecting its derivation from the Greek zeta. "Zed" comes from the original Greek zeta via Old French zede, and most English speakers worldwide pronounce it that way. The last letter of the alphabet was also pronounced "izzard" in Colonial America. It was the grammarian Webster who, in 1827, decreed "it is pronounced zee."

An Alphabet

Edward Lear

A was once an apple pie,
Pidy, Widy, Tidy, Pidy,
Nice insidy
Apple Pie!

B was once a little bear,
Beary! Wary! Hairy! Beary!
Taky cary!
Little Bear!

C was once a little cake,
Caky, Baky, Maky, Caky
Taky Caky,
Little Cake!

D was once a little doll,
Dolly, Molly, Polly, Nolly
Nursy Dolly
Little Doll!

E was once a little eel,
Eely,Weely, Peely, Eely
Twirly, Tweedy
Little Eel!

F was once a little fish,
Fishy, Wishy, Squishy, Fishy
In a Dishy
Little Fish!

G was once a little goose,
Goosy, Moosy, Boosy, Goosey
Waddly-woosy
Little Goose!

H was once a little hen,
Henny, Chenny, Tenny, Henny
Eggsy-any
Little Hen?

I was once a bottle of ink,
Inky, Dinky, Thinky, Inky
Black Minky
Bottle of Ink!

J was once a jar of jam,
Jammy, Mammy, Clammy, Jammy
Sweety-Swammy
Jar of Jam!

K was once a little kite,
Kity, Whity, Flighty, Kity
Out of sighty-
Little Kite!

L was once a little lark,
Larky! Marky! Harky! Larky!
In the Parky,
Little Lark!

M was once a little mouse,
Mousey, Bousey, Sousy, Mousy
In the Housy
Little Mouse!

N was once a little needle,
Needly, Tweedly, Threedly, Needly
Wisky-wheedly
Little Needle!

O was once a little owl,
Owly, Prowly, Howly, Owly
Browny fowly
Little Owl!

P was once a little pump,
Pumpy, Slumpy, Flumpy, Pumpy
Dumpy, Thumpy
Little Pump!

Q was once a little quail,
Quaily, Faily, Daily, Quaily
Stumpy-taily
Little Quail!

R was once a little rose,
Rosy, Posy, Nosy, Rosy
Bows-y - grows-y
Little Rose!

S was once a little shrimp,
Shrimpy, Nimpy, Flimpy, Shrimpy
Jumpy-jimpy
Little Shrimp!

T was once a little thrush,
Thrushy! Hushy! Bushy! Thrushy!
Flitty-Flushy
Little Thrush!

U was once a little urn,
Urny, Burny, Turny, Urny
Bubbly-burny
Little Urn!

V was once a little vine,
Viny, Winy, Twiny, Viny
Twisty-twiny
Little Vine!

W was once a whale,
Whaly, Scaly, Shaly, Whaly
Tumbly-taily
Mighty Whale!

X was once a great king Xerxes,
Xerxy, Perxy, Turxy, Xerxy
Linxy Lurxy
Great King Xerxes!

Y was once a little yew,
Yewdy, Fewdy, Crudy, Yewdy
Growdy, grewdy,
Little Yew!

Z was once a piece of zinc,
Tinky, Winky, Blinky, Tinky
Tinkly Minky
Piece of Zinc!

The Four Sentences

Dorothy Harrer

Commands

Listen to the night wind blow.
See the swirling flakes of snow.
Close the window. Shut the door.
Keep out the wild wind's angry roar.
Light the fire. Let it blaze.

Exclamations

How wonderful the morning is!
Oh, what a sparkling day!
Sky's blue around the golden sun!
The wind has died away!

Statements

The golden sun shines on the snow.
The trees blue shadows make.
The colors of God's own rainbow
Twinkle in each snowflake.

Questions

Where do snowflakes come from?
Why are they so white?
Who gives them each a separate form?
How far has been their flight?
And what creates the rainbow
In each which star of snow?

The Parts of Speech Verses

Virginia Field Birdsall

The Verb

I am a verb, I like to act,
To walk, to run, to dance; it's a fact.
To plow, to build, to work, to strive,
I like to feel that I'm alive!
But sometimes I just say, "I am,"
And act as meek as a little lamb.

The Noun

I am a noun; I give names to things,
To persons, from beggars to royal kings;
To animals also, great and small;
To flowers and trees that grow so tall,
To things like tables and chairs and sticks,
To houses and stone, concrete and bricks;
And to things you can't see or hear or feel,
Like goodness and truth and honor and zeal!
I like to be quiet; I don't run about,
I just sit still and let others shout.

The Pronoun

I am a pronoun; it isn't quite fair,
I'm only about when the noun isn't there!
Sometimes I'm "I" and sometimes I'm "you,"
Or "he," "she," or "it," or "they" or "them," too;
I change my form when it suits my whim,
Then she becomes her and he becomes him.

The Articles

The articles small are we;
We like to make ourselves known:
Fat A, an and the; but none of us three
Can stand for a minute alone.
Three small articles are we
And we keep nouns company.

The Adjectives

We are the adjectives; artists, too,
We stick to the nouns as your skin sticks to you.
I call the man great or good or sad.
I call the beast large or fierce or bad.
I paint the grass green and the flowers gay.
We dance through the world in our colorful way.

The Adverbs

We are the adverbs! We're lots of fun
Telling how, when or where the action is done;
Whether neatly, or carelessly, promptly or not,
We have you children right on the spot.
You act bravely and honestly, wisely and well,
Or falsely and foolishly, adverbs will tell.
Either now or later or sometimes or never,
Immediately, presently, soon or forever,
Either here or there or somewhere around,
Along with the verb the adverb is found.
But sometimes we go with the adjectives, too,
When the sun's very bright and the sky's very blue.
Or with other adverbs we sometimes mate,
When you walk very slowly and come very late.

The Preposition

A preposition small am I,
But others are not half so spry!
I'm up the mountain, down the glen,
Through the city, among the men,
Under the river, over the sea,
Or up in the tree-tops! There you'll find me.
I'm with and of and from and by,
Pointing always, low or high.

The Conjunction

I am the word that joins: conjunction,
I have a plain but useful function.
What would you do without your and?
Your or? Your if? I'm in demand,
Because, unless your work you do,
You're negligent and lazy, too!

The Interjection

I'm the interjection wild,
Dear to almost every child.
Oh! how lovely! Ouch! Take care!
Alas! Hurrah! Hello! Beware!
Oh! how noble! Look! red light!
My! you gave me such a fright!

Punctuation Verses

Dorothy Harrer

I am the period. I love to rest.
All sentences stop at my request.

I want to know
What is your name?
Where do you live?
What is your fame?
What answer will you give?
The question mark am I,
And can you tell me why?

Whoopee! Hooray!
Look out! Make way!
I'm here! I'm there! I'm everywhere!
Whatever the excitement rare,
The exclamation point is there!

When the sentences are long,
Running ever on and on,
I run with them, so nimble and merry,
To give you a breathing space,
Lest you grow weary.
I am the comma, so nimble and busy,
Without me some sentences might make you dizzy.

Mrs. Grammar's Ball

from Great Grandmother's Piece Book

Mrs. Grammar once gave a fine ball
To the nine different parts of our speech
    To the short and the tall,
    To the stout and the small,
There were pies, plums, and puddings for each.

And first little Articles came
In a hurry to make themselves known;
    Far A, AN, and THE—
    But none of the three
Could stand for a minute alone.

Then adjectives came to announce
That their dear friends the Nouns were at hand;
    Rough, rougher, and roughest,
    Tough, tougher, and toughest,
Fat, merry, good-natured, and grand.

The Nouns were indeed on their way,
Tens of thousands and more, I should think;
    For each name that we utter,
    Shop, shoulder, or shutter—
Is a Noun; lion, lady, or link.

The Pronouns were hastening fast
To push the nouns out of their places:
    I, thou, he, and she,
    You, it, they, and we,
With their sprightly, intelligent faces.

Someone cried, "Make way for the Verbs!"
A great crowd is coming to view."
    To light and to smite,
    To fight and to bite,
To be and to have and to do.

The Adverbs attend on the Verbs.
Behind, as their footmen, they run;
    As thus, "To fight badly"
    And "Run away gladly"
Show how running and fighting were done.

Prepositions came, in, by and near,
With conjunctions, a wee little band,
    As either you or he
    But neither I nor she,
They held their great friends by the hand.

Then, too, with a Hip! Hip! Hoorah!
Rushed in Interjections uproarious.
    Dear me! Well-a-day!
    When they saw the display,
"Ha! Ha!" they all shouted out, "Glorious!"

But alas what misfortunes were nigh!
While the fun and the feasting pleased each,
    Pounced on them at once
    A monster-a Dunce!
And confounded the nine parts of speech.

Help Friends, to the rescue! On you
For aid Verb and Article call.
    O give your protection
    To poor interjection,
Noun, Pronoun, Conjunction and all.

Subject and Object

Eugene Schwartz

When you speak or write in sentences,
Make them clear and make them true,
For confusing the SUBJECT and OBJECT
Is something you are not to do!

"Merton swiftly strikes the nail"—
Of this we can be certain;
But think how painful it would be,
If it were said, "The nail strikes Merton!"

"A strong horse pulled our heavy sled
Across the snowy course"—
But we'd not have gotten anywhere
If the sled had pulled the horse!

"Because he was so bad in school
His mother spanked poor Tom"—
It would not have been proper, though,
For Tom to spank his Mom!

I could tell so many tales
(But the tales could not tell me)
Of subjects turned into objects
And objects used subjectively,
Of a world tuned topsy-turvy
When grammar is ignored,
And how, through proper sentence form,
World Order is restored.

So keep the horse before the cart,
And make the hammer hit the nail,
Be sure to think before you speak,
And you'll speak well without fail!

Metrical Feet

Samuel Taylor Coleridge

Trōchĕe trīps frŏm lōng tŏ shōrt,
From long to long in solemn sort
Slōw Spōndēe stālks; strōng fōōt! yet ill able
Ēvĕr tŏ cōme ŭp wĭth Dāctyl trĭsÿllăblĕ.
Ĭāmbĭcs mārch frŏm shōrt tŏ lōng;—
Wĭth ă lēāp ănd ă bōūnd thĕ swĭft Ānăpăests thrōng;
One syllable long, with one short at each side,
Āmphībrăchys hāstes wĭth ă stātely stride;—
Fīrst ănd lāst bēĭng lōng, mīddlĕ shōrt, Āmphĭmācer
Strīkes hĭs thūndērĭng hōōfs līke ă prōūd hīgh-brĕd Rācer.

Shakespeare

Puck's Blessing

from A Midsummer Night's Dream

Through the house give glimmering light
By the dead and drowsy fire;
Every elf and fairy sprite
Hop as light as bird from brier;
And this ditty after me
Sing, and dance it trippingly.

First, rehearse your song by rote,
To each word a warbling note;
Hand in hand, with fairy grace,
Will we sing, and bless this place.

Aubade

Cloten from Cymbeline

Hark, hark! the lark at heaven's gate sings,
  And Phoebus 'gins arise,
His steeds to water at those springs
  On chaliced flowers that lies;
And winking Mary-buds begin
  To ope their golden eyes:
With every thing that pretty is,
  My lady sweet, arise:
    Arise, arise.

An aubade is a poem or song of or about lovers separating at dawn. It has also been defined as "a song or instrumental composition concerning, accompanying, or evoking daybreak". In the strictest sense of the term, an aubade is a song from a door or window to a sleeping woman.

The Fairies Sing Titania To Sleep

from A Midsummer Night's Dream

First Fairy:

You spotted snakes with double tongue,
Thorny hedgehogs, be not seen;
Newts and blind-worms, do no wrong,
Come not near our fairy queen.

Chorus:

Philomel, with melody
Sing in our sweet lullaby;
Lulla, lulla, lullaby, lulla, lulla, lullaby:
Never harm,
Nor spell nor charm,
Come our lovely lady nigh;
So, good night, with lullaby.

Second Fairy:

Weaving spiders, come not here;
Hence, you long-legg'd spinners, hence!
Beetles black, approach not near;
Worm nor snail, do no offence.

Chorus:

Philomel, with melody
Sing in our sweet lullaby;
Lulla, lulla, lullaby, lulla, lulla, lullaby:
Never harm,
Nor spell nor charm,
Come our lovely lady nigh;
So, good night, with lullaby.

When Icicles Hang by the Wall

Winter from Love's Labour's Lost

When icicles hang by the wall
    And Dick the shepherd blows his nail,
And Tom bears logs into the hall,
    And milk comes frozen home in pail;
When blood is nipt, and ways be foul,
Then nightly sings the staring owl
        Tu-whoo!
Tu-whit! tu-whoo! A merry note!
While greasy Joan doth keel the pot.

When all around the wind doth blow,
  And coughing drowns the parson's saw,
And birds sit brooding in the snow,
  And Marian's nose looks red and raw;
When roasted crabs hiss in the bowl—
Then nightly sings the staring owl
      Tu-whoo!
Tu-whit! tu-whoo! A merry note!
While greasy Joan doth keel the pot.

All the World's a Stage

Jacques from As You Like It

All the world's a stage,
And all the men and women merely players;
They have their exits and their entrances;
And one man in his time plays many parts,
His acts being seven ages. At first the infant,
Mewling and puking in the nurse's arms;
And then the whining school-boy, with his satchel
And shining morning face, creeping like snail
Unwillingly to school. And then the lover,
Sighing like furnace, with a woeful ballad
Made to his mistress' eyebrow. Then a soldier,
Full of strange oaths, and bearded like the pard,
Jealous in honour, sudden and quick in quarrel,
Seeking the bubble reputation
Even in the cannon's mouth. And then the justice,
In fair round belly with good capon lin'd,
With eyes severe and beard of formal cut,
Full of wise saws and modern instances;
And so he plays his part. The sixth age shifts
Into the lean and slipper'd pantaloon,
With spectacles on nose and pouch on side;
His youthful hose, well sav'd, a world too wide
For his shrunk shank; and his big manly voice,
Turning again toward childish treble, pipes
And whistles in his sound. Last scene of all,
That ends this strange eventful history,
Is second childishness and mere oblivion;
Sans teeth, sans eyes, sans taste, sans everything.

Blow, Blow, Thou Winter Wind

Lord Amiens from As You Like It

Blow, blow, thou winter wind,
Thou art not so unkind
    As man's ingratitude;
Thy tooth is not so keen
Because thou art not seen,
    Although thy breath be rude.
Heigh-ho! sing heigh-ho! unto the green holly:
Most friendship is feigning, most loving mere folly:
        Then, heigh-ho! the holly!
        This life is most jolly.

Freeze, freeze, thou bitter sky,
Thou dost not bite so nigh
    As benefits forgot:
Though thou the waters warp,
Thy sting is not so sharp
    As friend remember'd not.
Heigh-ho! sing heigh-ho! unto the green holly:
Most friendship is feigning, most loving mere folly:
        Then, heigh-ho! the holly!
        This life is most jolly.

Ariel's Song

Ariel from The Tempest

Come unto these yellow sands,
And then take hands:
Courtsied when you have and kiss'd
The wild waves whist,
Foot it featly here and there;
And, sweet sprites, the burthen bear.
Hark, hark!

Full fathom five thy father lies;
Of his bones are coral made;
Those are pearls that were his eyes:
Nothing of him that doth fade
But doth suffer a sea-change
Into something rich and strange.
Sea-nymphs hourly ring his knell:

Hark! Now I hear them,—Ding-dong bell.

To Be or Not to Be

Prince Hamlet from Hamlet

To be or not to be—that is the question:
Whether 'tis nobler in the mind to suffer
The slings and arrows of outrageous fortune,
Or to take arms against a sea of troubles
And, by opposing, end them. To die, to sleep
No more—and by a sleep to say we end
The heartache and the thousand natural shocks
That flesh is heir to—'tis a consummation
Devoutly to be wished. To die, to sleep
To sleep, perchance to dream. Ay, there's the rub,
For in that sleep of death what dreams may come,
When we have shuffled off this mortal coil,
Must give us pause. There's the respect
That makes calamity of so long life.
For who would bear the whips and scorns of time,
Th' oppressor's wrong, the proud man's contumely,
The pangs of disprized love, the law's delay,
The insolence of office, and the spurns
That patient merit of th' unworthy takes,
When he himself might his quietus make
With a bare bodkin? Who would fardels bear,
To grunt and sweat under a weary life,
But that the dread of something after death,
The undiscovered country from whose bourn
No traveler returns, puzzles the will
And makes us rather bear those ills we have
Than fly to others that we know not of?
Thus conscience does make cowards of us all,
And thus the native hue of resolution
Is sicklied o'er with the pale cast of thought,
And enterprises of great pitch and moment
With this regard their currents turn awry,
And lose the name of action.

FROM ANTONY'S FUNERAL ORATION

ANTONY FROM JULIUS CAESAR

Friends, Romans, countrymen, lend me your ears;
I come to bury Caesar, not to praise him.
The evil that men do lives after them;
The good is oft interred with their bones;
So let it be with Caesar. The noble Brutus
Hath told you Caesar was ambitious:
If it were so, it was a grievous fault,
And grievously hath Caesar answer'd it.
Here, under leave of Brutus and the rest—
For Brutus is an honourable man;
So are they all, all honourable men—
Come I to speak in Caesar's funeral.
He was my friend, faithful and just to me:
But Brutus says he was ambitious;
And Brutus is an honourable man.
He hath brought many captives home to Rome
Whose ransoms did the general coffers fill:
Did this in Caesar seem ambitious?
When that the poor have cried, Caesar hath wept:
Ambition should be made of sterner stuff:
Yet Brutus says he was ambitious;
And Brutus is an honourable man.
You all did see that on the Lupercal
I thrice presented him a kingly crown,
Which he did thrice refuse: was this ambition?
Yet Brutus says he was ambitious;
And, sure, he is an honourable man.
I speak not to disprove what Brutus spoke,
But here I am to speak what I do know.
You all did love him once, not without cause:
What cause withholds you then, to mourn for him?
O judgment! thou art fled to brutish beasts,
And men have lost their reason. Bear with me;
My heart is in the coffin there with Caesar,
And I must pause till it come back to me.

Polonius' Advice to Laertes

Polonius from Hamlet

Yet here, Laertes! aboard, aboard, for shame!
The wind sits in the shoulder of your sail,
And you are stay'd for. There; my blessing with thee!
And these few precepts in thy memory
See thou character. Give thy thoughts no tongue,
Nor any unproportioned thought his act.
Be thou familiar, but by no means vulgar.
Those friends thou hast, and their adoption tried,
Grapple them to thy soul with hoops of steel;
But do not dull thy palm with entertainment
Of each new-hatch'd, unfledged comrade. Beware
Of entrance to a quarrel, but being in,
Bear't that the opposed may beware of thee.
Give every man thy ear, but few thy voice;
Take each man's censure, but reserve thy judgment.
Costly thy habit as thy purse can buy,
But not express'd in fancy; rich, not gaudy;
For the apparel oft proclaims the man,
And they in France of the best rank and station
Are of a most select and generous chief in that.
Neither a borrower nor a lender be;
For loan oft loses both itself and friend,
And borrowing dulls the edge of husbandry.
This above all: to thine ownself be true,
And it must follow, as the night the day,
Thou canst not then be false to any man.
Farewell: my blessing season this in thee!

The Witches' Chant

The Three Witches from Macbeth

Round about the cauldron go:
In the poison'd entrails throw.
Toad, that under cold stone
Days and nights has thirty-one
Sweated venom sleeping got,
Boil thou first i' the charmed pot.

Double, double toil and trouble;
Fire burn and cauldron bubble.

Fillet of a fenny snake,
In the cauldron boil and bake;
Eye of newt and toe of frog,
Wool of bat and tongue of dog,
Adder's fork and blindworm's sting,
Lizard's leg and howlet's wing.
For charm of powerful trouble,
Like a hell-broth boil and bubble.

Double, double toil and trouble;
Fire burn and cauldron bubble.

Prospero's Farewell to His Magic

Prospero from The Tempest

Our revels now are ended. These our actors,
As I foretold you, were all spirits and
Are melted into air, into thin air:
And, like the baseless fabric of this vision,
The cloud-capp'd towers, the gorgeous palaces,
The solemn temples, the great globe itself,
Yea, all which it inherit, shall dissolve
And, like this insubstantial pageant faded,
Leave not a rack behind. We are such stuff
As dreams are made on, and our little life
Is rounded with a sleep.

Afterword

To a Poet a Thousand Years Hence

James Elroy Flecker

I who am dead a thousand years,
And wrote this sweet archaic song,
Send you my words for messengers
The way I shall not pass along.

I care not if you bridge the seas,
Or ride secure the cruel sky,
Or build consummate palaces
Of metal or of masonry.

But have you wine and music still,
And statues and a bright-eyed love,
And foolish thoughts of good and ill,
And prayers to them who sit above?

How shall we conquer? Like a wind
That falls at eve our fancies blow,
And old Moeonides the blind
Said it three thousand years ago.

O friend unseen, unborn, unknown,
Student of our sweet English tongue,
Read out my words at night, alone:
I was a poet, I was young.

Since I can never see your face,
And never shake you by the hand,
I send my soul through time and space
To greet you. You will understand.

Acknowledgments

Although every effort has been made to identify the authors of all poems, this has not been possible in every case. I offer my sincere apologies to anyone whose name I have not been able to put to their work. Omissions will be happily rectified in any future edition. While every effort has been made to trace the owners of copyrights, in a few cases this has proved impossible, and I take this opportunity of tendering my apologies to any owners whose rights may have been unwittingly infringed.

"Some Rivers" by Frank Asch: Reprinted by kind permission of Frank Asch.

"Dandelion, Yellow As Gold" by Noreen Bath: The author has made every effort to obtain permission.

"The Song of the Robin" by Beatrice Bergquist: The author has made every effort to obtain permission.

"The Parts of Speech Verses" by Virginia Field Birdsall: ©AWSNA Publications, reprinted by kind permission of the publisher.

"The Ten Amendments in Rhyme (The Bill of Rights)" by Carl Bridgman: Reprinted by kind permission of Carl Bridgman.

"Pirate Wind" by Mary Jane Carr: The author has made every effort to obtain permission.

"Sir Nicketty Nox" by Hugh Chesterman: The author has made every effort to obtain permission.

Notes on St. Martin from "Shaping the Flame" by Bob Clay: Reprinted by kind permission of Bob Clay.

"No Shop Does the Bird Use" and "The Rabbit's Song Outside the Tavern" by Elizabeth Coatsworth: Reprinted by kind permission of Kate Barnes.

"Goblin Gold", "Harvest", "The Knight", "The Owl", "The River", and "Seeds" by Molly de Havas: The author has made every effort to obtain permission.

"At the Keyhole", "Dream Song", "The Fairies Dancing", "Five Eyes", "Grim", "The Horseman", "I Saw Three Witches", "Ice", "The Listeners", "Nicholas Nye", "The Ride-by-Nights", "Silver", "Some One", "Tartary", "Unstooping", and "Wanderers" by Walter de la Mare: The Literary Trustees of Walter de la Mare and The Society of Authors as their representative.

"The Wolf" by Georgia Durston: The author has made every effort to obtain permission.

"Canticle to the Sun" translated by Lawrence Edwards: The author has made every effort to obtain permission.

"Poor Richard's Maxims" by Sverre Elsmo: The author has made every effort to obtain permission.

"Alms in Autumn", "The Fairies" and "Peacocks" by Rose Fyleman: The Society of Authors as the Literary Representative of the Estate of Rose Fyleman.

"November" by Elisabeth Gmeyner: The author has made every effort to obtain permission.

"Ancient Persia", "The Four Sentences", "Punctuation Verses" and "Time Rhyme" by Harrer, Dorothy: ©AWSNA Publications, reprinted by kind permission of the publisher.

"A Song of King Arthur's Castle", "Michaelmas Song" and "The Sun Is in My Heart" by A. C. Harwood: The author has made every effort to obtain permission.

"The Harvest" by Alice C. Henderson: The author has made every effort to obtain permission.

"To My Fellow Swimmers" by the Hopi Elders: The author has made every effort to obtain permission.

"A Sun Like Thee", "Hercules" and "Mother Earth" by Eileen Hutchins: The author has made every effort to obtain permission.

"Cosmic Dance" and "Soul Cricket" by Dennis Klocek: Reprinted by kind permission of Dennis Klocek.

"The Knighthood of the Present Age" by Dr. Karl Koenig: The author has made every effort to obtain permission.

"The Smithy" by Magda Maier: Reprinted by kind permission of the publisher. Christoph Jaffke (ed.): Rhythms, Rhymes, Games and Songs for the Lower School. Paedagogische Forschungsstelle beim Bund der Freien Waldorfschulen, edition waldorf, fourth, revised and supplemented edition, Stuttgart 2005, p. 77.

"Number Rhyme" by Joan Marcus: The author has made every effort to obtain permission.

"Sukkot" by R. H. Marks: The author has made every effort to obtain permission.

"A Ballad of John Silver", Cargoes", "The Rider at the Gate" and "Sea-Fever" by John Masefield: The Society of Authors as the Literary Representative of the Estate of John Masefield.

"Arthur the King" by Jehanne Mehta: Reprinted by kind permission of Jehanne Mehta, www.jehannemehta.com.

"A Winter Night" by Margaret Meyerkort: Reprinted by kind permission of Margaret Meyerkort.

"In Days Gone By" by Ida Mills: The author has made every effort to obtain permission.

"Cows" by Pelham Moffat: The author has made every effort to obtain permission.

"Alphabet", "Farming" and "Light-All Creating" by Margaret Morgan: Reproduced by kind permission of Floris Books, Edinburgh. Copyright 1987, 1998 Heather Thomas from Journey Through Time in Verse and Rhyme.

"A Mathematics Poem" by Michael Motteram: Reprinted by kind permission of Michael Motteram.

"The Highwayman", "The Moon Is Up" and "A Song of Sherwood" by Alfred Noyes: The Society of Authors as the Literary Representative of the Estate of Alfred Noyes.

"Spell of Creation" by Kathleen Raine: Reprinted by kind permission of Farrar, Straus and Giroux, LLC.

"An Old Rat's Tale" and "Antonio" by Laura E. Richards: The author has made every effort to obtain permission.

"Where the Rainbow Ends" by Richard Rive: The author has made every effort to obtain permission.

"The Forging of Thor's Hammer" by S. M. Ryan: The author has made every effort to obtain permission.

"Adventsong", "Ant, Bee & Butterfly", "In the Mountains", "Jack Frost", "Manahatta's Musings", "Number Verse", "Subject and Object", "St. George", "St. Jerome and the Lion" and "St. Martin" by Eugene Schwartz: Reprinted by kind permission of Eugene Schwartz, www.millennialchild.com.

"Seal" by William Jay Smith: Reprinted by kind permission of Farrar, Straus and Giroux, LLC.

"Gifts" by William Ward: Reprinted by kind permission of Andree Ward.

Wikipedia, wiki.com, for notes on the following poems: "The Charge of the Light Brigade" http://en.wikipedia.org/wiki/Charge_of_the_Light_Brigade, http://en.wikipedia.org/wiki/Battle_of_Balaclava, "The Destroyer of Worlds" http://en.wikipedia.org/wiki/J._Robert_Oppenheimer, "The Destruction of Sennacherib" http://en.wikipedia.org/wiki/The_Destruction_of_Sennacherib, http://en.wikipedia.org/wiki/Sennacherib, "The Fisherman and the Flounder" http://en.wikipedia.org/wiki/The_Tale_of_the_Fisherman_and_the_Fish, "Give Me Liberty, or Give Me Death!" http://en.wikipedia.org/wiki/Give_me_Liberty,_or_give_me_Death!, "In the Bazaars of Hyderabad" http://en.wikipedia.org/wiki/Sarojini_Naidu, "The Moon Is Up" http://en.wikipedia.org/wiki/Spanish_Main, "The New Colossus" http://en.wikipedia.org/wiki/Statue_of_Liberty, "Our Deepest Fear" http://en.wikiquote.org/wiki/Marianne_Williamson, "Ozymandias" http://en.wikipedia.org/wiki/Ozymandias, "Poor Richard's Maxims" http://en.wikipedia.org/wiki/Benjamin_Franklin, http://en.wikipedia.org/wiki/Poor_Richard%27s_Almanack, "Sympathy" http://en.wikipedia.org/wiki/Paul_Laurence_Dunbar, "This Land Is Your Land" http://en.wikipedia.org/wiki/Woody_Guthrie

"The Cow", "Fishes", "The Horse" and "Hymn to Prometheus" by Roy Wilkinson ©Reprinted with kind permission of Rudolf Steiner College Press, all rights reserved.

"Our Deepest Fear" by Marianne Williamson: Reprinted by kind permission of Marianne Williamson.

"The Daffodil" and "The Poem of Eva's Apples" by Isabel Wyatt: Reproduced by kind permission of Floris Books, Edinburgh. Copyright 1987, 1998 Heather Thomas from Journey Through Time in Verse and Rhyme.

"Fairy Shoes" by Annette Wynne: The author has made every effort to obtain permission.

Index of Titles, Authors & First Lines

David Kennedy has taught in Waldorf schools for over twenty years. He studied education and trained to be a teacher at Emerson College in Forest Row, England. David founded WaldorfToday.com, the world's largest weekly newsletter for Waldorf education.

Front cover art: "Michaelmas,", needle-felted wool tapestry, David Kennedy. "I was a first grade teacher in Bethesda, Maryland, only miles from the Pentagon, and was teaching on the morning of 9/11. I made this felt shortly after those events. St. Michael protects the town from the menacing dragon which would destroy that which is good."

Back cover art: Detail from "Madonna, Rainbow Bridge," needle-felted wool tapestry, David Kennedy.

Cover photographs of "Michaelmas" and "Madonna, Rainbow Bridge" by Bronwyn Fargo. www.bronwynfargo.com.

Front and back cover book design by Geri Shonka. gshonka@hotmail.com.

"The Waldorf Book of Poetry" was set in Minion Pro. Minion is a digital typeface designed by Robert Slimbach in 1990 for Adobe Systems. The name comes from the traditional naming system for type sizes, in which minion is between nonpareil and brevier. It is inspired by late Renaissance-era type.

Notes

Index

Printed in Poland
by Amazon Fulfillment
Poland Sp. z o.o., Wrocław

53492289R00209